Documenting the Image

A series edited by
Helene E. Roberts, *Harvard University Emerita, Cambridge, Massachusetts,* and Brent Maddox, *J. Paul Getty Center for the History of Art and the Humanities, Santa Monica, California*

Documenting the Image describes the history, influences, and implications of visual artifacts. Its goals include publishing monographs and reference books that promote visual collections around the world.

This book is part of a series. The publisher will accept continuation orders which may be cancelled at any time and which provide for automatic billing and shipping of each title in the series upon publication. Please write for details.

"Remove Not the Ancient Landmark":
Public Monuments and Moral Values

Discourses and Comments
in Tribute to
Rudolf Wittkower

Edited by

Donald Martin Reynolds

Gordon and Breach Publishers

Australia   Canada   China   France   Germany   India   Japan   Luxembourg
Malaysia   The Netherlands   Russia   Singapore   Switzerland
Thailand   United Kingdom

Emmaplein 5
1075 AW Amsterdam
The Netherlands

Cover: *Man Carving His Own Destiny*. Albin Polasek, sculptor. Limestone. 1961. Brookgreen Gardens.

British Library Cataloguing in Publication Data

Remove not the ancient landmark : public monuments and
    moral values. – (Documenting the image ; v. 3)
    1.Monuments – Moral and ethical aspects 2.National
    monuments – Moral and ethical aspects
    I.Reynolds, Donald Martin
    725.9'4'01

    ISSN   2–88124–602–8   (hardcover)
           2–88449–204–6   (softcover)

To the memory of
Samuel Dorsky

CONTENTS

INTRODUCTION
TO THE SERIES

Documenting the Image is devoted to describing the history, process, and use of visual documents. As many events and most artifacts are known and studied through images made of them, the study of the creation, collection, and use of these images becomes crucial to out understanding of the originals. *Documenting the Image* will provide an arena for discussion of the influence of visual documentation on culture, academic disciplines, and ways of thinking. It will inquire into how visual language is structured and how visual meaning is communicated. It will explore the visual documentation of artifacts through drawings, casts, facsimiles, engravings, and photography, and it will describe the effects of the new electronic technology on visual resources. Through the publication of catalogs of visual materials, it will seek to make these collections better known and more accessible to a wide range of potential users. In addition, the series will provide reference tools which support the description, organization, and use of visual collections.

ILLUSTRATIONS

Arch of Constantine. 312–315 A.D. Rome.

Column of Trajan. Marble. 106–113 A.D. Rome.

Equestrian Statue of Marcus Aurelius. Gilded Bronze. Over Lifesize. 161–180 A.D. Piazza del Campidoglio. Rome.

Australopithecus afarensis. John Holmes, sculptor. American Museum of Natural History.

Homo Erectus cranium. Don McGranaghan, artist. American Museum of Natural History.

Earliest known artificial shelter. Diana Salles, artist. American Museum of Natural History.

Earliest known representational art. Don McGranaghan, artist. American Museum of Natural History.

Monochrome rendering. Diana Salles, artist, after Abbé Breuil. American Museum of Natural History.

Tomb of Ilaria del Carretto. Jacopo Della Quercia, sculptor. Marble. 1406–1408(?). Cathedral, Lucca, Italy.

Logetta. Jacopo Sansovino, architect. 1530s. Venice.

Fighting Stallions. Anna Hyatt Huntington, sculptor. Aluminum. 1950. Brookgreen Gardens.

Diana of the Chase. Anna Hyatt Huntington, sculptor. Bronze. 1922. Brookgreen Gardens.

Narcissus. Adolph Alexander Weinman, sculptor. Marble. 1923. Brookgreen Gardens.

CONTRIBUTORS

James Ackerman, Harvard University, Cambridge, Massachusetts

James Beck, Columbia University, New York

Stanley Bleifeld, National Sculpture Society, New York

John J. Czaplicka, Harvard University, Cambridge, Massachusetts

Howard McP. Davis, deceased, art historian, New York

Wayne Dynes, Hunter College, New York

Jonathan Fairbanks, Museum of Fine Arts, Boston, Massachusetts

Oleg Grabar, The Institute for Advanced Study, Princeton, New Jersey

Eugene Johnson, Williams College, Williamstown, Massachusetts

Lenore Lakowitz, Raphell Sims Lakowitz Memorial Foundation, Douglastown, New York

Richard McDermott Miller, National Academy of Design, Washington, D.C.

Mary Mothersill, Barnard College, New York

Stephen Murray, Columbia University, New York

Ernst Neizvestny, Ernst Neizvestny Studio, New York

Joseph Veach Noble, Brookgreen Gardens, Murrells Inlet, South Carolina

Donald Martin Reynolds, The Monuments Conservancy, New York

David Rosand, Columbia University, New York

Murray David Schane, Creedmore Psychiatric Center, New York

Ian Tattersall, American Museum of Natural History, New York

Jean-Rae Turner, *The Elizabeth Daily Journal*, Elizabeth, New Jersey

Richard Wortman, Columbia University, New York

PART I

1. Introduction

Donald Martin Reynolds

"Remove Not the Ancient Landmark": Public Monuments and Moral Values explores the ways that public monuments symbolize and convey values. The essayists analyze the roles that monuments have always played and the influence they continue to exert on societies around the world. In Part I essayists explore the origins and nature of humanity in light of the monuments we have inherited.

From the ordinary human being's need to memorialize individuals to society's acknowledgment of noble ideas and great achievements, art historian E. J. Johnson, chairman, Department of Art at Williams College, illustrates the breadth and richness of the ways in which monuments operate. He scans the broad spectrum of traditional as well as avant garde forms to illustrate the variety of monumental expression throughout the world from antiquity to modern times. James Ackerman, professor of Fine Arts (retired), Harvard University, discusses three major forms of public monuments in antiquity—the arch, the column, and the equestrian statue—and their later adaptations. In view of their identification with autocratic power, he sees their demise as symbols a hopeful sign for the future of humanity.

In defining *monument*, Wayne R. Dynes, professor of art history at Hunter College, traces its origins to antiquity and its duality as written word and permanent structure. He shows that the monumental tradition answers a perennial need expressed in both physical and verbal monuments. Moreover, he shows that they both record the nobility of human action in ritual sanctified by the values of society, and they thereby assist our own survival.

Ian Tattersall, chairman, Department of Anthropology, American Museum of Natural History, explains that the urge to monumentality was born more than 100,000 years ago with the human species' achievement of anatomical modernity. Long dormant within the primitive psyche, the human capacity for creativity and self-expression awaited the appropriate cultural, technological, and economic stimuli. Among the earliest ritualized and symbolical activities were the burials of

3

Neanderthals. Demonstrating the human capacity of caring for another and suggesting the belief in an afterlife, Neanderthal burials may have been humankind's first monuments.

In developing a psychology of public monuments that articulates what monuments represent, how they are perceived and appreciated, why they are built, and what inspires their creation, Murray Schane, professor of psychiatry at Columbia University, illustrates the significance of that psychology today. Moreover, he shows that the dualism existing in the field of psychotherapy parallels the gulf between the individual and society that is expressed by public monuments. In his analysis of the monument to Raphell Lakowitz at Creedmoor Psychiatric Center in New York City, Dr. Schane demonstrates how that psychology explains the divide between the self as its own creation and the self as created and sustained by society.

Mary Mothersill, chairman, Department of Philosophy, Barnard College, explores what is asked of a public monument—what it conveys, and how and when its message is true or false. Establishing four categories in which to consider public monuments, she analyzes the Vietnam Memorial in Washington, D.C. as a successful example of what a monument is supposed to be: a beautiful memorial with an important message.

Art historian Donald Martin Reynolds, founder and director of The Monuments Conservancy, discusses the significance of public monuments as embodiments of human values and how monuments establish a continuity with the past and with the rest of creation. He relates how New York City's "Monuments to Neglect" inspired the establishment of The Monuments Conservancy, Inc., a not-for-profit foundation, whose mission is to perpetuate the integration of public monuments into the community through a policy of education and preservation.

Alarmed by the widespread destruction of objects by improper and irresponsible restoration sweeping the art world in recent years, James Beck, professor of art history at Columbia University, proposes a "Bill of Rights" for works of art to assure their protection. Citing examples of well-known works recently restored, Professor Beck shows the need for such guidelines.

David Rosand, professor of art history at Columbia University, focuses on the city of Venice as a monument whose survival is threatened by the elements as well as by improper restoration techniques. Ironically, Professor Rosand surmises, the lagoon that liberates its architecture from defensive responsibility allowing its unique openness of design is the ecological source of its ultimate disintegration. Discussions of Sansovíno's Logetta and frescos by such masters as Giorgione illustrate the vulnerability of Venice's monuments not only to the waters of the Adriatic but also to the devices of modern restoration.

In analyzing a selection of monuments erected in several new countries born since World War II, historian Oleg Grabar of the Institute for Advanced Study, links East and West, past and present. Many of those countries combined traditional forms or invented new ones in creating some outstanding monuments to express the aspirations, feelings, and needs of their existing societies. Thus, Professor Grabar reveals, it is possible to create a monument out of life and not only out of death. Moreover, monuments project social values within Third World countries in the same ways that they do in Western countries.

One of the most distinguished and impressive monuments to American sculpture is Brookgreen Gardens in South Carolina. Joseph Veach Noble, Brookgreen's chairman emeritus of the board of trustees, sketches the garden's history and discusses the display of the sculpture collection there and some of the major pieces and their creators.

Part I concludes with a tribute to Rudolf Wittkower, in which the late Howard McParlin Davis, professor of art history at Columbia University, analyzes the tomb of Urban VIII in St. Peter's in Rome, which links past expression to present day interpretations of values.

"Remove Not the Ancient Landmark . . ."

"Remove not the ancient landmark, which your fathers set up" is a biblical imperative from the twenty-second chapter of the Book of Proverbs, one of the sapiential books of the Old Testament. The verse refers to the piles of stones in ancient Palestine that served as fences or landmarks that defined each family's ancestral land claims. Removing those landmarks was a most serious matter then, as the neglect and destruction of our public monuments is today.

Part II moves from a concentration on the celebration and perpetuation of public monuments to a consideration of the neglect and destruction of our public monuments. The mass destruction of monuments in Russia following the dissolution of the USSR and the removal and transformation of monuments in twentieth-century Germany illustrate that alternative, while the creation of new monuments and the preservation of historical memorials and sites underscores the salutary benefits derived from their celebration and perpetuation.

In Russia the world was witnessing the most widespread revolution against totalitarian government it had ever seen. Many people are still destroying its monuments, as if to expunge the evil of atheistic communism from the face of the earth by removing its landmarks. A cluster of those broken statues lies on a lawn near Gorky Park in Moscow, where they were dubbed "Sculpture of the servants of the totalitarian regime."[1] They included the colossal bronze statue of Feliks Dzerzhinsky, founder of the State Police; busts of Khrushchev, Molotov, and Stalin; Sverdlov's statue from the Square of the Revolution; and a seated Kalinan from the Metropol Hotel. A few blocks away, Lenin towers over October Square. The future of his mausoleum, which has stood next to the Kremlin Wall in Red Square for six-and-one-half decades, is uncertain.

Destroying monuments is not new. Since ancient times, conquerors have destroyed their predecessors' icons and monuments. But because monuments are measures of humanity's journey along the road of civilization, cooler heads caution the iconoclast: "What is past is prologue," as Shakespeare reminds us with characteristic wisdom. There are those of us who ask that some of those monuments be preserved and that they become the subjects of ongoing research and study, so future generations will be reminded of the tyranny of atheistic communism in order to prevent its return.[2]

Looking at those "discarded monuments to lost ideals" piled up in Gorky Park, a Russian psychiatrist, Konstantin Danilin, said, "Of course, this is a disgrace. They should all be in some museum to the past, where something could be learned, not just discarded like this."[3] An old man with his grandson also examined the wreckage: "No, I can't say this is good. We trashed the old statues, now we've trashed these, then we'll be trashing the next ones. There's got to be a better way to do it. Toppling old statues is easy and satisfying. But, if they are simply added to the litter of history, nothing has been achieved."[4]

Richard S. Wortman, professor of history at the Harriman Institute of Columbia University, explains how the Russian autocracy used statues to present its changing imagery in the late 19th and 20th centuries. His examination of major monuments during that period provides useful insights into the current widespread demolition of public monuments in the former Soviet Union. Illustrating the remarkable ideological change now taking place in Russia, the Russian-American sculptor Ernst Neizvestny explains his monuments to the Russian martyrs under Stalinism currently being erected in the Ural Mountains. What will be the fate of these monuments should communism return?

Removing monuments to revise history is an action not relegated to the former USSR. John Czaplicka, assistant professor of fine arts at Harvard University, demonstrates that the monuments erected under the state socialist regime in the German Democratic Republic of this century were threatened or destroyed when that regime fell. Removing monuments is one way of revising history. If the monument no longer exists, perhaps the era it represents will also be forgotten.

Even cemetery monuments, usually the most endearing because they are personal rather than ideological, must be preserved through celebration. Jonathan Fairbanks, curator of American sculpture at Boston's Museum of Fine Arts, focuses on the eternal celebration he finds in America's funerary memorials. He analyzes the maturing of American sculpture expressed in the nation's funerary monuments in the Romantic cemeteries from 1830 to 1930, while journalist and author Jean-Rae Turner reviews key memorials in Evergreen Cemetery in Hillside, New Jersey. Her study led to the cemetery's designation as a National Historic Site. Lenore Lakowitz, founder and chairperson of the Raphell Sims Lakowitz Memorial Foundation, then shows how a monument can inspire the celebration and preservation of the values it embodies.

Sculptor Richard McDermott Miller, past president of the National Academy of Design, explores the coexistence of abstraction and representation in the Vietnam Memorial in Washington, D.C.; and Stanley Bleifeld, sculptor and past president of the National Sculpture Society, discusses his sculpture for the United States Navy Memorial in the nation's capital. Both of these monuments reflect the desire to find enduring expressions that will outlive ideology, history, and changing taste.

Stephen Murray, professor of art history at Columbia University, is concerned with the interaction between the idea of the unbuilt cathedral as monument and the reality of construction, essential components in the celebration of the great Gothic Cathedrals of the Middle Ages. He addresses the dialectics of the social, economic, and political burdens that come along with that interaction.

* * *

By commemorating specific people, deeds, and events, monuments symbolize and convey systems of values. To encourage the exploration of the dynamic between monuments and values, on March 21, 1991, a symposium in New York convened authorities from various fields. This book is derived from that and the 1992 symposium. The symposium is now held annually, thanks to the generosity of Samuel Dorsky,[5] and it meets on the first day of spring to symbolize the role of public monuments in the life of society.

Conceived and organized by the editor, the annual symposium is dedicated to the eminent authority on Baroque art and architecture, Rudolf Wittkower. The first symposium was held on the twentieth anniversary of his death. Because public monuments are interdisciplinary by nature, the symposium is an appropriate tribute to Rudolf Wittkower, who decried specialization.

Wittkower encouraged interdisciplinary collaboration throughout his career, which followed his interests from Quattrocento painting to Baroque sculpture and the history of architecture. His spirit of collaborative scholarship dates from his very first publications. Indeed, his first five books were the work of collaboration. He wrote two books, *Born Under Saturn* (1963) and *The Divine Michelangelo* (1964), with his wife Margot, his lifetime helpmate and partner. The last course he gave at Columbia University, just before he retired in 1969, was "The Impact of Non-European Civilizations on the Art of the West."

It is that spirit of collaborative inquiry, so much a part of Rudolf Wittkower's life and work, that infuses this book.

NOTES

1. Serge Schmemann, "The Old Order, Like Its Idols, is Toppled, but the Victors Find Words of Bereavement," *New York Times,* September 4, 1991, p. A13.

2. One effort is being organized by two Russian-American artists, Vitaly Komar and Alexander Melamid. They are developing a program to save the monuments but to change their meaning. They wish to leave the monuments at their sites but to transform them through art into history lessons, which show the evils of the totalitarian tradition they symbolize. (Author's interviews with Vitaly Komar, during the spring and fall of 1992; see also Vladimir Ryabsky, "Varied Approach to the 'Iron Felix'," *New Times,* p. 46–47). Along these lines, concerning the continued maintenance of Lenin's body, see Serge Schmemann, "Preserving Lenin, the High-Tech Icon," *New York Times,* December 17, 1991, p. A14.

3. Schmemann, "The Old Order. . . ," p. A13.

4. Ibid. See also Craig R. Whitney, "Russians Are at a Loss For a Respectful Word," *New York Times,* September 9, 1991, p. A8. For international implications, see Clifford Krauss, "Ethiopians Rejoice at Fall of Rulers," *New York Times,* May 24, 1991, p. 1, and "In Former East Berlin, It's Off With Lenin's Head" *New York Times,* November 14, 1991, p. A3.

5. Samuel Dorsky operated his own art gallery in New York City from 1964 until his death in 1994. In addition to dealing in contemporary art, he contributed works to

universities and colleges to provide students with close and ongoing exposure to contemporary art. He supported many artists over the years in a variety of ways, from direct purchase of their works to underwriting their living expenses, so they could concentrate on their art.

2. Do You Know a Monument to Modesty or Mirth?

E. J. Johnson

Making monuments is serious business. The title of this chapter—"Do You Know a Monument to Modesty or Mirth?"—came long before the chapter itself was written. It grew out of the hardly startling realization that there are essentially no monuments to either. Monuments are raised to heroines and heroes, not jesters, and they deal with noble ideas and great achievements, not jokes. Let us look at some ways in which monuments operate.

As we can see in two American cemeteries—one in Grand Butte, Colorado, and the other in Cooperstown, New York—ordinary human beings feel the need to memorialize individuals, to mark tiny spots on the globe with their names, to insert into the vastness of nature some small shape that challenges the forces of time. The richer and more powerful the person remembered, the larger the shape planted in the void. For some, such as an Egyptian Pharaoh, it is possible to build a form that rivals those of nature itself, be that a mountain or, as one colleague suggested, a giant sand dune. But the desire to erect monuments is as strong in the humble as in the rich and famous. Only the means are different. Walker Evans's photograph of a child's grave in Hale County, Alabama, published in 1936, shows a low mound that will flatten out after the first good rain, marked at both ends by pieces of scrap lumber that hardly have the staying power of the Pyramids at Gizeh. The child's bowl, perhaps its only possession other than clothes, lies atop the mound.

We also mark places where people have died, as the battlefields of Vicksburg and Gettysburg show. Indeed, a trip through these battlefields today is a trip through a host of monuments, in a park-like setting, that chronicle lives lost, blood shed, suffering endured. We are asked to ponder mud and gore while looking at green grass and white marble. I'm not convinced that turning battlefields into monument parks is a good idea; they become too sanitized.

We also build monuments to groups of people, in which the single life is honored as one among many. One of the most successful and moving of these is the monument at the Fosse Ardeatine outside Rome, designed by a group of Italian architects and opened in 1949. The outside reveals a simple, rectangular concrete slab rising above a berm of earth. Passing beyond that berm, we enter a large, dark chamber, filled with more than 300 individual sarcophagi, each the final resting place of an Italian killed in the last days of the war by the Germans who occupied the city. The Italian partisans had slain some 30 SS troops in the city. The SS, in turn, took 10 Italians for each German to the Ardeatine caves south of town and slaughtered them. The rows of grey granite sarcophagi are moving enough in themselves, but, as you become accustomed to the low, dark space, you realize that the concrete slab that floats above your head is a giant sarcophagus lid. You are in a grave on which the top is being lowered.

The word *monument* comes from the Latin, *monere*, which means to remind. A monument to George Washington in Milwaukee makes this point with particular clarity. In a photograph in Lee Friedlander's splendid book, *The American Monument*, the stone woman is using the monument to remind a stone child of the importance of the father of our country. Not everyone, of course, cares to be reminded of greatness, however, as Freidlander's photograph of a bust of John F. Kennedy in Nashua, New Hampshire, makes clear.

Monuments set out to address us, so that we will pay attention to their reminders. More often than not, monuments make use of a combination of visual object and words. The Washington monument in Milwaukee has Washington's name on the base, so that the woman can point to it, and so that we can know whom she is singling out. Sometimes the monument itself uses words to talk to us directly. The inscription on a sixth-century capital from the Greek island of Corfu reads: "I am the column of Xenvares, son of Meixis, upon his grave." Others use words to speak to us through the mouth of the donor, as in the inscription, on the left, on a capital, c. 500 B.C., found near the Argive Heraion: "I, Cosina, have buried Hysematas near the race course and provided a memorial for many, even in future days, of a brave man who died in battle and surrendered his young life. He was prudent, winner of victories, and wise among his fellows." Thus we know what Cosina thought of Hysematas, or at least what she wants us to think she thought of him.

In other cases, such as in the Mary Dyer Monument in Boston, the inscription assumes the voice of the omniscient narrator, giving us in a few stark words and phrases the outline of the action by Mary Dyer that makes her life and death worth remembering. At the bottom, the narrator quotes Dyer's own words. The automobile has played hell with such texts, which are meant to be read by a pedestrian. At Ft. Ticonderoga, New York, to keep you from missing the grave of Ephraim Williams, founder of Williams College, a billboard has been erected beside it. Eph's headstone lacks sufficient monumentality, or even readability, for the automobile age. Many such insufficiently monumental monuments require a bit of help. Consider Plymouth Rock, hardly bigger than a good sized pebble. A temple is placed over it to provide the monumental presence the stone itself lacks.

We all have a clear idea of what the standard forms for monuments are. An illustration from *Webster's New International Dictionary of the English Language*, published in 1933, gives us most of them: triumphal arch, dome, column, obelisk, pyramid, tumulus and sculpture, both allegorical and representational, at a grand scale.

All of these monuments stand tall, and some stand taller than others. The importance of this fact is made brilliantly clear by a couple of drawings from David McCauley's book, *Great Moments in Architecture: The Arc de Defeat*, which he describes as a project proposed in 1783 for Paris, Maine, and almost immediately abandoned, and the Tour I-Fell, complete with sideways diner and waiter at the restaurant on the *deuxieme étage*.

All of these monuments have a high degree of seriousness. I realize that's an obvious statement, but I feel it has to be stressed, if only because monuments that unintentionally strike us as funny, because they lack solemnity and solidity, or include some form that can be read in a dubious way, fail as monuments. The monument to Leif Eriksson in Boston, for instance, presents us with a figure of the hero on top of a sturdy pedestal. The sculptor, unable to restrain a delight in historical detail, added the prow of a Viking ship at the base of the pedestal. The ship looks as if it might float away, carrying Leif and his pedestal into the nearby Charles. Of course, it is also possible deliberately to make fun of monuments, as Claes Oldenburg did with his lipstick of 1969. This columnar form, mounted on tank tracks, moves up and down in a thoroughly disturbing reminder of, well, the sexiness of war. Or, in this drawing of 1966, he proposed to substitute a gear shift for the Nelson Column in Trafalgar Square, thus honoring the arm movements of millions of motorists in Morris Minis charging through central London. Oldenburg's proposed monuments are really anti-monuments.

The persistence of these monumental forms through time is remarkable, as we all well know. Rudolph Wittkower himself traced the progress of the obelisk through much of western civilization. The same can be done for the triumphal arch, which we now find in St. Louis, designed by Eero Saarinen, at great height and in stainless steel. Down the Mississippi at Memphis, stands a thirty-six storey pyramid, also clad in stainless steel. Unlike the original pyramids near ancient Memphis, this one contains a sports arena and an observation platform.

These forms crop up in unlikely places, such as Bennington, Vermont. As part of the celebration of the 100th anniversary of Vermont statehood, a 300-foot obelisk, a monument to the Revolutionary War Battle of Bennington, was dedicated on August 19, 1891. The rusticated obelisk, designed by J. Philipp Rinn, rises at the end of a grand street, called Monument Avenue. The original choice for the Bennington Battle Monument had been a sculptural group, but that idea was thrown out in favor of "an architectural monument of lofty and massive, yet simple proportions." For the dedication there was a grand parade which wound its way from an old soldiers' home to the monument under a series of temporary triumphal arches. We tend to think of monuments as permanent things, but actually history is littered with the literary, and sometimes even the visual, remains of monuments meant to remind only for a brief time.

Fortunately, a photograph of one of the arches at Bennington has been published. The arch stood at the most important corner in town. Made of wood and canvas, it was painted so convincingly to resemble the rusticated masonry of the obelisk that gentlemen reportedly tapped it with their canes to see if it were real. Arranged across the arch were almost 200 young ladies and even younger boys, all identified by an inscription which read, "The Best Legacy of Vermont's First Century. Her Sons and Her Daughters." Those on the lower level personified the 13 original states, while the young woman under the canopy at the top was costumed as Liberty. When the carriage containing President Harrison approached the arch, Liberty stood to greet him, he tipped his hat to her, the young women and boys showered the presidential party with roses and, with childish voices, burst into singing "America." What a way to bring an old form to life!

Although they were separate forms at Bennington, the obelisk and triumphal arch have been known to join into a combination form, the Eiffel Tower. This is hardly a unique example of the way architects and sculptors have been able to bend monuments to their wills. These forms can change their meaning as well as their shape. Take, for instance, Constantin Brancusi's Gate of the Kiss at Tirgu Jiu, Rumania, completed in 1938. Brancusi was commissioned to make a memorial to Rumanian soldiers killed in World War I; he turned it into a triumph of love and regeneration. The posts have giant eyes of kissing couples, while a frieze of full length kissing pairs runs around the entire lintel. Actually, the pairs on the lintel have gone beyond the kissing stage. The American sculptor Malvina Hoffman once said to Brancusi, regarding the Gate of the Kiss: "I see the forms of two cells that meet and create life, the beginning of life . . . through love. Am I right?" "Yes, you are," Brancusi replied.

A similar case is I. M. Pei's steel and glass pyramid that forms part of the new entrance to the Louvre. The monumental form is the one we know from Egypt, but the materials and the function, and thus the meaning, are entirely different. Egyptian pyramids were not meant to be entrances and exits for large groups of people. Once the Pharaoh went in, he wasn't supposed to come out. Moreover, the pyramids are solid. You can't see through them. Egyptian pyramids are extraordinarily forceful symbols of an autocratic society that put a lot of its resources into the final resting place of a single leader. I believe that Pei had a specific meaning in mind when he opened up the pyramid visually and physically. When he was an architecture student at Harvard, he was on the editorial staff of a short-lived magazine called *Task*. For that magazine Hannes Meyer, the socialist architect who succeeded Walter Gropius as head of the Bauhaus, wrote a piece called "The Soviet Architect." In that essay, Meyer spoke of an eighteeth-century design by Claude Nicholas Ledoux for a Woodman's House at his salt works at Chaux. Meyer saw this log hut, in the shape of a pyramid, as a revolutionary social statement, in which a form designed to serve absolutism had been given over to the well-being of a modest workman. Pei must have known this article, and I suspect it was somewhere in the back of his mind when he made a pyramid that still retains its autocratic aura but is open to the people. In so doing, he surely served the architectural ambitions of François Mitterand, who has more than once been called the socialist sun-king.

Modern technology and materials offer a range of new possibilities for the monument, just as twentieth-century sensibilities have reworked its purely formal properties. Electricity, I believe, made its monumental debut in 1889 on the Eiffel Tower. In earlier times, monuments were either entirely invisible at night, or else they had to be lit, inadequately, by candles, lamps, and torches. Electric light allowed the monument not only to have a new life in the dark, but even to extend its reach into the surrounding space by means of searchlights. The skeletal structure of the Eiffel Tower presents little mass to reflect light, and so the effect is more one of rows, points and beams of brightness. The white stone faces of the Washington Monument, on the other hand, present the lighting designer with the opportunity to turn it into a glowing needle of light that can be doubled in the reflecting pool to make an image that might almost bring to mind Barnett Newman.

Newman, of course, did a famous obelisk himself, but a broken one that was conceived only as a piece of free-standing sculpture. One version of the Broken Obelisk, however, ended up in Houston, where John de Menil set it up in a pool as a memorial, and thus a monument, to Martin Luther King, Jr. This brings up another point about monuments. They didn't always start out as monuments. For instance, on our page of monuments in *Webster's Dictionary*, the Church of the Invalides in Paris is labeled Tomb of Napoleon. That was hardly the function Louis XIV had in mind when it was built as a hospital church for his soldiers and stood as a monument to his military might. When the dome began to shelter Napoleon, the meaning of the monument changed, just as Newman's Broken Obelisk acquired a new significance in that pool in Houston. We might also recall that Trajan's triumphal column in Rome was transformed into a monument to the triumph of Christianity over paganism by Pope Sixtus V, who, in the late sixteenth century, had a statue of St. Peter placed atop it.

We should also consider how all these monuments are placed, at the centers of large spaces, or at the ends of long vistas, where they can be seen and appreciated in all their magnificence. The Statue of Liberty has perhaps the most challenging task: commanding the whole of New York Harbor, and welcoming those who sail into it. The purport of her position and gesture were not lost on Claes Oldenburg, who, in 1969, made a drawing for a "Proposed Colossal Monument, Fan in Place of Statue of Liberty." That outrageous machine would have blown your tired, your poor, your huddled masses back whence they came.

Monuments, set out in the weather, are attacked by numerous antagonistic forces. Beset by pigeons, they look slightly ridiculous, as in the fountain in Detroit photographed and published in *The American Monument* by Lee Friedlander. Monuments also have to compete with the man-made environment, as well as with nature. The best can hold their own, even in New York, illustrated by Friedlander's shots of Father Duffey and George M. Cohan in the Times Square area. Cohan seems more at home. I'm not sure that's because it seems right for him to be giving his regards to Broadway, or because of the formal properties of the statue. Even though he's oversized and up on a pedestal, he's still strolling down the street, just like the people who pass him by.

Where a monument is placed, of course, is crucial. You have to wonder who made the decision to put a battling Doughboy alongside the main street of Stamford, Connecticut. He seems completely out of place. And the Boy in Blue in Milton, Vermont, stands at a forlorn intersection where no one can approach him to contemplate the heroism for which he stands. Why was he put in such an unpromising spot?

Sometimes some careful digging will reveal why a monument is placed where it is. One of the most startling, in terms of placement, is the Ames Monument, which rises at the top of Sherman Pass, between Cheyenne and Laramie, Wyoming. Designed by Henry Hobson Richardson and built between 1880 and 1882, this pyramid of rusticated local stone originally rose alongside the tracks of the Union Pacific Railroad, whose route, the first to cross the continent, had been completed ten years before. Passengers traveling Union Pacific must have been shocked to see, in the middle of the now vanished little town of Sherman, such an enormous sign of civilization. On two of the faces of the pyramid are portrait busts of the brothers, Oakes and Oliver Ames, whose names are recorded on a plaque on a third face. These men were heirs to a fortune made from manufacturing shovels. Shrewd New Englanders, they tried to parlay their millions, through complex financial manipulations, into even more, created out of the building of the Union Pacific. Oakes was a congressman from Massachusetts. His attempts to obtain protection from investigations into his financial activities by giving stock to his fellow members of Congress backfired. He was condemned by the House, and he voluntarily retired to his home in North Easton, where he died in 1873. Oliver died four years later. The railroad set out to rehabilitate the brothers' reputations through this pyramid, a defiant gesture of corporate pride set at the highest point of the railroad, 8,275 feet above sea level. There, at Sherman, all trains paused to be inspected before descending the steep grades to east and west. In its first years, the railroad ran in each direction, one passenger train a day, with the capacity of about 100 people. Perhaps, then, some 60,000 viewers annually saw the pyramid when the trained stopped at the top of the pass.

The setting is as dramatic as it is remote. Way to the south rise snow covered peaks of the northern Colorado Rockies. From a distance, the Ames pyramid joins those peaks as part of the panorama of nature, its truncated shape echoing the far mountains. That is clear enough from the numerous published views of it. What you can't see are the natural rock formations that populate the area near the monument. Of the same yellow-brown stone, these rocks break the horizontal line of the land just the way the pyramid breaks it. To many Americans of the late nineteenth century, the geological formations of the continent were seen as our monuments, our antiquity. We may not have had pyramids that dated from 2500 B.C., but we had great mountains and canyons and natural bridges that were far, far older. The Ames Monument partakes of that sensibility. It is a new work of man, set in the grandeur of the geologic past. In its form, it connects its heroes, those shovel makers and money manipulators who financed one of the great feats of the age, the transcontinental railroad, to that grandeur and that past. Through this pyramid, the work of the Ames brothers is compared to nature. It would have been impossible to make quite this same statement by building the pyramid in the Jersey Meadows. Following this vein, we should note that the United States is the only country in the world to designate natural phenomena of the second rank as National Monuments. Those of the first rank, such as Yosemite and Yellowstone, are National Parks, whereas sand dunes and singular shafts of rock, such as The Devil's Tower in Wyoming, are Monuments. They, too, act as reminders of the wondrous formal inventiveness of nature, and, once again, they are our antiquity.

Between 1877 and 1881 the children of Oakes and Oliver Ames built a library, a town hall, and a rockery back home in North Easton. The buildings were designed by Richardson, but the rockery, which I am not going to discuss, was laid out by Frederick Law Olmsted. I bring these structures up because they make a useful point for our purposes. The library and the town hall are memorials, the former to Oliver and the latter to Oakes. On the town hall are a number of decorative devices that take up a subject often discussed on memorials and monuments: time. On the left-hand side of the facade is a sundial, while the tower to the right is decorated with signs of the zodiac. In the dormer are the initials OA, for Oakes Ames. But the intertwined letters can also be read as AO, a romanized version of Alpha and Omega, beginning and end. These memorials are not monuments. They are functional structures in which the business of every day life can be conducted. Monuments, in general, are largely useless. They instruct and remind us, but they do not provide spaces we need to live our lives.

The Ames Monument in Wyoming is a rather modest example of the nineteenth-century passion for monuments. Indeed, I doubt that any other century in human history was responsible for so many enormous and totally useless structures, mostly dedicated to national pride.

The mother of all nineteenth-century monuments is that dedicated to Victor Emmanuel II, first king of a united Italy. After his death in 1878, an international competition was announced to design a monument to honor his achievements and celebrate the unification of the country. The history of this competition is particularly instructive for our purposes, because the terms of the competition ignored so many issues that we might consider fundamental in the design of buildings, but may not be fundamental in the design of monuments. Almost the only specific terms laid down were the dedication to the late king and the location of the monument in the city of Rome. No particular site or function was specified. The budget was to be lavish. That suggests that the Italian government felt that all that mattered, beyond a handsome design, was that the monument be in the capital city, and that it be expensive and useless. Projects that offered functional solutions, such as the one by Becchetti, got nowhere. Quite sensibly, Becchetti proposed placing an equestrian monument to the king in front of the Pantheon and flanking it by needed buildings for Parliament, buildings that Rome still lacks. The original winning entry—there were two competitions in the end—was submitted by a young French architect, Paul Henri Nénot, who proposed to erect a semicircular structure at Piazza Esedra, on top of the foundations of part of the Baths of Diocletian. Nénot was not insensitive to the history of the city of Rome. He saw his monument as a symbol of a new, third Rome that would rise alongside the great monuments of the earlier Imperial and Christian Romes. For him, Christian Rome was represented by St. Peter's, and ancient Rome was represented by the Capitoline Hill, at the bottom of the Corso, almost the only long, straight street to be found in town. The site at the Baths of Diocletian, nicely complemented and balanced those two locations, and it suggested the development of a new governmental quarter in largely empty land to its east. The eventual winner of the second competition, an unknown from Umbria named Giuseppe Sacconi, also chose the Piazza Esedra site for his entry, which was far inferior to Nénot's skillful Beaux Arts concoction.

When a scandal erupted over the choice of the foreigner Nénot, the whole competition was thrown out, a new competition announced, the entrants restricted to Italians, and the site specified as the northern slope of the Capitoline Hill, facing up the Via del Corso. That site had been chosen by the architects Piacentini and Ferrari for their entry in the original competition. The jury liked their location, the most visible place in the whole city, but not their design.

In the second competition of 1884 Sacconi won out over Manfredo Manfredi and over the German Bruno Schmitz, who somehow managed to get into the competition, even though foreigners were supposed to be excluded. All featured terraces, steps, and colonnades climbing the hillside and framing a colossal equestrian monument of the king. How big that monument turned out to be is shown in a wonderful photograph, taken as workmen celebrated the completion of the casting of the bronze horse by having some wine in its belly.

The surfaces of the monument abound in sculpture, all related to the Italian nation. The wall behind the king was supposed to be enlivened by enthroned figures of great men of Italian history, with pride of place on the central axis given to Garibaldi himself. Fortunately, someone was smart enough to nix that part of the project. No one, he argued, could imagine Garibaldi sitting still for eternity. Worse, Garibaldi would forever look at the king's horse *a posteriore*. No monument can afford such high risibility. Sacconi's design was superior to its competitors in at least one respect. It provided broader staircases and landings on which elaborate ceremonies of national pride could take place. The lessons of the grand staircase of the Paris Opera by Charles Garnier had not been lost on the obscure Umbrian nobleman. Indeed, one might see Sacconi's monument as the greatest of all nineteenth-century opera sets. Imagine, if you will, a chorus of a thousand voices standing on it to sing Verdi's *Va pensiero* from Nabucco, the piece that became the theme song of Italian unification. You may not recall the tune, but those of you who saw *Godfather III* heard it played by a sad little oompah band at the arrival of Michael Corleone in Sicily.

How we use and view monuments, of course, is a crucial question to keep in mind. Lee Friedlander's photograph of two middle-aged tourists at Mt. Rushmore brings the viewing issue into sharp focus, because it allows us to see the viewer and the thing viewed simultaneously. A few years ago I acquired a placemat at the gift shop in the building that stands behind the tourists. The quotation on the placemat tells us what the sculptor, Gutzon Borglum, hoped to achieve:

> I want, somewhere in America, a few feet of stone that bears witness to the great things we have accomplished as a nation, carved high, as close to Heaven as we can, then breathe a prayer that the wind and rain alone shall wear them away.

The image of the monument on the mat provides a reminder of what those few feet of stone look like. In the Friedlander photograph, viewers try to come to grips with the distant sculpture through binoculars, as if looking at details of the four heads might add to their understanding of it. Clearly, the monument is close to heaven; they have to bend their necks to see it. Having to look up at things almost always makes them seem more important. The tourists are also kept at a distance from the monument, and that distance can also make a monument seem more important, as long as you can grasp its totality from afar. Moreover, if a monument rewards close inspection—and I'm not sure that the heads of Mt. Rushmore do—then the experience of it can be all the more moving and enlightening. At the site, but not on the placemat, the monument has to work without the help of words. Borglum depended on the fact that the presidential faces are sufficiently well known to be recognized without clues from texts.

If a monument is a piece of figural sculpture, the question can arise, "Who is looking at whom?" In a 1982 project for the city of Mantua in north Italy, the contemporary Italian architect Aldo Rossi has taken up that theme. In one of Rossi's drawings, the architect shows a bird's-eye view of the proposal, which includes a semicircular arena looking out onto the harbor of lake-encircled Mantua. In front of the seats is a colossal statue of the poet Virgil, who was born nearby. Below is a drawing of a Roman gem, in which a man looks at a statue, and the statue looks back. The implication is perfectly clear, and certainly not innocent of the influence of a particularly famous drawing by one of Rossi's favorite architects from the past, the late eighteenth-century French neo-classicist, Claude Nicholas Ledoux. Ledoux's elevation of the interior of his theater at Besançon shows the theater reflected in an eye, which has to be the eye of a statue standing on stage. Perhaps the implication is that the work of art reflects the life lived by the people who look at it. We might carry this further and say that the good monument is one whose designer is observant of the ways of those folk the monument is intended to admonish.

Rossi has designed a series of monuments that take up issues involving the relation between viewer and monument. For the unbuilt Monument to the Resistance in Cuneo, 1962, Rossi proposed a semicircle of seats focused on a masonry cube. In this sense, the monument itself becomes the focus of a theatrical event. The cube can be entered by means of a pyramidal staircase that leads to an interior platform. In the wall opposite the staircase, a slit is cut in the wall to allow the viewer inside the cube a view of a ridgetop on which members of the resistance fought the Germans. The slit is angled toward the circular seats, so that a few people, sitting on the far right seats, might be able watch a viewer inside the cube look across the landscape at the site. In that way, they would be reminded of the hallowed site and the importance of the act of looking at the site by the performance of the viewed viewer in the memorial cube. Or, even if most people in the seats couldn't see a viewer inside the cube, she or he should become aware of the fact that the cube was more than a pure form, that it is also a kind of *camera obscura* that focuses our attention on a site where heroic deeds took place. The audience in the seats contemplates a device for contemplation and thus, in a larger sense, contemplates the very act of contemplation.

In his Monument to the Resistance at Segrate, 1965, Rossi placed an oversized, abstract sarcophagus in front of a set of steps on which viewers can sit and look at the monument. The lid of the sarcophagus is drawn back to rest on a column, and a set of steps leads up to a platform inside. A visitor to the monument can walk up into the ready sarcophagus, a foretaste of his or her own future, and then turn to face the audience in the seats, who can see in the visitor's action a preview of their own destinies. Here you might say death contemplates life, as life contemplates death.

The Vietnam Memorial in Washington, D.C., both continues and changes the things I have discussed in this chapter. The aerial view of the dedication ceremony in 1982, in contrast to the view taken in Rome in 1919, makes clear what the Vietnam Memorial lacks, and what you can't do there. Unlike the Lincoln Memorial or the Victor Emmanuel Monument, it is not axial, so that great processions of soldiers cannot march up to it, nor do ordinary visitors approach it on axis. It has no Altar of the Fatherland at its center, at which elaborately choreographed ceremonies can take place. It has no classical architectural forms, and no colossal sculpture, although the first scheme of its designer, Maya Lin, included an over-life-size figure of a man in agony standing at the angle where the two walls meet. She wisely took the advice of her teachers at Yale to eliminate him. Most importantly, the memorial does not rise up; uncharacteristic of all the monuments we have viewed today, it sinks into the ground. Instead of a great erection to national pride, Maya Lin envisioned, as she is reported to have put it, a scar on the land which would heal around the edges but would forever remain a scar.

In the history of architecture this memorial is of enormous importance for at least one reason, and this reason may explain some of the differences we see. As far as I know, it is the first major national monument designed by a woman. It is easy enough to do a pop Freudian analysis of the difference between Maya Lin's design and the Washington Monument—a difference that her own drawing makes manifest in the way she has shrunk and, in contemporary jargon, marginalized the "father of our country." As yet we have no significant literature on the differences, if there be any, between buildings and monuments designed by women and men. Thanks to a particularly brilliant seminar report two of my students did a few years ago, I am inclined to believe such differences may exist. These two young women, one now an architect and one now doing graduate work in art history, set out to study work by contemporary women architects. In spite of themselves, they began to see differences in the way men and women think about buildings. They tried their hypotheses out by studying a group of roughly 80 house models that had been submitted as final projects for another course I was teaching. They looked at the models and tried to decide which had been designed by women, and which by men. They were right, they told me, 85% of the time. Among the points they made were that women tend to place entrances at corners, rather than on axis; that women tend not to use the standard angles of 30, 45, 60 and 90 degrees in their geometry; and that, given the opportunity, women tend to integrate their buildings more fully into the landscape. I keep hoping that someday they will publish their hypotheses, because I think they would serve as a very useful basis for further discussion and study; their work has helped me to understand differences that a lot of us have felt we shouldn't even be looking for. If they are right, probably no man could have arrived at the Vietnam Memorial design, a complexly powerful and moving comment on that particularly equivocal event in our national history.

You might say that the Vietnam Memorial is a limited monument, its shape controlled by powerful objects outside its own borders. The two arms of the monument are aimed directly at the Washington Monument and at the Lincoln Memorial. As you walk up out of the center of the monument, your attention is focused on those two national icons. But you are flanked by that black wall of names, 58,000 of them, so many that you can never hope to read them all, or to come to grips with the loss of each individual life recorded there. The Vietnam Memorial overwhelms you by sheer numbers of names. At the same time, the shiny surface of that wall of words reflects the life around it: the trees, the sky, the Lincoln Memorial, even jets coming in for a landing at National Airport. The reflections fuse the dead with the continuous flow of life. Visitors, seeing their own reflections superimposed on the lists of names, become aware of their own act of witnessing those countless dead. People come to the wall to search for the names of those they knew. Theirs are not elaborately choreographed public rituals, but private acts of remembrance. 58,000 names bring back memories to a lot more than 58,000 people. The wall is also a place for something like public offerings. When I was there last month, I saw a crumpled fatigue hat, a big hole in its crown, laid at the base of the wall. On the brim of the hat someone had written, with ballpoint pen in capital letters, the words: "CHRIST YOU KNOW IT AINT EASY." That is the first line of a Beatles song, from their album *Let It Be*, that came out at the height of the war. The complete stanza—and you can be sure a lot of visitors to the wall remember the song—reads:

Christ, you know it ain't easy.
You know how hard it can be.
The way things are goin',
They're gonna crucify me.

Because of its shape, its words, and its placement, I would argue that for the brief time it remained in front of the wall, that hat became a monument. Although small of size and perishable of material, it was a potent reminder.

3. The Power of the Classical Tradition

James S. Ackerman

The basic forms of the public monument—the triumphal arch, the commemorative column or obelisk, and the equestrian statue—were established in Rome in antiquity and have persisted to an extraordinary degree in modern times. They were adapted in a variety of ways by later societies and differed a great deal in their aims, both from the original models and from each other. In contrast to Professor Johnson's incisive review of the monument in history, my triad of forms includes the distinction between male (column/obelisk) and female (arch).

Most of the ancient examples celebrated triumphs in war. The triumphal arch, memorializing various conquests, is best known through those raised in and near the Roman Forum by the emperors Constantine, Titus, and Septimus Severus (Fig. 3–1). The column of Trajan (Fig. 3–2), in the Forum of that emperor, is wrapped in reliefs celebrating a military campaign; equestrian statues such as the Monument of Marcus Aurelius (Fig. 3–3), placed by Michelangelo at the insistence of Pope Paul III on the Capitoline Hill and recently removed, represented the Emperor as a triumphant military leader. The appearance of even a kindly despot such as Marcus Aurelius as the centerpiece of the piazza of a communal government seems incongruous, but this government was not autonomous *de facto*; it was entirely dependent on the papacy.

The triumphal arch reappears in the "Torhall" at Lorsch, the entranceway to a monastery, during the ninth-century Carolingian revival of the antique. The arch does not have the superficial appearance of an ancient monument, but the three-arched passageway could not have come from any other source.

During the Renaissance, the appropriation of ancient forms and decoration was the norm. Equestrian statues were taken over and became a major type of public monument, as in the statues of the Gattamelata by Donatello and of Colleoni by Verrocchio, which stand on high pedestals in squares before major churches. As in antiquity, they celebrate military successes, in these cases of hired *condottieri*, and

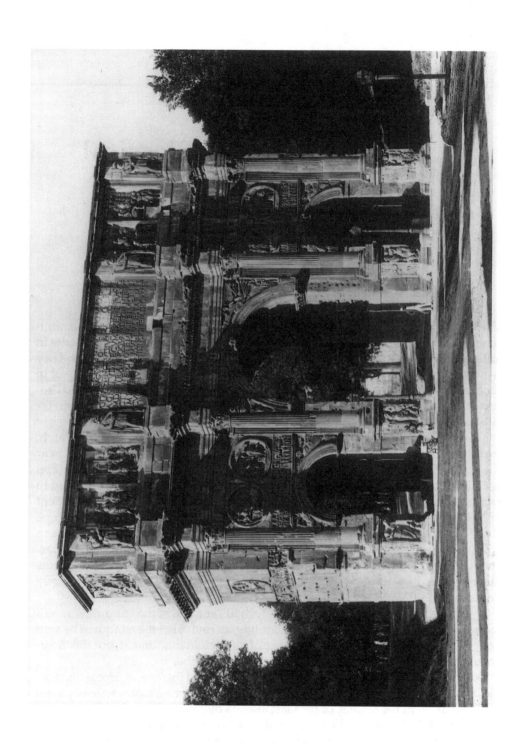

elsewhere often of heads of state. But Renaissance rulers rarely raised their own permanent columns or triumphal arches. Rather, they built temporary structures for festive occasions, such as the welcome of high-ranking visiting dignitaries. When wars were fought by hired help, conquest was not itself a great priority, except as it provided greater security. There was less need on the part of rulers to celebrate publicly.

To leap a couple of centuries, the centerpiece of the *Place des Nos Conquêtes* in Paris (later the *Place Vendôme*) of the 1690s was an equestrian statue of Louis XIV which overtly referred to his European conquests. The statue was destroyed in the Revolution a century later, and Napoleon renamed the square and placed a triumphal column in the center which imitates that of Trajan in Rome both in form—the spiralling reliefs—and function, recounting *his* conquests. The column in turn was toppled by revolutionaries during the nineteenth century as a tribute to the potency of the traditional message of power.

With Napoleon's destruction of the Parisian *Barrières*—customs collecting offices at the city gates—space was allotted to triumphal arches, such as that at the *Étoile* (1806–1836), which emulates the Roman antecedents but at the same time celebrates freedom from the old regime. At the opposite terminus of the axis (the *Champs Elysées*) from the *Étoile* is a remarkable conglomeration of monuments that brings together my three types: the arch of the Carroussel at the entrance to the Tuilleries gardens, an obelisk at the center of the Place du Carroussel, and an equestrian statue of Louis XV.

In London, two of the three types join in Trafalgar Square: the column raised in 1840–1843 to the memory of Nelson (a naval hero) and an equestrian statue of King George IV, built in 1843. The column is not Trajanic but Corinthian, taken from one of the temples in Rome.

The Corinthian form became popular in the United States: there is a column in Baltimore dedicated to Washington, who was the cause of numerous columns memorializing his dual role as general and first president. In Washington D.C., the Washington Monument on the Mall was initially an obelisk. The original project of 1841 envisioned a much less Egyptian design, with a flattened pyramid at the top and a large round columnar structure at the base. It is perhaps to be expected that Boston's first commemorative column, by Charles Bulfinch on Beacon Hill, was dedicated to an abstraction, Liberty, and that it was torn down not by revolutionaries but by real estate developers. Even at the height of the romantic vogue for the picturesque in American design, classical models persisted: Andrew Jackson Downing, the prophet of the picturesque, designed an informal landscape layout for the Washington Mall in 1851 that proposed a one-passage triumphal arch as the Pennsylvania Avenue entrance to the president's house. Washington Square in New York has another one-passage arch dedicated to Washington (1895). By this time, Roman architecture was the principal model for all public building, and the architect, Stanford White, was considerably more accomplished than Downing at

Figure 3–1   Arch of Constantine. 312–315 A.D. Rome.

Figure 3–2   Column of Trajan. Marble. 106–113 A.D. Rome.

Figure 3–3 Equestrian Statue of Marcus Aurelius. Gilded Bronze. Over Lifesize. 161–180 A.D. Piazza del Campidoglio. Rome.

recalling ancient antecedents. Yet White also designed a wooden forerunner to the masonry Washington Square Arch, which was Renaissance in form.

The equestrian statue celebrating Northern military leaders of the Civil War appears in many parts of the country. It declined as a type with the rise of the automobile, which makes a poor model for sculpture.

The arch, on the other hand, has retained its hold during the twentieth century. Perhaps the best known arch in this country is the one celebrating Jefferson in St. Louis, facing the Mississippi River and symbolizing the entrance to the Western frontier. It is entirely modern, though without quite abandoning classical roots.

Nonetheless, the classical tradition has been terminally stricken in our time, due in part to our loss of contact with ancient languages, literatures, and ideas, as well as with classical architecture. Attempts by postmodern architects to make ironic and superficial use of ancient motifs have probably quickened rather than retarded the decline. With respect to monuments, the celebration of military victory associated with the classical tradition is no longer welcome, given the mechanized and nuclear elements aspects of war. The Vietnam Memorial, which could be interpreted as an acknowledgment of defeat, may be the paradigmatic war monument of the late twentieth century; it might well be classified, as my wife suggested to me, as a wailing wall.

The era of the column, the triumphal arch, and the equestrian statue has neared an end; not only did it have an illustrious life in the ways that other classical survivals have, but it was more closely married than the others to autocratic power, and we should greet the close of its long life as a hopeful sign.

4. Monument: The Word

Wayne R. Dynes

Discussions of the monument by modern historians of art and architecture show a general agreement on the meaning of the term. In papers and lectures on the subject the word is not commonly defined, but a broad consensus appears to obtain that a monument is a tangible, material construction, usually of stone, brick, or metal, that serves to remind passersby of some person, event, or concept. There is, however, another main sense of the word monument: a written record. Thus when the Victorian scholar Mark Pattison wrote of the critical study of the monuments of Roman and feudal law he was not referring to the material monument as we usually think of it, but to written texts.

The English word monument entered our language from Old French, which inherited it from Latin.[1] The classical Latin noun already had the dual sense found in modern languages: a permanent and imposing structure erected to commemorate a person or event, which functions as a continuing reminder to passersby; and a noteworthy writing, or collection of writings, as the annals of a kingdom. This dual sense was buttressed by the derivation of the word from the verb *monere*, to remind, recommend, or presage. The Roman scholar Marcus Varro connected *monumentum* with *memoria*, memory.[2]

During the Middle Ages the meaning of the word tended to narrow, so that without qualification it means a tomb or a complex of buildings marking the *memoria* of a saint.[3] However, monumentum could also be used metaphorically to refer to the virtues of a good person that live after him or her as a continuing reminder. During the later Middle Ages, the popes, concerned about the threatened patrimony of ancient monuments in the Eternal City, began to refer to them in the old way as "Urbis monumenta."

It was the French antiquaries of the seventeenth and eighteenth centuries, with their concern for all kinds of material remains of the past, who most enlarged the meaning of the term. Bernard de Montfaucon includes in his landmark *Les Monumens de la monarchie françoise* (1729–1733) statues, reliefs, paintings, manuscript illuminations, textiles, coins, medallions, gems, seals, arms, tombs and regalia (such as crowns, scepters, robes, and rings). Other books of this period make it clear that noteworthy buildings of all kinds also fall under the rubric of "monument." In a work published in Italian, *Monumenti antichi inediti* (1767), the archaeologist Johann Joachim Winckelmann protests against what he regards as the magpie approach of the indiscriminate Montfaucon; instead of recording all and sundry, one should discipline one's taste so as to concentrate on the beautiful. What persists in all this semantic iridescence is the core Latin meaning of "reminder."

This duality expressed in the original Latin sense of the word—physical object vs. written text—underlies one of the most famous Roman poems, a text by Horace. This poem, which belongs to the last years of the Republic, I will compare with two other writings, one much earlier, the other belonging almost to our own day. But first the testimony from Horace. The concluding lyric of the three books of Odes that the poet published in 23 B.C. follows an established Greek custom whereby the last poem in a cycle ranks as the "seal" (*sphragis*), decisively concluding the whole. There are eighty-eight poems in the three books, covering an enormous range of moods and topics. The valedictory poem opens with the words "Exegi monumentum," I have completed a monument. Here is an English rendering of the text:

> More durable than bronze, higher than Pharaoh's
> Pyramids is the monument I have made,
> A shape that angry wind or hungry rain
> Cannot demolish, nor the innumerable
> Ranks of the years that march in centuries.[4]

Horace says that he has completed something more durable than bronze (*aere perennius*), higher than the pyramids. For his carefully wrought collection of lyrics he claims the two hallmarks of physical monuments: permanence and imposing size.

Thus Horace is not satisfied, as well he might, with the second meaning of the word—a written record—but goes further, invoking the architectural sense, specifically in the form of a pyramid. Moreover, though his monument rivals such works, what he has wrought is even more durable. Copied and recopied, memorized by countless admirers, his own construction will not be affected by the erosive force of the elements: angry wind or hungry rain.

It is a striking fact that this boast was anticipated in the record left by an Egyptian scribe writing some twelve centuries before the Roman poet:

> The names of the learned scribes of the age after that of the gods . . . remain preserved forever, although they departed once their life was ended and their next of kin are entirely forgotten. For themselves they have not fashioned brazen pyramids with iron funerary plaques. They left behind no heirs or children to preserve their names. As their legacy they have created texts, the Instructions. They made the papyrus roll their funerary priest, the writing tablet their beloved son. *Their teachings are their pyramids* [emphasis added], the pen their child, and the inscribed stone their consort. For them were gates and strongholds prepared, but these have gone to dust; their funerary priests have disappeared; their gravestones are buried in earth, their habitations for-

gotten. But their names are known through their books, since they were outstanding, and the memory of their maker will remain forever. Be a scribe and mark well that your name also be one of these.[5]

To be sure, this admonition originated long after the age of the pyramids was over, but still the claims advanced for the written word are extraordinary.

This is one of those instances of the influence (by whatever channels) of East over West, of which the artistic counterpart was surveyed by Rudolf Wittkower in the lectures so ably brought to publication by Donald Reynolds.[6] The Egyptian scribe anticipates Horace not only in the reference to the pyramids, but in the *aere perennius* theme—written words last longer than material monuments which the harshness of the elements and human carelessness will ultimately efface.

In a period in which literacy was very restricted, the prestige of the Egyptian scribe was considerable. When one adds to this near monopoly of craft the role that hieroglyphs played in assuring immortality, the claims of the scribe seem more comprehensible, though still grandiose.

Horace's reference to the pyramids shows the likelihood that he was influenced by such an Egyptian source, doubtless through the intermediary of Greek poetry from Alexandria in Hellenistic Egypt. Recently, very large claims have been made for the Egyptian origins of Western civilization. I refer, of course, to Martin Bernal's widely noticed book *Black Athena: The Afroasiatic Roots of Classical Civilization.*[7] Current disputes about multiculturalism are too broad and polemical a subject to be discussed here. But it does seem that the opening image of Horace's monument poem has an Egyptian origin.

The third text to be examined comes from a somewhat surprising source, the Russian poet Alexander Pushkin (1799–1837). Pushkin's poem "The Monument" was written in 1836 but was not published until after his death.[8] "I have erected a monument made by no human hands," he says, "the people's path thereto shall not be overgrown; it has risen higher with its unsubmissive head than Alexander's column." For Horace's generic reference to the pyramids, Pushkin substitutes a specific monument in St. Petersburg, the column honoring Tsar Alexander. The poet bore a grudge against Alexander as the persecutor of his family and the man responsible for his own temporary exile.

Tsar Nicholas erected the Alexander Column to commemorate the rule of his father Alexander I, who reigned from 1801 to 1825 and was victorious over Napoleon. The column was raised in Winter Palace Square by the neoclassical architect Auguste de Montferrand. The granite monolith, the largest in the world, was meant to surpass all other memorial columns, whether in Rome, Constantinople, or Paris. Dedicated in elaborate ceremonies in 1832 (which the poet contrived to miss), the Alexander Column marked one of the last achievements of neoclassical taste in the Russian capital, for under the influence of the Romantic movement aesthetic interests had shifted away from the universal values derived from the classical world to a new interest in the nation's past. Time proved Pushkin the winner, for his poem, in its splendid Russian original, is known by heart by millions of Russians, far more than know about the Column.

More generally, the Alexander Column stands in the twilight of the old monumental tradition of art in the service of the state. This tradition increasingly clashed with modernist ideals. Permanent celebrations of state power are out of step with the critical oppositionalism of so many modernists, and the imperative of irony, such a key modern concept, has no place for them. And yet, as we have seen, the monumental tradition answers to some perennial need, so that it did not die, but sought to adapt itself to a changing mental climate.

It was not just a mental climate that it confronted, for there is the logocentrism of our own culture. Even in the age of television, this deeply rooted attitude continues to grant a privileged place of authority to the written word. The comparisons just presented took us 1200 years before Horace's pivotal poem and and 1800 years after, spanning three millennia.

These specimens show the intersection of the two meanings of the word: the physical and the verbal monument. They also reflect something broader: a *bellum perenne*, the clash in our civilization of the verbal and visual semiotic systems.

Such is the result of a comparison of what all three texts have in common. But it would not be right to leave the matter in this state of conflicted suspension. If we return to the Horace's poem we will find—a few lines farther on—a different answer. For he evokes another image, the progress of the ancient Roman priest, accompanied by a Vestal Virgin, through the Forum to sacrifice on the Capitol. Such ritual observances had taken place for centuries and would continue, Horace believed, into the foreseeable future. Perhaps they did not endure as long as he would have liked. Yet the poet touches here on a more general pattern: the stability of human action sanctified by the values of the society. This continuity of meaningful action and custom, which anthropologists designate as human culture, is the social ecology in which both poems and monuments are embedded and on which they depend for their life support.

How important such support is we can recognize when we think of the threat to our own New York City monuments through a combination of neglect and vandalism. This process began, as a function of sudden social change and ideological conflict, in the 1960s. Yet the deterioration is not irreversible as a growing response of civic-minded individuals and groups has shown. Like other public inheritances, monuments require a "survival triad" of observation, contemplation, and preservation. Employed meaningfully in combination, this triad assures the restoration of the community of care which our monuments need to live in good health. In assuring this continuity we assist our own survival.

NOTES

1. For the range of meanings and usage in older French, see Walter von Wartburg, *Französisches Etymologisches Wörterbuch* (Basel: Zbinden, 1967), 6:2, 121–22; for Latin senses, see P. G. W. Glare, ed., *Oxford Latin Dictionary* (Oxford: Clarendon Press, 1982), 1132.

2. Roland G. Kent, ed. and trans., *Varro on the Latin Language* (Cambridge: Harvard University Press, 1938), 216–17.

3. On the postclassical development of the word, see Norbert Wibiral, "Ausgewaehlte

Beispiele des Wortgebrauchs von 'Monumentum' und 'Denkmal' bis Winckel-mann," *Oesterreichische Zeitschrift für Kunst and Denkmalpflege* 36 (1982): 93–8.

4. The translation is by James A. Michie, *The Odes of Horace* (Harmondsworth: Penguin Books, 1967), 217. The Latin text of these lines is:

> Exegi monumentum aere perennius
> regalique situ pyramidum altius,
> quod non imber edax, non Aquilo impotens
> possit diruere aut innumerabilis
> annorum series et fuga temporum.

A recent commentary is Hans Peter Syndikus, *Die Lyrik des Horaz: Eine Interpretation der Oden* (Darmstadt: Wissenschaftliche Buchgesellschaft, 1973), 2:272–7. Of considerable general value is the older standard work by Eduard Fraenkel, *Horace* (Oxford: Oxford University Press, 1957).

5. This connection was pointed out by Harald Fuchs, "'Nun, o Unsterblichkeit, bist du ganz mein . . . : Zu Zwei Gedichten des Horaz," in *Antiphron: Edgar Salin zum 70. Geburtstag* (Tübingen: J. C. B. Mohr, 1962), 149–66. The apparent borrowing is connected with Augustus' Egyptian politics by I. Borzsák, "Exegi monumentum aere perennius . . . ," *Acta Antiqua Scientiarum Hungaricae*, 12 (1964): 137–47 (the excerpts cited above are translated from the German text given in this article). In the same periodical, see also I. Trencsényi–Waldapfel, ". . . Regalique situ pyramidum altius," 149–67.

6. *Selected Lectures of Rudolf Wittkower: the Impact of Non-European Civilizations on the Art of the West* (Cambridge: Cambridge University Press, 1989).

7. Volumes I, II (New Brunswick, N.J.: Rutgers University Press, 1987, 1991).

8. See Waclaw Lednicki, "Grammatici certant: Puskin's "Aleksandrijski stolp," *Harvard Slavic Studies* 2 (1954): 241–63. For this reference, and other bibliographical assistance, I am indebted to my research associate Warren Johansson.

5. The Evolution of Humanness

Ian Tattersall

The reader may wonder what a biologist might conceivably contribute to a volume devoted to monuments, that most culturally driven of all expressions of the human spirit. I wondered, too, when I was first asked to provide a biological background to the subject. But then I realized that this issue of monuments impinges squarely on a central question that must ultimately face all students of human evolution: the problem of recognizing how, when, and, if possible, why humans first acquired the traits that make them so remarkably distinct from any other of the many millions of living species that populate the earth. As long as we accept that *Homo sapiens* did not spring fully fledged into being in September, 4004 B.C., but is instead the result of a long and complex evolutionary history stretching back ultimately to over 3.5 billion years ago, then we must, at least in principle, be able to identify some point, or points, at which our lineage acquired our distinctive characteristics—among which we must number that urge and those abilities that have produced monuments ever since population sizes and technologies burgeoned to the point that made this activity possible.

This, then, is my purpose: to examine the human fossil and archaeological records, at least in a preliminary way, with the aim of identifying just when it was that members of our lineage became human in the sense that they possessed the cognitive capacities—if not the economic means—that underlie the creation of monuments. This will at least help provide some perspective on what it means to be human, and on what it signifies when we use this singularly ill-defined term.

Let us start, then, at the point at which our precursors diverged from the ancestors of our closest relatives living today. For the paleontologist such as myself, tracing the origins of the human lineage is a comparatively straightforward task, if not necessarily a simple one. In essence, over the past century the attention of those who study the human fossil record has focused on one or another of four character complexes. Each of these is reflected to one extent or another in human

skeletal anatomy, and is thus at least to some degree accessible in the paleontologi-
cal record. They comprise the large and internally reorganized human brain; bipedal walking, which involves considerable modification throughout the
skeleton; reduction of the face and (particularly) the canine teeth; and our unparalleled manual dexterity, which is directly, if subtly, reflected in the structure of the
bony elements of the hand.

Over the years opinions have varied as to which of these complexes is para-
mount. Back in the 1920s Sir Arthur Keith chose brain size as the critical factor in
determining human status, with his "cerebral Rubicon" of 700 ml of brain volume
(later raised to 750 ml: apes average around 400 ml, while the modern human
mean is about 1400 ml). In the early 1960s attention was very much on canine reduction (now generally given less weight since it is clearly not correlated with
tool-use) and, as reflected in the specific epithet *habilis* given to the claimed early
Homo from Olduvai, on manual dexterity, even though these two attributes were
never quite so baldly presented as boundaries to be crossed. Today's Rubicon
seems to be the fourth member of the quartet, the acquisition of upright posture.
This is less a matter of assumed theoretical importance, as brain size was to Keith,
than one of chronology: in effect the general belief among human paleontologists
seems to be that the possession of any one of these complexes by a hominoid pri-
mate may be taken as evidence for inclusion of that form in the human family (or
subfamily, or tribe, depending on your classificatory taste;[1] for the sake of simplic-
ity I will here refer to a family *Hominidae*, containing *Homo sapiens* and its close fossil relatives); and upright posture appears to have been the first of them to emerge.

But there is a certain narrowness to viewing human evolution simply as a matter
of the acquisition within the human lineage of various bony structures. Of course,
to allocate a species to the zoological family Hominidae, to which among living
organisms *Homo sapiens* uniquely belongs, is undeniably to say that it is "human"
in a sense. Nonetheless, ever since it became apparent with the advent of evolutionary thought that *Homo sapiens* is not separated from the rest of nature by a narrow but bottomless divide, it has been clear that the adjective "human" lacks
precise or even adequate definition. This vagueness notwithstanding, it still
seems to me highly dubious that we would intuitively recognize our most ancient
ancestors as "human" were we to meet them in the flesh, or could under those circumstances justify using this term to describe them as functioning beings.

What, then, do we mean by "human"? Where in our lineage do we start to pick
up evidence of "humanity" of the kind that we might recognize intuitively in the
living being? And, in the context of this symposium, what early evidence might
we expect to find preserved of that particular aspect of the human makeup which
impels the building of monuments? There exists today no absolute answer to the
first of these questions, and the prospect of attaining one seems increasingly remote as scrutiny of the great apes reveals ever more details in which they resemble
us, particularly in aspects of cognition. I personally find the second question easier, if only because of its intuitive aspect; but because of that aspect others might
well draw the line differently. Surprisingly, the third question is perhaps the most
broachable of the three, for reasons which will emerge later. Let us, then, look

briefly at the record of human physical and cultural evolution to see what of relevance to the latter two questions may be extracted from it.

Before about 4 or 5 million years (myr) ago, human ancestry is effectively undocumented. Most anthropologists reckon that the ancestral human species diverged from the ancestor of one (more likely than both) of the African ape genera in the period between about 6 and 9 myr, but substantial fossil evidence is lacking until about 4 myr, when eastern Africa begins to yield fossils generally ascribed to the species *Australopithecus afarensis* (Fig. 5–1). These hominids were small-bodied, the males standing about four feet, six inches tall and the females perhaps a foot shorter; their brains were relatively larger than those of the living apes, but not by much; they had large chewing teeth with substantially reduced canines housed in a projecting face; and their body proportions were completely different from ours, with long legs and short arms compared to trunk length. But they had crossed the bipedal Rubicon: these early hominids walked upright, as attested not only by numerous details of their skeletal structure, but by the famous fossil footprints, some 3.6 myr old, found at Laetoli, in Tanzania. These prints, made in a light volcanic ash dampened by rain and preserved by a subsequent ashfall, show a generally human gait and footform, even though anatomical studies on fossil bones suggest that *A. afarensis* may have retained a substantial climbing component in its behavioral repertoire. There is no evidence, however, that these primates made tools, which only begin to turn up in the geological record well over a million years later. They were, thus, human only in the narrow sense that they were hominid, belonging in our own zoological family; it seems unlikely to me that, meeting them in the flesh, any of us would recognize them as human in any functional, particularly cognitive, sense. There is, indeed, a growing tendency among paleoanthropologists to emphasize the "apelike" characteristics of *Australopithecus*. Here, though, it is only fair to add that the concept of "apeness" is even more poorly defined than that of "humanness," and that what we are seeing in these creatures is the overwhelming of the few evolutionary novelties that they share with later hominids by the preponderance of retained primitive characters.

Sites in southern and eastern Africa from the period between about 3 and 2 myr have yielded remains of the slightly more lightly-built *Australopithecus africanus*, while a (cranially at least) more robust lineage whose members are increasingly allocated to the closely related genus *Paranthropus* are known in the region from about 2.6 to 1.0 myr. It is possible that *Paranthropus* was a slightly more dedicated vegetarian than *Australopithecus*, and it has recently been argued, very controversially, that it made tools; but in all likelihood early hominid lifestyles did not change much between 4–5 and 2.5 myr ago. During this period small bands of hominids roamed the African savannas supporting themselves by foraging and perhaps some scavenging: it has even been argued recently that the early hominids developed behaviorally as they did in order to exploit leopard kills, often dragged into the trees that dot the savanna and then left unguarded for hours at a time.

It is not until about 2.5 myr that we find evidence for any major behavioral innovation, with the production of the first stone tools. These are pretty miserable affairs, it's true (and remained so for a million years): small pieces of stone chipped on one side or occasionally two to produce a cutting edge; indeed, many feel now-

Figure 5–1   Two bipedal *Australopithecus afarensis* at Laetoli, Tanzania, as shown in a diorama at the American Museum of Natural History. Original sculptures, by John Homes, are life-size, the male (left) about four feet, six inches tall.

adays that it was probably the simple flakes knocked off in this process that were actually used for cutting. What may be most important in the present context, however, is that the earliest toolmakers showed evidence of foresight, carrying appropriate materials with them to be shaped into tools as needed, in places where the kind of rock involved was not necessarily to be found. In a strict sense, apes make tools (stripping twigs to extract termites from their mounds, for instance), but they do this in an ad hoc way, picking up materials at the place of end use. Anticipating one's material needs seems to be a behavioral attribute that is unique to our lineage, and one of the first to be acquired. What its behavioral corollaries were among the earliest toolmakers remains anyone's guess.

What is missing at these earliest eastern African tool sites, however, is any evidence of the beings that made them. Not until a little over 2 myr ago, still in eastern and southern Africa, do we have any evidence of a new kind of hominid with whom stone tools can be associated. This new form is widely known as *Homo habilis* ("handy man"), but over the quarter century that has elapsed since its initial description, this species has acquired a motley assortment of fossils. I have no doubt that this assemblage will be broken up over the next few years; at this point it is simply worth mentioning that the few postcranial elements that have been associated with *Homo habilis* do not suggest any major change in body size or proportions from the primitive condition of *Australopithecus*, even though in some cases, at least, there is evidence of some increase in relative brain size: for instance, the famous 1.9-million-year-old ER-1470 skull from Kenya, which is now widely attributed to a different species, *H. rudolfensis*, has a brain volume estimated at about 750 ml.

For true innovation it was not necessary to wait long, however. At around 2 myr ago or slightly less we begin to encounter, still in Africa, fossils usually ascribed to the species *Homo erectus* (although perhaps better allocated to a different, albeit closely related, species *H. ergaster*). *Homo erectus*, first described on the basis of Javanese fossils under a million years old, is the first early hominid to have displayed effectively modern body size and proportions and to have dispersed (earlier than 1 myr ago) beyond Africa. But at around 1000 ml its brain was no more than intermediate in relative size between those of its antecedents and modern humans, and it was housed in a flattish skull overhung in front with prominent brow ridges (Fig. 5–2). Its face projected somewhat, and housed chewing teeth much smaller than those of its predecessors but still of substantial size. Moreover, for some time after its appearance in Africa *Homo erectus* produced crude stone tools of the kind also associated with *Homo habilis*. When technological change occurred it was not correlated with any detectable biological change, reflecting a pattern that is standard throughout human evolution. It was thus at about 1.5 myr ago, well after *Homo erectus* (or its close relative) was established in Africa, that it began to make more sophisticated tools of "Acheulean" type, typified by the large, bifacially-flaked pointed "handaxe" and the straight-edged "cleaver."

It is with *Homo erectus* that we encounter hominids who might begin to fit a functional definition of "human," certainly in the sense that they cannot be considered "apelike." Nonetheless, although there is growing evidence of the use of fire by *Homo erectus*, the trend among archaeologists today is to play down the behavioral

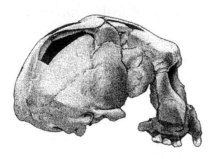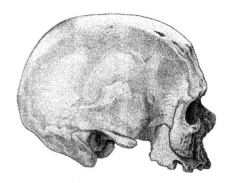

Figure 5–2 The best-preserved *Homo erectus* cranium (*Sangiran 17*) from Java (left), compared to the "Old Man of Cro-Magnon," an anatomically modern *Homo sapiens*. The Java fossil, with a relatively small braincase and large face, may be over 1 million years old; the large-brained, small-faced Cro-Magnon cranium is about 30,000 years old. Both scales are 1 cm. (Drawn by Don McGranaghan.)

sophistication of these hominids, once considered to have been skilled hunters but now widely thought still to have been principally scavengers, at least of medium-sized and larger game. Had we been around to do so, perhaps we would have thought these creatures pretty human, or at least humanlike, until we tried to talk to them.

Homo erectus persisted until perhaps only about 200 thousand years (kyr) ago in the Far East (where stone tool types remained crude throughout, perhaps due to the use of bamboo as an alternative material). It was, however, replaced in Europe around 500 kyr ago by a larger-brained form usually viewed as an "archaic" variant of *Homo sapiens*, but clearly deserving its own specific status, as (probably) *Homo heidelbergensis*. By this time the current cycle of climatic deteriorations or "Ice Ages" in northern latitudes was well underway. Cold phases ("glacials") marked by expansion of the ice cap at approximate 100 kyr intervals were interspersed with warmer "interglacials," with many minor oscillations in between. The stone tools initially associated with these earliest Europeans were remarkably crude, but at some time over 200 kyr ago a new technological innovation appeared. This involved the production of fully shaped stone "cores" from which an almost completed tool could be detached with a single blow. In this general time period we also find the first evidence for artificial shelters (Fig. 5–3). These were simple frameworks of saplings presumably covered with hides; we know from studies of the wear on stone tools of this period that hides were being scraped to make them usable in this way. There is also some evidence for an improvement in hunting techniques, but the archaeological record does not yet contain anything suggestive of ritualized or symbolic activities. In other words, while successive hominid species were steadily acquiring traits in common with us, at this point they had yet to show evidence of those more abstract qualities of the mind of which almost everyone thinks first when compiling lists of attributes that distinguish us from our closest relatives alive today.

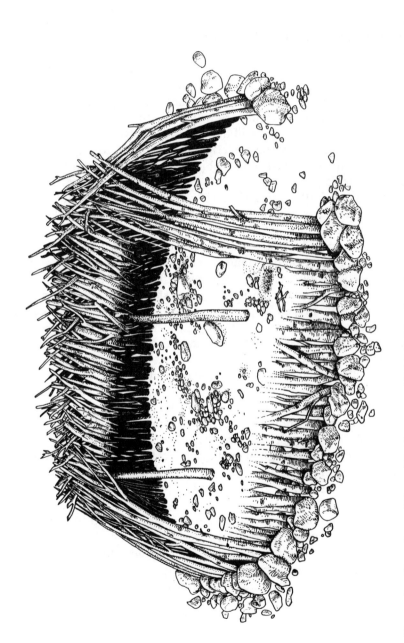

Figure 5–3 Reconstruction of one of the earliest known artificial shelters from Terra Amata, southern France, about 400,000 years old. The side has been cut away to show the interior, with a hearth in the depression at right. Original shelter was about 25 feet log. (Drawn by Diana Salles.)

The "prepared-core" stoneworking technique was taken to its zenith by *Homo neanderthalensis*, a distinctive form conventionally but erroneously viewed as a subspecies of *Homo sapiens* and known from Europe and western Asia in the period between 150 (or perhaps even 200) kyr and about 32 kyr ago. Modern *Homo sapiens* replaced them rather abruptly in western Europe at the end of that period, though as we will see the situation was more complex elsewhere. Although the Neanderthals had brains fully as large as our own, these were rather different in external shape. The Neanderthal skull was long and low, in contrast to the short high vault of *Homo sapiens*, and the Neanderthal face was large, hafted in front of rather than beneath the braincase, and curiously projecting in the midline. These people lacked a chin but possessed well defined brow ridges, and also differed from us in a number of details of the postcranial skeleton, including robusticity. Modern humans are, in fact, rather remarkable for the lightness of build of their musculoskeletal systems.

Behaviorally, the Neanderthals are an interesting case: they made beautiful stone tools, but, as the late François Bordes once remarked, they did so "stupidly." They made tools of many kinds, but their "Mousterian" toolkit was uniform everywhere the Neanderthals occurred. This by itself is very different from what we find among the Upper Paleolithic ("Cro-Magnon") modern humans who eventually replaced them, and indeed it is probably easiest to understand the Neanderthals by contrasting them with the Cro-Magnons. Neanderthals made stone tools, almost exclusively,[2] and held them directly in their hands; the people of the Upper Paleolithic used bone, antler and ivory as well as stone, and commonly hafted their tools. Caches of pigments, such as ochre, have been found at Neanderthal sites, but we are forced to conclude that they were used for body painting, since the decorative works for which the Upper Paleolithic is famous—carved, engraved, drawn, painted—are virtually absent at Neanderthal sites. Neanderthals, whose time on earth spanned both an interglacial and the rigors of a glacial, and who lived in northern latitudes, virtually certainly wore hide clothing; but it was not the tailored clothing permitted by the Upper Paleolithic invention of the bone needle.

We can make such contrasts over and over again, yet I must confess to difficulty in refraining from referring to the Neanderthals as "people" (yet another undefinable term!). Perhaps this is because there is undisputable evidence that they cared for each other in a social as well as individual sense. At the cave of Shanidar in Iraq, for instance, were found the remains of an oldish man who had been disabled since childhood, and who could not possibly have survived all those years without the constant support of his group (which must have led at least a partially nomadic existence). And perhaps most significantly of all, the Neanderthals practised, at least sporadically, the deliberate burial of the dead. This, of all rituals, is perhaps the one that most closely reflects the ambiguous human attitude to individual extinction; which hints at a belief in an afterlife, or (which is almost the same thing) at the presence of an ego that is reluctant to acknowledge its own ephemerality. It has recently been argued that all of the presumed Neanderthal burials are in fact artifacts of excavation or interpretation; and misinterpretation certainly appears to explain many alleged instances of Neanderthal ritual, such as the "bear cults" of the Drachenloch and Regourdou, or the interment of the Monte

Circeo Neanderthal skull within a ring of stones. Yet, although none is as elaborate as some of those carried out by Upper Paleolithic people, many instances of Neanderthal burial simply cannot be explained away, and we have to conclude that at least on occasion the Neanderthals did indeed bury their dead—with all, whatever it may be, that this implies (and to the extent that monuments and memorials are the same thing, burial may have a special significance in the context of this text) about their perceived relationship to the world.

This tantalizing glimpse of the Neanderthal psyche aside, it is undeniable that these people lacked that spark of inventiveness and creativity which—along with ego and its alter ego, spiritual awareness—distinguishes modern humans. Would Neanderthals have built monuments if they had possessed the technology and the economic infrastructure? I don't know, but I'm highly dubious. Could they have produced the technology and the economic infrastructure? Frankly, I doubt it. But before we conclude on this shaky basis that anatomy—Neanderthal or modern?—provides a convenient measure of the achievement of fully human status in a behavioral as well as a physical sense, we need to consider one further factor. While Neanderthals were replaced in western Europe toward the climax of the last glacial by people who were physically, artistically, and technologically distinct from them, Neanderthals coexisted with anatomically modern people in the Near East for a long time: the earliest dates for sites containing "modern" fossils hover around 100,000 years, while the latest Neanderthal dates are not far off 40,000 years. More significantly for present purposes, though, the earliest anatomical "moderns" in the Levant were culturally indistinguishable from the Neanderthals of the region. Thus indisputable moderns from the Israeli cave site of Jebel Qafzeh, almost 100,000 years old, were found in association with archetypical Mousterian tools, and totally without any of the testimonies to the creative human spirit—the engravings, the notations, the figurines, the simple joy in the manipulation of multiple materials—that are present in such abundance in the Upper Paleolithic sites of western Europe. In this context it's thus perhaps significant, that the last documented occurrence of a Neanderthal skeleton in the Levant is penecontemporaneous with the first occurrence of Upper Paleolithic toolmaking cultures in the region.

To be fair, of course, such manifestations are not typical of all times and places in which the cultural remains of modern humans have been found, in Cro-Magnon days or since. Nonetheless, their absence is suggestive: it hints that our vaunted creativity and self-awareness, what Alex Marshack has termed the "human capacity," is a cultural rather than a biological acquisition. Or at least that its expression is (Fig. 5-4). So does the fact that the great art of the Upper Paleolithic, epitomized by such astonishing sites as Lascaux, or Niaux, or Altamira, represents the exception rather than the rule in cultural expression, the world over. The only alternative is to believe that a speciation event has taken place in the human lineage subsequent to the original acquisition of our modern cranial and postcranial anatomy. In principle, this might not be surprising: my own work shows that the anatomical innovations distinguishing two daughter species of the same parent species are highly unlikely to exceed the variation that can accumulate within a species in the form of geographic variation. The steps of anatomical evolution must thus be incremental, and rather small. But the first well-documented expres-

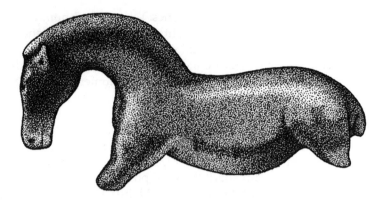

Figure 5–4   The earliest known example of representational art. Carved in mammoth ivory, this tiny horse from Vogelherd, Germany, is about 32,000 years old. Wild horses of the time were rather stocky; this image distills the graceful essence of the horse. Scale is 1 cm. (Drawn by Don McGranaghan.)

sion of the human capacity, namely the astonishing outpouring of Upper Paleolithic creativity, occurred relatively late (about 34,000 to 11,000 years ago), and in an unimportant geographical dead end in the far west of Europe. This argues strongly against the idea of a later speciation; for if this creative disposition were really a specific biological heritage of these early Europeans, their descendants would have had to have spread rapidly throughout the globe, and we know this did not happen. Besides, in a rather poor record there are hints of similar early expressions elsewhere on earth.

So, if we must conclude that the creative spark, the egotism that builds monuments or scrawls graffiti, was indeed inherent if unexpressed in the earliest people of modern form, why was it so long dormant (and why, indeed, has it been so sporadically expressed in the ten millennia since the end of the last glaciation)? Clearly, this vaunted quality is something totally unrelated to the basic business of making a living. If it were, it would have been expressed regularly and routinely ever since the origin of our kind. Rather, it has to be an unpredictable emergent quality, a byproduct, an accident, an exaptation if you wish. Also it has to be something that is spurred occasionally by social, economic, or environmental circumstance. Modern human cognition and its correlates are obviously a function of our large and complexly-organized brain; we certainly did not evolve this remarkable organ in order to send rockets to the moon, or to compose symphonies, or to browse through mail-order catalogues. Perhaps its acquisition was no more than pure accident; evolutionary novelties must after all arise before they can acquire a function. But enlargement and, presumably, elaboration of the brain have been continuing themes in human evolution ever since the beginning. I emphasize that the emergence of the human capacity is not simply the culmination of an inexorable trend; however, there is nonetheless something in the way in which hominids interact with nature or with each other that has predisposed our lineage to cortical elaboration (Fig. 5–5). I doubt strongly that we will ever be certain of what it is: if

Figure 5–5 Monochrome rendering of a now badly faded polychrome wall painting probably about 14,000 years old, from Font de Gaume, France. A female reindeer kneels before a male, who leans forward and delicately licks her forehead. (Drawn by Diana Salles, after rendering by the Abbé Breuil.)

pressed, most paleoanthropologists would probably mumble something about language or our complex social milieu, but these, too, are as likely to be effects as causes.

Well, if we'll never know for certain why we have our remarkable capacities, can we know why they are normally expressed in ephemeral ways such as the astounding skills of the Bushman tracker (in which we might, perhaps, usefully look for their functional basis), but sometimes in the construction of the great pyramid of Khufu? Here an economic element surely enters in. In the Upper Paleolithic of France cold times were not necessarily hard times: when the steppes crept southward to the latitude of the Dordogne they brought with them vast and varied herds of large-bodied game: a resource base of unparalleled richness. Of course, there is obviously much more to it than simple material abundance: no one can enter a decorated sanctuary inaccessible within an Upper Paleolithic cave without a sense of wonder at the impulses, so evidently noneconomic, that propelled men and women deep into the recesses of the earth by the feeble light of guttering fat lamps. Nonetheless, it is hard to imagine that the thousands of carved figures and plaques of sites such as the Mas d'Azil, or the elaborate decorations of a cave such as Lascaux, would ever have been made had the societies that produced them not been running sizable economic surpluses. Monumental architecture, of course, required larger populations and surpluses, possible only after the introduction about 10,000 years ago of settled agriculture, which in turn permitted the development of complex economies and societies.

It is almost invariably religion, spiritual or secular, that has been harnessed in such societies to focus the energies necessary for the creation of monuments; this brings us back to ego, for religious belief is probably the most universal expression among people of the ego, that consciousness of self which resists the notion of human ephemerality. Yet ego (perhaps unlike superego, which we share with dogs, also social carnivores) is surely the ultimate exaptation.

All this, of course, begs the issue of the origins of the urge to create monuments. I am pretty convinced that the uniquely human capacity that permitted the Cro-Magnons' outburst into art, music, notation, symbolism, ingenuity, technological advance and spiritual awareness following 34,000 years ago was acquired as a single package. And despite the apparent remarkable lag in its expression it is highly improbable that the acquisition of this creative capability and its associated impulses did not coincide with the achievement of anatomical "modernity" in the last speciation event we know of in the human line. If so, the urge to monumentality was born over 100,000 years ago—but simply as a potential that long lay dormant within the human psyche, awaiting the appropriate cultural, technological, and economic stimuli to express itself.

NOTES

1. It is now generally acknowledged that *Homo sapiens* is almost certainly not equally related to all of the great apes, but is more closely related to one of them (which one is debatable) than to the others. In a roundabout way the classificatory problem thus

posed has profoundly affected paleoanthropologists' views of what is properly called "human." Clearly, we cannot continue to use the traditional device of classifying all of the great apes in the family Pngidae on the one hand, and *Homo sapiens* and its fossil relatives in the contrasting family Hominidae on the other. Hominidae as formerly conceived has to be reduced not simply to the subfamily Homininae, but to the tribe Hominini. Because the dysphonic "hominin" sounds alien to the ears of all, there has been a tendency to substitute "human" for "hominid." The unintended (and unperceived) consequence of this has been the broadening of the meaning of the adjective "human" beyond all functional reason.

2. I refer here to durable materials; evidence from microwear analysis of Mousterian implements indicates that some Neanderthal stone tools were used to shape wood.

6. The Psychology of Monuments

Murray Schane

In the mid-1960s a major—one could say, *majestic*—cleavage occurred in the domain of the psychotherapies: with its full maturation and wide dissemination, family therapy came to occupy an equal but wholly opposed intellectual and clinical camp from the previously dominant and individually focused psychoanalytic psychotherapies. This fracture probably represented an extension or modern localization of ancient and familiar dualisms: the mind-body problem; nature vs. nurture; the concept of the mental apparatus as either being an endowment or an acquisition. Within philosophy, Locke, Hume, Mills, and the logical empiricists represent an externally determined, *exogenic* view of mind as having been formed, even created, out of encounters with an organized real world; whereas Spinoza, Kant, Nietzsche, and even Chomsky represent an *endogenic* view of mind as so innately organized and structured that it creates knowledge of the world out of unordered, naturally occurring data. Thus we have two opposite concepts of mind: one as formed by experience and the other as taking experience into its own preexisting form.

In psychotherapy a parallel dualism is represented, on the one hand, by psychoanalysis, which views the self as a mental structure ontogenetically unfolding and organizing it*self* through time and experience. Family systems theory, on the other hand, would view the self as a culturally localized referent, an element in a social system, and therefore the enactment of an externally originated concept about the self as a unit organized and arrayed within the total system of selves. Psychoanalysts therefore consider society to be the creation of developed, self-realized individuals; family therapists see the self as a product of society, an operative concept generated and sustained within a hierarchy of social contexts.

This dualism, threaded through the long history of Western civilization, surely must also wind through the history of monuments: what they represent, how they are perceived and appreciated, why they are built, what inspires their creation. A "psychology" of monuments, of course, refers ultimately to the mental representations of these objects by the self and by a society of selves. In considering how such representations enfold into our language, our perceptions, our conceptions, our understanding, we must examine the ways we delineate the self and honor its categorical importance both in the immediacy of sensation and cognition as well as in the various historical extensions through acts of remembering and memorializing. Thus the psychology of monuments requires us to track individual apperception along with social and aesthetic appreciation and thereby discover a reciprocating or reverberating duality perhaps not unrelated to the current duality within psychotherapy. Exploring the one may help illuminate aspects of the other and may also explain, at least in part, the factors and forces which maintain these dualities. First, we might examine how the division in psychotherapy functions.

Psychoanalysts assume that the self is an early life achievement—like language acquisition—and is formed out of learned paradigms of social expectation and self-presentation. To achieve change in the self, psychoanalysis must facilitate a reworking of these mental representations outside the real family, long after the "crimes," the acts, of familial interaction have been committed. Psychoanalytic therapy takes place within a kind of sanctuary formed between patient and therapist, a refuge which now functions as a laboratory for the controlled recapitulation and reconfiguration of early, formative family life.

Family therapy, by contrast, operates by focusing on social interactions which maintain individual family members as a functional, unitary system. Like cells of a body tissue, these individuals derive their identity and active existence—their *meaning*—from the whole they interactively compose, while that entire system also collectively contains and defines their individuality. In family therapy personal restructuring would be said to occur as the system changes, with behaviors and relational patterns providing a reconstitution of collective family existence. In this light the self may be seen as a contextually driven subset of that collective, a kind of dependent social variable. Family therapy therefore assumes that the self changes as the whole family system redefines, restructures, redistributes, and realigns individual roles, personal attributes, social agency, and autobiographical recall. Thus the self is held on the one hand to be a fixed primary structure modified by past confrontations with the family, and on the other to be a kind of individually localized, secondary derivative of continuous family process. This distinction between self and social determination and between a fixed past and an eternally fluid present is largely what monuments are all about.

Monuments, of course, are defined as things that remind: either by their mere survival and ensuing appreciation, or as things *intended* to commemorate. Here, then, is the beginning of a restatement of that old dualism: between a prior intention or preconfiguration and a later or subsequent recognition. Monuments may begin with an intent to realize through concrete objects the remembrance of such persons or historical events or abstract ideals as somehow deemed worth honoring and committing to perpetuity. From the moment of intent the monument then passes through an act of commission, a creation identified with the chosen object, and then achieves its function as a monument either in the immediate recognition of that object or in an induced or even fantasized remembrance of what the object may have been. Either we know the object memorialized—at least knew of it—or we construct the object from our own associated memories. Either we know the Burghers of Calais as Rodin intended us to know them and remember them (which knowledge and memory we would acquire quite differently from Rodin), or we inflame and inflate the monument with our own regard, with inventions out of a memory that extends perhaps *here* but not *there*. In effect, monuments are built (psychologically) over the gulf between the intentional, identifying constituents of one self and the collectively cognizing and recognizing selves of others. Moreover, we know this, we expect this of monuments: a self knows that there are others, that there are past lives and distant events and old ideals and that these, however remote, however unfamiliar, form and inform our sense of self. The appreciation of a monument entails this peculiar reshaping of the self around an abstraction of loss. We cannot know, cannot predict, can never anticipate how far the original intentional self may deviate from the receptive other. This psychological gulf, even if it primarily refers to one individual's time in death, is the acute and enduring poignancy of monuments. It is the function of monuments to be a permanent context for the idea of the self forever doubling back over ideas or examples or exemplifications about the self. In this way a monument, like a cultural idea (like a psychotherapeutic idea of the self), shadows its origins and its destinations and its own definition.

On the grounds of Creedmoor Psychiatric Center, which is a state mental hospital in Queens, there exists a monument erected in the form of a statue and a fountain (Fig. 9-1). The hospital itself was built in the 1920s on land granted to the state by the Creed family. State mental hospitals in that era were conceived as vast, long-term residential facilities for the chronically mentally ill who failed to recover from symptoms involving hallucinations, delusions, and publicly intolerable behaviors. By the mid-1960s Creedmoor had a stable population of over 5,000 patients. But in the 1970s a reform swept through state hospitals all over the country in the form of de-institutionalization. At that time, the predominating psychoanalytic view of madness had fixed its origins in the very earliest period of self-formation, during the "symbiotic" phase of mother-infant attachment in the first year of life. Failing to resolve that attachment and achieve a complete differentiation of self from the primordial (maternal) other, such individuals, it was thought, can never maintain adequate boundaries around the self and cannot consistently and reliably distinguish their own perceptions and experiences as separate from those of others. Intense thoughts and feelings would be misperceived and misread and misattributed. Mental patients then became tormented by thoughts and feelings from which they were alienated and by relations with others whom they experienced as invasive, engulfing, and frighteningly inconstant. Psychoanalytic treatment was available for very few such patients and seemed to work only rarely. The hospitals, as residential institutions, inadvertently provided a reduced environment for the repair of the self. Instead, they tended to foster a de-differentiation of individuals so that basic self-maintaining skills and ordinary social presentations of the self came to be lost.

De-institutionalization, by integrating mental patients back into the community, provided the possibility, with requisite supportive community services, of re-
storing and maximizing the recovery of the self. Medications like Thorazine,
introduced in the mid-1960s, ameliorated many of the symptoms of alienation and
misattribution and thus were seen to facilitate the process of de-institutionalization. Such drugs, however, led to subsequent—and now ongoing—studies of the
biology of mental illness. And this caused a radical shift away from the psychoanalytic view to an organic, medical one: that madness is a chronic biological disease,
like diabetes, and is therefore imposed on the self through externally originating
distortions of the mind. With such a disease model psychiatry has lost much—
some might same most—of its interest in the psychology of self and the indivi-
duating forces of social context. Thus, the state hospital itself has become a kind of
monument to a double loss of self: by the dehumanizing effects of institutions (with
or without walls) and by the lack of interest in issues of self-development and self-
realization.

For a psychiatrist, or any one familiar with this history and these issues, walking
on the grounds of Creedmoor Psychiatric Center invokes only an abstract, vague
sense of that loss, even as one watches the progression of stiff, vacuous patients
out on a pass, or as one declines to give a cigarette in response to a request which
seems as depersonalized as any beckoning vagrant hand. Indeed, this almost inex-
pressible, monumental sense of personal loss needs—*demands*—an edifice. And
Creedmoor has one.

The monument is a fountain occupying the center of a round reflecting pool,
centered in the oldest part of the hospital grounds. Around this pool clusters of
two- and three-storey brick buildings radiate. Most of these had been long-term
residential treatment wards, each series of buildings with its own iron-fenced
walkways enclosing open air gardens or pens with grass, shrubs, and trees. There
is also the central administration building on the west side of the pool and, opposite it, a "community center" that once was a hub of activity for the thousands of
patient residents. In 1969, soon after the massive discharge of some four thousand
patients, a twenty-one-year-old Queens College student, Raphell Lakowitz,
asked to become a volunteer at Creedmoor Psychiatric Center in order to enhance
her studies of psychology. Over the next few years she helped develop a program
of student volunteers working with patients in the hospital. That was a time of
great excitement and optimism in the field of mental health, as new hope for the
cure and rehabilitation of the insane seemed possible and imminent. In 1978, at the
age of twenty-nine, Raphell Lakowitz died suddenly of an aneurysm only a few
months before she was to be married. Within the next year her parents began planning a monument, with support from the Creedmoor administration. A fountain
was commissioned and finally dedicated in 1983.

Standing on a boulder which forms part of a raw, towering elevation of rock—
perhaps a mountainside—is a statue of Raphell, standing and apparently playing
with the stream of water that flows from the top. She is barefoot; her simple summer frock stirs in a breeze; her hair falls long and free over her shoulders. She is
smiling and seeming to delight in watching the water dapple through her out-

stretched hands. This statue is arresting because it portrays aliveness and spontaneity and even joy.

But it is seen, it is identified on first sighting, as a monument. First, because of its placement: all monuments seem fixed within (usually upon) a context that signals their purpose, their monumental nature: often this is a massive, sarcophagal pedestal. "Raphell" occupies the focal point of a formal surround: a radiating walkway and garden centering on the pool and its sloping, low pedimental wall. The statue seems isolated, unreachable, hauntingly unconnected. It seizes our attention but remains, despite the representation of the figure as moving and only momentarily dallying at that fountain, forever frozen and banished across a body of water like the mythical river that separates the living from the dead.

To most who see this monument, Raphell Lakowitz is a stranger, an unnamed object who may not have existed except as a sculptor's model. Thus the name "Raphell" is inscribed on the rock at her feet: just the first name, written in her own script. That signature both reveals her identity and further portrays the summary, monumentalized moment of her life: her youth, happiness, grace, and liveliness. On the pool wall is a large bronze plaque with Raphell's full name and a formal inscription:

Raphell

"As we give love, so shall we receive love"
"As we give strength, so shall we receive strength"

This statue honors Raphell Sims Lakowitz (1948–1978)
A volunteer whose radiant spirit fills our hearts with love

A gift of the Raphell Sims Lakowitz Memorial Foundation

Sculpture by Bruno Lucchesi
From a concept by Lenore Lakowitz

This plaque completes or rather, fully establishes the monument. Now the statue comes to represent the life—the once living person—so inscribed. In effect the monument serves to thrust that biographically, identifiably, characteristically unique self into the memory of a public, who having been introduced to Raphell, are also made to know her as a woman who lived and died and should be remembered. At the very moment that one perceives this structure, recognizes this pool and fountain and statue and plaque as a monument to Raphell, one passes through the divide between the self as its own creation and the self as one created and sustained by others.

The monument summons us, the others, to bear witness to the self, to particularize a life, a person; in effect, to rework our deeply formed concept of personal being upon the few, conventionally selected and highlighted traces of this once real self (such traces as her name, physiognomy, her role or life career as a hospital volunteer, and herself as object of the eponymous foundation). In this way we may re-create and thereby perpetuate her existence. And we achieve this, for her and for ourselves, by doubling back and forth between the general, even abstract, cultural concept of personal existence and the specific times and events and physical embodiment and real acts that constituted Raphell's life. The general concept serves as a base upon which we may project our own identification of and with the person that we must imagine had been Raphell. Such projection truly memorializes her and carries her life forward through a permanent, publicly reflective domain. And such a memorial also serves all of us, we the public witness, by reifying the possibility of all remembrance, the promise fulfilled of personal being encountered, perpetuated, and continually re-remembered as someone's life. The power of monuments, their psychological force, derives from this slippage over the dual poles of the self manifested in life and the self reinstilled, almost materialized, in those who look on, who reconstitute that life out of the known context of possible lives, out of the abstraction of personal being. In that act of renewal we also recognize our selves, our own lives readying for the sculptor's tool and preparing for remembrance.

7. Public Monuments

Mary Mothersill

What makes the topic of public monuments philosophically interesting is the demand that a public monument meet two independent requirements: we ask that it be beautiful but also that it make a point. Public monuments are assertoric: they convey messages and teach lessons. Assertion requires a language and hence every monument has a title, a label, an accompanying text. Architecture in general is often characterized as didactic: a severely modernist building will be said to "make a statement," but here the phrase is a metaphor. What it means is that the building suggests—perhaps is meant to suggest—thoughts of a general kind about art, the human condition, the meaning of life, and related conceptions. But no monument can, in this metaphorical sense, make a statement unless it is tagged with what is literally a sentence, or at least an identifying phrase, in English, French, or German. A pyramid, an obelisk, a tholos may be in itself an imposing structure but does not count, one might say, as a monument until a verbal message is affixed.

There is a bronze statue of a gentleman in a frock coat near where I live on Riverside Drive. I have looked at him for years without ever taking the trouble to find out who he is. Well, he is Samuel J. Tilden. That is something—but not much. (I associate the name with New York politics, and his outfit places him in the nineteenth century.) But the legend goes on to give an identifying description: Samuel J. Tilden was a "patriot, statesman, lawyer, philanthropist, and the Democratic nominee for the presidency in 1876." (His motto was "Trust the people," so it must have been a blow to him not to win the election.) Now at least I know what *sort* of thing I am supposed to be impressed by, but the tacit injunction to reflect on the merits of Samuel J. Tilden still lacks force since I do not know whether his reputation was justified by his achievements.

Another neighborhood monument, one that I like, is the memorial to Isadore and Ida Straus in a little triangular park at 106th Street and Broadway. There is a reflecting pool—or what was intended to be one, since it is seldom cared for—and behind it a classically draped female figure reclining on a low stone wall and looking pensively towards the water. Then there are benches and a curved background wall that tells us that the couple were among those lost on the *Titanic* in 1912 and a commemorative verse from 2 Samuel, "lovely and pleasant in their lives . . . in their death they were not divided." From Donald Reynolds' excellent book,[1] we learn that Ida Straus refused to join the other women in a life-boat but elected to stay and face death with her husband. The female figure depicts Memory and the sculptor was Augustus Lukeman, a Virginian who studied at the *École des Beaux Arts* in Paris and worked as assistant to Daniel Chester French. In contrast to the Tilden statue, neither the couple memorialized nor the sinking of the *Titanic* is depicted. There is no reason to think that Ida Straus resembled Memory, and the overall mood is one of tranquility rather than of violence and disaster. The message, as I read it, is that affection and fidelity can triumph over panic and confusion. I think that message is true (or sometimes true) and that it is a valuable thing to remember. Although it is not high art, the Straus memorial is graceful and unobtrusive and, in conjunction with the legend, teaches a lesson that is worth learning.

A monument is not a story but, in one way or another, an illustration of a story. Think of it like a sentence: once the subject has been fixed—and this is something that can be done only in words—then the structure functions as something analogous to a predicate. Marble, granite, and bronze cannot be true or false, but it is characteristic of predicates to be either true or false of their subjects. Hence it is possible for a monument to convey a message that is false, misleading, or morally objectionable. This potential is most obvious where representational or figurative sculpture is involved. Suppose that I erect a monument to Columbus, say, or Vasco da Gama or Cortez, and that on an accompanying bronze relief I show the hero surrounded by naked figures in attitudes of submission and adoration. What I thereby suggest and what is open to challenge is that the indigenous people of the land that was "discovered" were happy and grateful to the forces that invaded and conquered them.[2]

Not only depictive and narrative sculpture can be mendacious. A monument of abstract or allegorical design dedicated to the memory of someone not worth remembering is a kind of lie. Often such monuments are commissioned and certified by the subject himself. (Think of the Victor Emmanuel Monument in Rome.) Overt falsehood inspires indignation and rage. A monument is not only didactic but aggressively so. I could write a sonnet or compose a tone-poem in honor of the emperor: those who do not admire the emperor need pay no attention. But if I build a huge structure and put it in the middle of the public square, then no one can avoid looking at it or having to walk around it every day. Sometimes this visibility gives rise to iconoclastic violence. The first things to go in eastern Europe were the statues of Stalin and his regional representatives; the zeal with which the Berliners dismantled their Wall shows that they perceived it not just as a barrier and a source of frustration but as the assertion of a thesis that they wished to deny.

Here there may arise an interesting conflict. The Berlin Wall was not beautiful and there is no aesthetic reason to regret the destruction of the Stalin statues. But there do exist beautiful monuments designed to honor unjust, cruel, disgraceful persons or regimes. Their false message are overlooked and forgotten: they stand on their own feet and are admired not for what they teach but for what they are.

The Medicis, for example, had money and power but were not admirable people, except perhaps by virtue of their taste in sculpture and architecture. What happens then is that the project, as it were, misfires: when a person or a cause that is unworthy or obscure is memorialized by an artist of genius, then what people come to love, admire, tell their children about, is not the historical subject but the work itself and if any name is immortalized it is that of the artist, not that of the prince. (There are parallels in literature. The leitmotif of Shakespeare's *Sonnets* is the desire to enshrine the subject in verse, to defeat old age, decay, death, oblivion. But we can hardly keep green the memory of Mr. W. H. when nobody even knows who he was. What stands the test of time is the poetry and the name of the author of the sonnets.)

Assume then that there are monumental structures that are well-designed and visually beautiful; assume that corresponding to the distinction between worse persons and wicked ones, worthy causes and ignoble ones, there is a difference between true monumental messages and false ones. Then four combinations are possible, and I believe that without much research one could find examples of each. You can have an ugly monument with a false message, a beautiful monument with a false message, an ugly monument with a true message, and a beautiful monument with a true message. What one hopes for is the last of the four possibilities, and that hope is not empty. You will have your own examples. One of mine would be the Vietnam Veterans' Memorial in Washington.

Set in two open acres on the Mall in sight of the Washington Monument and the Lincoln Memorial, it is a polished black granite wall, sloping, angled, sunk in a broad trench, and inscribed with the names of the 58,000 men and women who died in Vietnam.[3] It was designed by Maya Ying Lin, an undergraduate architecture student at Yale: her plan was the first choice of the jury of professionals in an open competition in which there were 2,421 submissions. The eight million dollars that it cost to build it was raised from private sources—650,000 contributions—in a drive headed by Jan Scruggs, a thirty-year-old former rifleman with the U.S. Army, 199th Light Infantry Brigade. He began his fund-raising in 1979, and the Memorial was opened in November, 1982. Although it had been explicit from the beginning that the message of the Memorial was to be one of reconciliation, that it should, in the words of the committee, "heal the nation's wounds," at every step—fund-raising, congressional approval, design, location, the very idea that there should *be* such a memorial—met with bitter opposition; it seemed an occasion for reopening old wounds. There was, for example, the question of which names to include, and this issue depends on how you date the beginning of the Vietnam war and how you delimit its geographical boundaries. Why honor only those who died in action and not those who were (and are) dying of war-related injuries in veterans' hospitals? Why not honor those brave enough to go to jail for draft-resistance during what they took to be an immoral war? Why not honor everyone who served? (This last was a question with an answer: 2.7 million names was too many to have engraved.) As for the design, *The National Review* described it as "Orwellian glop" and said that the veterans deserved better. Tom Carhart characterized it as "A black gash of shame."[4] When it was worked out as a sort of compromise that a representational sculpture of three American soldiers should be erected nearby—a work designed by Frederick Hart that was completed and dedicated in 1984—the pro-Maya Lin committee members dismissed it contemptuously as a "Starsky and Hutch" production, and the name-calling continued.

I have a student who was in Vietnam and has been active in veterans' affairs. He tells me that he and his friends began by thinking badly of what they referred to as "The Wall" but were completely won over when they actually saw it and noted the responses of visitors. In the first two years, between 5 and 6 million people came—an average of about 20,000 a day. Many, even those not looking for names they know, touch the wall; many are moved to tears.

What accounts for the power of this monument? I do not think that it is the purely visual aspect, although that is striking enough. As for listing names, that is a commonplace: every war memorial has its roll of honor. One thing that is important in what I have called the message is that there is something that is left out. Jan Scruggs and his colleagues were clear from the beginning that the memorial was to be apolitical—it would, in his words, "say nothing" about the war. This position shows a reticence that is rare in war memorials. Remember that they are a species of funerary art:[5] they acknowledge and articulate private grief, honor, and devotion to duty, and they provide a focus for memory. But often they attempt to do more: it is terrible and sad to die, like Isadore and Ida Straus, in a shipwreck, but to die in battle is something different. Wars are not natural disasters; they are planned activities initiated and carried out by responsible agents. Hence the question of justification or excuse arises. If my child is killed in a war—bear in mind that the *average* age of those listed on the Wall is nineteen—then I can hardly help asking what was gained at the expense of my loss. Monuments that presume to provide an answer to that question are likely to strike us as offensive. Perhaps there are just wars (although I doubt it): the Vietnam War was, to say the least, open to challenge. But *no* war licenses the survivors to announce that it is sweet and fitting to die for one's country. Nor can allegorical representations—Victory in classical garb with her sword or her laurel wreath, Peace with her palm and olive branch—strike us as other than tasteless.

A final word about the Memorial: the names are listed chronologically by date of death rather than alphabetically—which would make it like a phone book. This design means that the Memorial can be read like an epic poem, that the names one knows will be grouped together. A second point is that the black polished granite acts as a mirror: in seeing the incised names, you see your own face and the sky behind you. Here is a reminder that you, the onlooker, have been and are involved in the death of these soldiers—a true and important message.

NOTES

1. Donald Reynolds, *Monuments and Masterpieces: Histories and Views of Public Sculpture in New York City* (New York: Macmillan, 1988), 213.

2. I once thought that the relief on the south face of the monument to Columbus in Columbus Circle provided an example. On more careful inspection I see that the kneel-

ing figure who appears to be kissing the border of Columbus' cape is in uniform and so must be a European. What he is doing and why are unclear to me.

3. The following facts and figures come from J. L. Scruggs and J. L. Swerdlow, *To Heal a Nation* (New York, Harper and Row, 1985). See also J. L. and S. S. Strait, *Vietnam War Memorials* (Jefferson, N.C.: McFarland Inc., 1988).

4. Carhart had been one of the ones to submit a design of his own. It was to depict in bronze an officer the body of a dead G.I. up to heaven as though in sacrifice; the officer was to be standing on a Purple Heart.

5. See Reynolds, op. cit., 9ff.

8. The Value of Public Monuments

Donald Martin Reynolds

Monuments are often simply perceived as another form of public sculpture, but they are more than that. Monuments are first and foremost reminders. They are embodiments and symbols of our traditions and values.[1]

We build monuments to people and events because those people and events are important to us for the values they possess or represent. In addition to communicating our traditions, beliefs, and values from generation to generation, monuments also help us to come to terms with the unknown, the unexplained, and the mysteries of life. They express our deepest emotions, both social and personal, such as the pain we feel at the death of a loved one.

In his discussion of the history of monuments, E. J. Johnson includes a picture taken in 1936 by the famous photographer Walker Evans of the grave of an unknown child in Hale County, Alabama.[2] The grave was marked with two pieces of scrap lumber and the child's cereal bowl; the arrangement of the lumber and the relic of the dead child was the family's memorial. With this monument the family came to grips with the separation and isolation connected with the death of their child. Because of the impermanence of the materials, however, that monument soon withered and disappeared. We do not even know the child's name.

The eighteenth-century monument to four-year-old St. Claire Pollock that stands near Grant's Tomb at 122nd Street and Riverside Drive in New York City is another matter altogether.[3] A marble base supporting a classical funerary urn, it is set picturesquely on a high bluff overlooking the Hudson River. Wild strawberries grew so abundantly there that it was known as Strawberry Hill, and it was St. Claire Pollock's favorite place. While playing there one day, he lost his footing and fell to his death in the Hudson River, two hundred feet below.

Because St. Claire so enjoyed Strawberry Hill and because the site was so serene and beautiful, his family buried him there and marked his grave with the marble monument. They inscribed it:

To the Memory of an
Amiable Child
St. Claire Pollock
Died 15 July 1797
In the Fifth year of His Age

That monument to an Amiable Child so endeared itself to the hearts of New Yorkers that a century later, when the city tried to remove the little monument and the child's grave to make way for Grant's Tomb, the citizens of New York rose up and said NO! "A monument to an Amiable Child, 'Who led no cause/Who only lived and died,' is as important to us as a monument to a national hero."[4]

And so Grant's Tomb was erected where it is today, and the monument to an Amiable Child remains intact. A newspaper reporter who witnessed that ground-swell of civic indignation expressed its essential meaning when he noted that the presence of that monument "is so fine a tribute to the gentleness that underlies the apparent brutality of a great city that the little stone monument [on Strawberry Hill] has come to be almost a national institution."[5]

The essential difference between the monument to the Amiable Child near Grant's Tomb and the monument to the unknown child in Hale County, Alabama, is that the material of one has lasted longer. St. Claire Pollock's monument, howev-er, is not going to last forever. But we want it to because of what it stands for: all that we cherish and respect in the innocence of childhood, with its beauties, hopes, and dreams. So we make our monuments as permanent and as beautiful as we possi-bly can because they symbolize the values we honor, cherish, and wish to pre-serve. These values give vitality to our cultural heritage.

Survival through Celebration

"The past is not dead history," the eminent scientist and Pulitzer Prize-winning author René Dubos writes, "it is the living material out of which man makes him-self and builds the future."[6] From our past come the timeless, universal, and ele-mental truths that governed our earliest evolution and determined our gradual development as human beings. By means of these truths we slowly achieved the intellectual and spiritual potential that has enabled us produce symphonies and conquer disease, as Ian Tattersall points out in his discussion of the origins of hu-mankind. With them we have pierced the cloud of unknowing that surrounds our universe.

When we lose touch with the past, Dubos believes, we lose touch with the inner self. We are cut off from what he calls "the deepest layers" of our natures, a kind of genetic and cultural memory bank. This repository of experiences and images en-ables us to understand the mysteries of the past that keep us in tune with our ori-gins and the rest of the cosmos.[7]

Dubos maintains that that sense of continuity with the past and with the rest of creation, which is served by our public monuments, not only enhances life but "is also essential to sanity" because it keeps us mentally and emotionally intact.[8]

In prehistoric times, primitive peoples believed that all of nature was interwo-ven into a single pattern and that they were a part of that pattern. These beliefs gave rise to complex rituals and taboos, the forerunners of our public monuments. Those who violated taboos or disparaged rituals did so at their own peril.[9] That primitive imperative resounds with meaning today for us, who neglect and destroy our public monuments at our own peril.

"In assuring continuity with the past through our public monuments," art historian Wayne Dynes writes, "we assist our own survival" by means of the "triad of survival—observation, contemplation, and preservation."[10] The social anthropologist Francis Huxley would say that monuments objectify those truths, which constitute our cultural heritage, and so provide us with permanent and tangible means to study and analyze them.[11]

"The wise man preserves that which he values and celebrates that which he preserves."[12] The key word in this adage is *celebrate*. It is not enough to gather at the base of a monument once a year and engage in religious, commemorative, or other ceremonies in which we honor the person or the event. Those ceremonies are important, to be sure, for they contribute to our edification and enjoyment as we join with others to honor the values that we wish to preserve.

Celebration in the fullest sense, however, is not restricted to formal ceremonies. The word comes from Latin and means "much frequented," suggesting continuity of involvement. To celebrate a monument properly, then, is to incorporate it into the everyday life of our society at all levels. Monuments should inspire us to study the people and events they commemorate and to contemplate the values they perpetuate. The monuments in our neighborhoods, for example, should be part of our grade school curricula, and they should be the objects of continuing study at colleges and universities. Monuments should be mini-laboratories of human values and the objects of interdisciplinary study and research. It is through celebration in this fullest sense that monuments become living forces that demonstrate the power of human values.

We should preserve our public monuments and integrate them into our society through programs of education and communication so that we might revivify the human values that they embody.[13] Art critic Hilton Kramer once took issue with this proposal. He said I was a dreamer, and how could I expect New York City to preserve its public monuments while encumbered with ravaged spaces such as the South Bronx. I pled guilty to the charge of being a dreamer, and in my defense I conjured up the testimony of Eugene O'Neill, who reminds us "It's the dream that keeps man fighting—willing to live." I answered Mr. Kramer's second charge with a case history.[14]

My wife recently visited a South Bronx shelter. One of the pupils pointed to a hole in the woodwork and said, "That's a bullet hole." He knew all about that bullet hole and the circumstances surrounding it. Yet that child knew nothing about the land on which his building was built—the country villages that existed there in colonial times and that persist today only in name. Landmarks are overlooked where he lives. These landmarks, if celebrated through Wayne Dynes' triad of survival—observation, contemplation, and preservation—would introduce that youngster to the glories of his past and his cultural heritage and just might inspire him to achieve his intellectual and spiritual potential.

Unfortunately, the South Bronx is not unique, as the murder of the two Jefferson High School students by a fellow classmate in Brooklyn reminds us. The principal of Jefferson High wants to raise a monument not just to those two students, but to the more than 20 other students who have met violent deaths in the halls and classrooms of that school. She wants the monument to be rows of trees flanking Pennsylvania Avenue and exist as living reminders of those tragedies and memorials to those youngsters. As trees are added, she hopes that perhaps someone will pay attention.

While the principal's plans are laudable, Hilton Kramer's attitude toward public monuments is not exceptional. There are people in responsible positions in city and national governments who feel the same way. For example, $2.1 million was budgeted to restore the *Firefighter's Memorial* at 100th Street and Riverside Drive. The Parks Commissioner, however, lamented the use of that money for restoring that or any other monument, saying, "I think [that] money should be spent on things that have more practical use."[15]

If by being practical the Commissioner means the application of our tax dollars to useful ends that realistically deal with the pressures of drugs and violence, then there could be nothing more practical than the preservation and celebration of our public monuments. They embody the values that decry destructive behavior and offer hope not only to New York City but to the nation and the world. The values of honesty, integrity, justice, personal commitment, dedication to higher purpose, and duty as expressions of conscience, kindness, and goodness not only ennoble the human spirit but also deserve our respect and admiration. There is no better way to revive and perpetuate those values than to preserve and celebrate our public monuments that symbolize and embody them.

Monuments to Neglect

If we do not integrate our monuments into our daily lives through preservation and celebration, we forget, neglect, and even destroy them with improper maintenance. Witness the tragedy of the Washington Arch in Greenwich Village, not only one of the nation's most important tributes to George Washington, but also one of the architectural and sculptural gems of the City Beautiful Movement. It deserves preservation for both its significance and its artistic merit. Yet the monument is disintegrating because of generations of neglect and destructive cleaning practices. The City of New York has been forced to erect a fence around it to protect the public from falling pieces of statuary and ornamental marble. What is most pathetic, however, is that the Washington Arch is not unique. New York City has 1,512 public monuments in its 1,000 city parks. Of that number, some 800 have major sculptural elements—statues, carved reliefs, and ornamental embellishments, as well as architectural components and landscaping. Most of those monuments are disintegrating. We have created what I call "Monuments to Neglect."[16]

If we are to reclaim New York City's and the nation's Monuments to Neglect and prevent their deterioration and destruction, we must adopt a philosophy of celebration that fully integrates our public monuments within the community. This philosophy must acknowledge that monuments are primarily symbols and embodiments of traditions and values before they are public art and components of urban planning. Monuments are the tangible and permanent means by which we perpetuate those traditions and values. We must develop a policy of education and preservation to implement that philosophy.

Our preservation policy must assure that we maintain and preserve our public monuments in perpetuity. Such a policy requires that standards and guidelines be established and supervised by professionals in dialogue with the community. There must be full and open disclosure of all conservational methods and techniques.

Our policy of education should take the form of instructional programs at the elementary and high schools. These programs should produce citizens who are familiar with our public monuments and instructed in the historical, cultural, and aesthetic principles they embody.

Our colleges should expand their liberal arts curricula to include the interdisciplinary study of public monuments. Classroom and laboratory work should be supplemented by internships.

Curriculum development in public monuments at the university level should encourage research and publication. Chairs should be endowed to assure continued research and development in the field of public monuments.

Through symposia, lectures, special programs, and publications, the general public should be informed of the various aspects of our public monuments and the timely issues pertaining to them.[17]

NOTES

1. This paper, which combines my remarks from both symposia, is drawn from my book *Masters of American Sculpture, the Figurative Tradition from the American Renaissance to the Millennium* (New York: Abbeville Press, 1993). See also Donald Martin Reynolds, *Monuments and Masterpieces: Histories and Views of Public Sculpture in New York City* (New York: Macmillan, 1988), xi–xii.

2. E. J. Johnson, "Do You Know a Monument to Modesty or Mirth?" *"Remove Not the Ancient Landmark": Public Monuments and Moral Values* (New York: Gordon & Breach, 1995), p. 9.

3. Reynolds, op. cit., 13–4; and Gerard Devlin, "Ceremony Honors an Amiable Child," *The News World* (July 16, 1981), 1A. See also the St. Claire Pollock Archives, Museum of the City of New York.

4. Devlin, 1A.

5. Ibid.

6. René Dubos, *So Human an Animal* (New York: Scribners', 1968), 242.

7. Ibid., 76.

8. Ibid., 201.

9. Ibid., 235.

10. Wayne Dynes, "Monuments, the Term," *"Remove Not the Ancient Landmark": Public Monuments and Moral Values* (New York: Gordon and Breach, 1995), p. 30.

11. Francis Huxley, *The Way of the Sacred* (London: Bloomsbury Books, 1989), 60.

12. Reynolds, op. cit, xii.

13. Donald Martin Reynolds, "Celebration or Neglect? The Future of America's Monuments," *American Art Today: Today and Tomorrow*. Hastings-on-Hudson, 1992, 6–9, 24. Published by The Newington-Cropsey Foundation.

14. Ibid., 24.

15. "The Fireman's Memorial," *New York Times* (February 24, 1991), A22.

16. Donald Martin Reynolds, "Monuments to Neglect?" *Newsday* (April 18, 1989), 60.

17. To achieve those objectives, The Monuments Conservancy, Inc., a not-for-profit corporation, was established by the author in 1992.

9. A Bill of Rights for Works of Art

James Beck

The final years of the twentieth century have seen an outburst of restoration that has reached near epidemic proportions. In Florence I am constantly amazed to see in every corner of the old city on the Arno scaffolds all over the place, and niches, sculptures, and paintings being cleaned. I think something has gone amuck. In a virtual orgy, paintings on canvas, wooden panels, and walls executed in diverse techniques—oil, tempera, watercolor, wax, true fresco, mosaic, stained glass, marble inlays, and drawings—are all being subjected to the grand treatment. However, a state of near anarchy exists in terms of standards, methods, techniques, and philosophy. Furthermore, two-dimensional works comprise but a small portion of the restoration effort. Sculptures of every kind, stone ranging from marble to granite, various woods, terracotta, coated ceramics, and precious metals are also undergoing a kind of Renaissance of restoration.

Nor should we forget that the most vast and expensive area of modern restoration is for architecture; that is, building restoration, which is truly big business. While one might think initially of the Ilaria Monument, the Brancacci Chapel, or even the Sistine Chapel, entire downtowns all over the world are being facelifted.

The reach of restoration activities spreads widely. Museums have thriving restoration and conservation departments that execute work not only for their collections but for other museums and individuals. There are considerable vested interests. Universities and colleges teach restoration and have restoration schools, and philanthropic foundations are often deeply committed to restoration. Sponsors are aware of the public relations value of the restoration of famous works. Suppliers of material, often international chemical corporations, recognize a lucrative future. Book publishers have a good deal of interest too, for the new, the recently discovered. Many individuals, often powerful and prestigious persons, are directly concerned, including chemists, museum directors, curators, superin-

tendents of art, art historians, critics not to mention restorers themselves, in an activity that as yet has very few controls.

Every treatment or restoration inevitably has negative side effects. That is a gen-
eralization I am prepared to stand on: even in the best of conditions and assuming
the most ethical intentions. In less favorable circumstances, losses can be enormous. Mistakes can be irreparable. The Giottesque frescoes in the upper church of
Assisi, Correggio's in Parma, and Piero della Francesca's in Arezzo are Italian examples. The tragic results of the radical cleanings that took place at the London
National Gallery in the later 1950s and 1960s are still with us. Also Yale University's Jarvis collection underwent a very "hard" cleaning a generation ago, over the
objections of many critics even then. There have been voices objecting, but for the
most part they have been dismissed. Lamentations come from practicing artists,
sculptors, and painters more generally; art critics and art historians have tended to
keep silent.

Many people question the so-called scientific operations at the Metropolitan
Museum of Art and at the National Gallery in Washington, as well as the Getty
Museum in California, all three favoring a radical approach. Frequently new techniques, procedures, and products are employed quickly without long testing. The
results of relatively untested glues, detergents, and solvents have proven to be
damaging and dangerous to the art, in some cases. Hope for discovery sometimes
seems to be the justification for certain interventions as if the tail is wagging the
dog. Claims of preventive treatment are heard, which at best offers more employ-
ment in the field, at worst, has objects undergo risky interventions.

The removal of countless fourteenth- and fifteenth-century frescoes from their
original walls and the division of the fresco surface from the under drawing layer,
the so-called sinopia, was widely advocated a generation ago, and with euphoric
pronouncements about discoveries everywhere, even in New York with the mem-
orable fresco show at the Met. Now there are serious doubts about the desirability
of removing the frescoes at all. That both the outer painted surface and the sinopia
were indiscriminately transferred to masonite supports by the thousands has
caused enormous headaches for this generation of conservators, since it turns out
that masonite is an inappropriate support in the first place. They watch the surfaces flake off under their very eyes.

These days artworks, including the most rare and treasured, are permitted to
travel to an extent unknown a generation ago. The mega exhibitions, the block-
busters, require a gathering of objects from diverse locations scattered around the
world. They are brought together for a fixed period, for months or even years
when the show may be sent from one center to another—lock, stock, and barrel—
even from one continent to another, and back again. Yet, at least in principle, I suggest that art objects should not be required to undergo the indignities of being
bound and packaged, tied, bracketed, wrapped in polyester, and sent on risky
voyages by ship, train, and plane, hundreds and sometimes thousands of miles
where there are temperature shifts and all kinds of other possible dangers. Problems related to shipment, for example, are very important for contemporary art as
well as for objects from the more distant past. Indeed, contemporary artists have
lamented to me the state in which they find their works when returned from ex-

hibition. Sometimes they have been repaired (poorly) without the artist's knowledge, much less thier consent, and in ways they would not approve.

Market conditions have encouraged various barbarous acts as well. It is common knowledge among art specialists that heads and torsos of ancient statues can fetch more on the art market when sold separately than when sold together. That is also true of medieval statues where sometimes arms that are outstretched have been judged as unattractive and have been lopped off. Furthermore, significant changes have been made in paintings to make them more saleable, like the elimination of certain ill-looking features. Illicit exportation and trade in art objects have gone on for centuries and continue to flourish. Due to the clandestine nature of the business, invaluable archaeological and art historical evidence is often destroyed at the same time that objects are being mishandled.

About half a year ago a sculptor, a friend of mine who works in Pietrasanta, called me in despair and said that "they" had restored the Ilaria Tomb Monument (Fig. 9–1). The Monument is private, located in the Cathedral of Lucca, and was made by Jacopo della Quercia for the second wife of the Lord of Lucca. She died at the end of 1405. A work of great beauty, it is very well known and highly regarded. It has not come down to us in its original state, but is now a sarcophagus with putti below and the figure of the deceased above. It has become a public monument, even though it was not created as a public monument. It has even come to symbolize the city of Lucca, and one of the local banks uses Ilaria as a monogram for its advertising. Ilaria, who died in childbirth, has given rise to countless number of Italian children with the name "Ilaria." I have at least two close friends who have children named Ilaria, and they represent but a small sampling. The English equivalent is "Hilary."

Because of the sheer beauty of this figure and the ways it fits into the tradition of Italy and Italian art, and more specifically Renaissance art, this precocious type has become emblematic of Renaissance Art. The putti down below are the earliest fully stated nude, winged, boy children of the Renaissance. Quercia used putti here ten or more years before Donatello was to appropriate the motif. Therefore, from an art historical point of view, this element and the entire monument are very early examples of the new style which became dominant for at least the next 400 years.

When my sculptor friend said they have done something awful to the monument, I reacted rather indifferently because I knew that the work was in excellent condition. So I failed to pay much attention to my friend's invitation to look at it. But she insisted, "You've got to come," and when I was in Italy for my sabbatical leave I went straight away to Lucca. Aware of my explosive nature with regard to such matters, my friend invited two local journalists to watch my reactions. Predictably, I was shocked to find that the work had indeed been "restored," and I said some unpleasant things about the results of the restoration. Consequently, I am now being sued by the restorer for criminal defamation because of what I said.[1]

Before speaking out, I asked what good it would do to speak out after the damage is done and what effect could I have on society? I pondered the matter. Several points occurred to me: If I do not speak out, and I have been studying the artist for nearly thirty years, who is going to address the problem? I am, for better or worse,

Figure 9–1　*Tomb of Ilaria del Carretto*. Jacopo Della Quercia, sculptor. Marble. 1406–1408(?)
Cathedral, Lucca, Italy.

a world expert on Jacopo della Quercia. Then I thought that although this monument has been "restored," others should not be similarly treated. Besides, there were plans to restore other works by Jacopo della Quercia and paintings by others of the same period. For example, I learned of the possibility that, following the much-heralded restoration of the Brancacci Chapel in the Carmine Church in Florence, plans were set in motion to attack the Trinity in Santa Maria Novella. This possibility upset me very much because I was aware of the delicacy of that fresco's surface. It had been transferred at least twice; it had been covered with whitewash that had evenually been removed; and it had been cleaned a few times, most recently about thirty years ago. The plans worried me a great deal, making me realize that it is not enough just to complain. One needs a plan, program, or series of suggestions that might win the approval of the art community.

I confess not to liking the Brancacci fresco restoration either. On the other hand, what differentiates the Brancacci Chapel from the Ilaria is that it really needed treatment, while the Ilaria did not need anything except a dusting. The walls of the Brancacci Chapel were full of moisture and there was mold on the surface. No doubt some intervention was required. I had seen a whitish veil expanding over the surface in recent years and I was concerned about it.

The results of the restoration nevertheless disturb me deeply. Some surface and tactile qualities are gone. In fact, that is not even the worst of it. You cannot see any of the details now because of the repainting. In a damaged area on the left side of the Tribute Money that was dark there is now a nice, bumpy, stone wall. I was on the scaffolding, saw this new "wall," and said to one of the young restorers, "how wonderful, you've discovered Masaccio's wall. I never saw that before." He replied somewhat defensively, "well, not really; actually, we painted that wall. However, it is just like the wall Masaccio would have painted." This incident should give you an inkling of what has been motivating me to take a firm stance on these issues.

Part of that same scene, the Tribute Money, depicts the story of Christ and the Apostles going through a foreign land and the messenger demanding a tax. The Apostles gather around Christ, asking what to do. Christ tells Peter to go to the water and catch a fish; what Peter finds in the mouth of the fish he should give to the messenger. There was a lot of shrubbery behind Peter in the segment with the fish, on the left side of the painting. There is no more shrubbery since the cleaning. Now, you might say that the shrubbery was a restoration of the seventeenth or eighteenth century, which has now been happily removed, since to leave it would have provided an incorrect impression; I am sure the restoration team makes precisely this claim. But what motivation could a restorer have had to paint in the shrubbery? Why should he paint leaves there when they were not there in the first place? In my opinion, the missing green areas were not a previous restoration, for there would have been no motivation. Everything in art and life has to have some sort of motivation. Here it is very difficult to reconstruct a situation in which those leaves would have been painted in by anybody but Masaccio. And now they are gone. To my eyes the painting looks the worse for the missing leaves and for much else. I would not like to see similar things happen for the Trinity.

There are encouraging signs, however. I found out that the director of the Uffizi Gallery acted courageously in protecting Leonardo da Vinci's *Adoration of the Magi*, as we all know an unfinished painting. A donor came along and said his organization would pay for the restoration, every penny. "Here is the money, let's go to work," he said. The director refused, saying in effect that the object is too delicate to touch. I too am reluctant to see the *Adoration* undergo restoration, and I think that the director's action was exemplary. That is the kind of position we must applaud.

The case of Raphael's *Madonna of the Granduca*, housed in the Pitti Palace, is another interesting as well as curious example. For this famous painting, most art scholars have long thought that there was a landscape beneath the dark background application. Some ten years ago the work was x-rayed, and low and behold there was indeed a landscape with a window behind it. The director of the Pitti Gallery wrote a paper suggesting that Raphael definitely painted the background landscape and it was apparently his intention to show the landscape, which is in the tradition of Leonardo da Vinci. But more recently the same scholar has concluded that Raphael created the overpainted background, representing a change of mind, a pentimento. Had the black background been removed, we would have lost Raphael's final idea about his painting. Luckily there were no funds available for the quick fix before minds were changed. This type of situation also forms part of my motivation for seeking a larger statement.

The Bronzes from Riace provide another example. Those exceptional Greek statues were recently discovered, then restored and exhibited with great fanfare to mobs of visitors. Every one of these restorations is among the "greatest," promising new discoveries while miraculously appearing to be old works. It turns out that the Bronzes from Riace, which, as many of you know, were rescued from maybe twenty or more centuries under water, were in respectably good condition. They were cleaned and treated, but now we learn that they have developed some unexplained, strange disease, and the specialists are completely bewildered. The objects are again being taken back for restoration. As a general principle I suspect that there are good reasons to do as little as possible with all the objects in our custody.

In view of all these considerations, I have written a Bill of Rights for a work of art. There are 11 "rights."[2] There probably should and will be more as time passes. They are not written in stone; they are suggestions that can be altered and changed:

1. All works of art have the inalienable right to live an honorable existence.

2. All works of art have the inalienable right to remain in their original abodes, whenever possible. They should be permitted to rest in their acquired homes without being moved to distant places: in galleries and museums, in private collections, in houses of worship, in public spaces, under protected and controlled situations as removed as much as possible from pollution, excessive variations of climate, and all forms of degradation.

3. Works of art recognized as the highest order should be regarded as belonging to the entire society of the world, the "global cultural patrimony," not to a

single entity, either local, institutional, or national, although the "owners" would continue to have full custodial responsibility.

4. The "owners" of the paintings and sculptures, as well as other art objects, hold them under an enforceable constructive trust, for the benefit of the public.

5. In the process of conserving works of art, ample room must also be provided for the new as well as for the conservation of the old, for otherwise we would risk fossilizing ourselves to the past. Decisions affecting art held in trust should be reviewable.

6. The most distinguished art objects shall be specifically designated "world-class masterpieces," representing, perhaps, one object in a hundred among the finest cultural treasures (somewhat in the way that buildings are selected for "landmark" status). Prior to the restoration of any in this group of masterpieces, all proposed procedures would be subject to review by a court of competent jurisdiction after hearing testimony from specialists and representatives of the culture. Second opinions and sometimes third opinions would be sought.

7. Under no circumstances should preservation and conservation techniques be employed that are essentially experimental in nature, except where the artwork is in imminent danger. In all other cases carefully controlled, fully documented testing is a prerequisite; findings, including photographs, must be made publicly available in a timely manner and at a reasonable expense. No restoration should be undertaken for the sake of curiosity or profit. If scholarly or scientific "discoveries" result from conservation techniques, they should be regarded as fortuitous by-products, not as the *raison d'etre* of the intervention, as the artwork must not be considered an "experimental laboratory." Since every treatment, cleaning, or restoration has the potential of negative side effects, interventions should be taken sparingly, and with reversible techniques if possible, recognizing implicitly that in the future more effective and less damaging procedures may be devised. Restoration techniques should be subject to review before any restoration is undertaken.

8. Masterpieces of the past should not be reproduced without clearly distinguishing original from copy, so that the integrity of the original is preserved. Efforts should be made to protect artists and their estates from violations of their intentions.

9. Unified artworks should not be divided, dissected, altered, or mutilated; e.g., predella panels should not be separated from their altarpieces and individual pages should not be removed from a book of drawings. In principle, subsequent transformations, adjustments, and reformulations added to the original statement should be left intact as marks of history.

10. The stewardship of works of art, especially masterpieces of noted historical significance, should be subjected to free and open debate and appropriate judicial review.

11. The examination and maintenance of works of art must be provided on a regular basis and carried out by dedicated, trained professionals, certified by national and international standards when feasible, after any objector has been given the right to be heard.

NOTES

1. Professor Beck was acquitted by the Florence court of aggravated slander on the basis of the fact that there was no crime committed.
2. This version of the Rights was revised on December 8, 1992.

10. Venice—Time and Conservation

David Rosand

Of all the definitions of "Monument" in the *Oxford English Dictionary*, the fourth, "anything that by its survival commemorates a person, action, period or event," describes the meaning that will be addressed in this paper. What I want to focus on is the city itself as the monument—not only in the physical sense but as an expression of values, to go back to Don Reynolds' remarks in Chapter 1. The city that I want to focus on is indeed Venice, the city that I began to work with under Rudolf Wittkower. In fact, the problems that I want to deal with have everything to do with the physical aspect of the city. In 1966, as a young instructor at Columbia, I had just returned to Venice—this is after the floods—and I came running to Rudi Wittkower crying, "Venice is sinking, Venice is sinking, we have to do something." He patted my head and said: "Oh, tush. Venice will be there as long as you need it." He always had one's professional advancement in mind.

However, Venice is indeed flooded. It is, in effect, more or less there, and the survival of the city of Venice, the situation of its special dilemma, in fact epitomizes itself in being absolutely unique, and we tend to accept its self-celebration. Insofar as it is a city built upon water, on mud flats, it rises miraculously out of the water. Indeed, the water itself takes the place of the crenelated walls that would have protected most medieval cities. It is the water that makes Venice unique and that defines the primary element of its ecology. Venice is a city founded on inhospitable and insecure ground, at least for durability: on mud, into which supporting piles were driven, and the water itself, a constant wash upon the foundations of its fabric.

The water itself then is a major threat to the monuments along the Grand Canal, such as the Ca' d'Oro. These are the monuments that make the city unique, the monuments that are themselves made possible, in the openness of their design, by the water: the lagoon liberated their architecture from defensive responsibility, permitting such lightness. But even these palaces are built of stone. They sit like

73

sponges, constantly absorbing water. The effect of the water that is constantly present in the atmosphere is a major threat to the stone itself. (I will refer to some experiments that were done here at the Ca' d'Oro a little bit later in this chapter.)

The Fondaco de' Tedeschi, the great German warehouse, was rebuilt in the early years of the sixteenth century after it burned down, between 1506 and 1508. It was covered with decorations, external frescoes primarily by Giorgione. Those frescoes, which we know only in a few poorly preserved fragments, tell us an awful lot about this particular city. Their condition epitomizes the kinds of problems that it faces. By the eighteenth century, they were already almost impossible to read. The fate of Giorgione's frescoes is a natural consequence of their situation. Fresco is a painting technique in which the plaster wall itself effectively becomes the binding agent of colors. So long as that plaster dries properly, fresco is as durable as its architecture. Built upon salt water, however, plaster can hardly set properly in Venice, and fresco has a very difficult time of it. Eventually, the Venetians abandoned it, though not completely, and in the fifteenth century began to develop on a monumental level an alternative support for painting, painting on canvas. In a certain way, when we look at this fragment of Giorgione's frescoes, we are looking at what Jim Beck might call the "natural death" of a work of art; in a sense, that it was part of its own environment, the external circumstances were the circumstances themselves into which this painting was introduced from the very beginning.

But there are other kinds of problems. Again, Venice continues to serve as a kind of laboratory. I introduce the four horses from an ancient quadriga that were brought back from Constantinople in the fourth crusade and were used to crown the facade of the basilica of San Marco as war monuments, as trophies. Indeed, they had been monuments of victory in antiquity and continued to function as such when the Venetians appropriated them. These horses are no longer there. The bronzes were being infected, and the horses are now housed inside. Their place has been taken by copies, good copies, but still copies. This in itself raises fundamental issues about the survival of works of art and the responsibility that any society has toward their survival. What has been happening, too slowly perhaps, is the recognition that the contemporary situation, that is, the contemporary ecology of a city like Venice, no longer corresponds to what it once was. Venice, the most delicate urban environment that one can imagine, is now cheek-by-jowl next to one of the largest oil refinery complexes in all of Europe. Here, too, water is responsible: the direct access to the sea through the lagoon made the development of Marghera, at least from an economic point of view, inevitable—however unfortunate for the survival of Venice. A whole set of consequences went along with that, including the opening of deep water channels for large petroleum tankers. All of these wreck havoc with the city itself. But most of all, of course, the havoc comes from the pollutants in the air. Venice, which might otherwise have been free of automobile pollution, is absolutely covered by the residue coming from the industrial plants and water rails along the coast of Marghera.

Taking the horses of San Marco inside is a very weak step. However, that step reminds us of other horses that are still out in this polluted pasture, including, of course, Verrocchio's Colleone. This monument, too, should have been taken in, protected, and a replacement put up outdoors. This is exactly what was done with Michelangelo's *David* in front of the Palazzo Vecchio in Florence. Why not a great campaign to save these Italian monuments? The only answer is of course that it would take a certain amount of money. We can push this even further by asking questions about—again to go back to Jim Beck's bill of rights for monuments— what happens indeed once the dirt is taken off the frescoes, the dirt that presumably has in some ways been protecting those frescoes against pollutants that they originally never had to face.

All of this is by way of a prelude, for there is one monument I do want to focus on because it raises still other problems. It is the monument at the base of the Campanile of San Marco in Venice, the little porch that was built by Jacopo Sansovino in the 1530s (Fig. 10–1). The Logetta is a monument by any definition in so far as, even though appearing as a piece of architecture, it is in effect without function. It served as a gathering place for nobles at times, but essentially it is there as a public declaration of values. We know a fair amount about those values precisely because Sansovino's son, Francesco, in his famous guidebook to Venice, offers his father's programmatic statement. The program itself involves a series of bronze statues in niches representing figures of Mercury, Minerva, Apollo, and Peace, clearly as allegorical figures in the system of state values. According to this program, Mercury is there to celebrate eloquence; Minerva stands for wisdom, the music that Apollo represents is the harmony of the Venetian state; it is the harmony of its construction. The whole metaphoric message is the declaration of values of this particular society. However self-serving the rhetoric and transparent the propaganda, these values were indeed taken at face value, as it were, by the rest of Europe in various ways. What we are dealing with here is indeed a monument to an abstract idea, the idea of the state. No leaders are portrayed here. Rather, what we have is the celebration of abstractions that equate with the very notion of the Venetian state, which is embodied primarily in a set of laws, in a constitution. And above in the attic, in the very center, is the figure of Venetia herself. We are dealing with the personification of the state, a personification that owes its inspiration to the figure of the goddess Roma; we are still very much involved, not architecturally but iconographically, with the legacy of ancient Rome. And we are also confronted by another major issue, that of the female figure on the public monuments: the figure of Venice is indeed a most beautiful woman, a composite made up of a variety of elements from Dea Roma to the Virgin Mary to the figure of Venus. Sansovino's Loggetta is the epitome of civic values. It stands opposite the Doge's Palace, seat of government, directly across from the basilica of San Marco itself, which is, in effect, the ducal chapel. It is in the center of the city, in a very fundamental sense. It makes a declaration. It figures values of the Venetian constitution as they have come to be interpreted.

Some years ago, this monument too underwent restoration. There is no question but that intervention was needed and is still needed. Unfortunately, the intervention involved a process that was irreversible. Following the advice of a group from the Victoria and Albert Museum in London, a system of stone impregnation was used to consolidate the stone. The stone itself was literally being pulverized inside. Preliminary tests had been run on balusters of the Ca' d'Oro. The technique

works to a depth of about half an inch. What you have is a kind of eggshell situation, a solidified outer layer surrounding a core of sand. This was supposedly corrected in the efforts taken on the Loggetta. No sooner had the operation been completed, however, when we all watched as the balusters around this particular monument began to bleed, turning themselves into the T'ang vases. Something was going wrong very clearly. When the whole thing was revealed, one's first reaction to Sansovino's stone sculpture was: "My God, these pieces look like they have been carved out of soap, ivory soap, pure white!" Something was wrong, and it wasn't merely, I think, a question of aesthetic habit, that we were used to the dirt on the marble. Something had happened to the surfaces. They have been coated; they have been protected; presumably they have been consolidated internally, but basically they look as though they have been covered. There was not a public outcry about that then.

For years, Venice has been talking about establishing a laboratory devoted to stone conservation. The plight of the Loggetta confirms the need for such a center, a place where the special and complex problems of treatment might be seriously studied. Such preliminary study might have saved the Loggetta itself from becoming an experiment in stone conservation—and another witness for Jim Beck's case for a monumental bill of rights.

Figure 10–1 Logetta. Jacopo Cansovino, architect. 1530's. Venice.

11. Monuments in New Countries

Oleg Grabar

A few comments are in order concerning material covered thus far. One is the question of feminine patronage and of "feminine" architecture—a very interesting phenomenon which can be identified through a separate series of features. In addition, somebody mentioned earlier the absence of monuments to abstractions. It is curious that nearly all abstract notions are feminine nouns. I cannot think of one that is masculine. It would have been very embarrassing to the macho world of the eighteenth and nineteenth centuries to have too many great "Liberties," "Charities," and so on as public monuments representing women. The same is true of the names of most countries, especially in Latin forms: Britannia, Gallia, and the like. Only recently I learned that the nineteenth century avoided representations of women in official images of states' victories.

The theme that I would like to explore comes from Don Reynolds' book and from the many conversations with Rudi Wittkower about East and West and the relationships between Oriental and Western themes. He was fascinated by these subjects. I am sure that he would have reacted with great interest to developments during the past thirty years in our knowledge and sensitivities about them.

The key point is simple. Since the Second World War, about 100 new countries have been born. All these countries have needed images. All these countries have needed memories and ways to commemorate those memories. These 100 countries can also be identified with what I call "a cult of the dead." They are steeped in pain, misery, blood, and dissensions. Only two, Israel and Algeria, can be considered to have achieved something militarily. That dearth of achievement is very important. We have to realize that something like nine-tenths of humanity lives surrounded by memories of martyrs: people killed, assassinated, murdered, and executed in one way or the other. Or, as in the African countries, the memory is that of slavery, which is again not a happy one. At the same time we are dealing with 100 countries that are trying to develop national glory, prestige, greatness, and a sense of their own real or invented past. How can they resolve that conflict? How can they create identity, express expectations, and distinguish themselves from their neighbors when they have barely existed and their pasts have been so difficult?

Since I have not studied these problems in depth, I am going to discuss only a series of impressions. In fact, interesting solutions have emerged in some of these new countries. Let me give you some examples. First, all of these countries have employed universal, Roman-inspired systems. It was a great experience to arrive ten years ago in Kashgar (or Kashi), which is the westernmost city of China, practically at the frontiers of Afghanistan, China, and the Soviet Union. As one enters the main street, one encounters a huge statue of Mao Tse Tung, not on horseback, but standing like Augustus of Prima Porta. Such statues abound, although many have been destroyed, as in Iran. Differences do occur, however. One very interesting difference is in Jakarta, where there is an enormous oversized statue of the Java Man, a prehistorical hero transformed into the national hero through an oversized sculpture that stands in the middle of Main Square.

Other examples are from two cities that have extraordinary modern buildings. One is Dhakka in Bangladesh, which is one of the poorest countries in the world but has one of the most vibrant architectures. The other one, if anything remains after the recent bombings, is Baghdad. Baghdad is probably the richest Third World city in contemporary architecture. There have been more fascinating buildings built in Baghdad over the past thirty years than any place else except Saudi Arabia, Singapore, and the oil countries of the Gulf.

Specific themes appear in both of these cities. Both have monuments to the dead or to martyrs. For instance, there was an arch (now replaced) in Baghdad that was a memorial to unknown soldiers. This arch was an imitation of the celebrated Sasanian Ctesipkon vault of the sixth century. Historically it was a rather simple work of architecture, but it was interesting because it fit with all the traditions of copying in monumental architecture. Sculpted onto another arch in Baghdad is a message about what free people do, how they work, and so forth. There is also a new memorial to the dead in Baghdad built about ten years before the war. It houses a military museum—a museum to the history of Iraq. This museum attempted to create a completely new ideology of commemoration without reflecting an older example. Another monument is rather like an egg cut in half, with each half switched and moved from the other. Instead of using a traditional form—the typical dome of Iraq or Iran—in the old fashioned way, the architect cut it in two, moved those two halves, and created two separate sculptures that sat next to each other.

These three examples in Baghdad, and a similar one in Dhakka, are all attempts to create a different iconography of memory: to create for memory formal themes that would not repeat those in Rome, so that the memory is not associated with an alien past but is created by local needs, local features, and local characteristics. This is the first idea I want to outline: the idea of trying to use the same ideas, memory, victory or defeat, the dead, the heroes, the martyrs, but avoiding the vocabulary that had been imposed by Rome and seeking a genuine vocabulary that is modified either locally or through the schools, usually in Britain, where these designers were trained. There were many attempts to do abstractions in architecture, for abstraction is the new universalism. It can be done in any country, in any place.

There are other, more interesting examples. The first is known to every student of architecture: the Parliament building in Dhakka, designed by Louis Kahn. It is truly one of the masterpieces of the architecture of the twentieth century. What is extraordinary about this building, aside from its inner qualities of design and construction, is that it is so paradoxical. In the poorest, most miserable country in Asia, Dhakka is one of the most depressing capitals. Its true poverty hits you the moment you leave your hotel. Yet, here is this luxurious, magnificent thing. Leftist critics have often asked why such a beautiful building was constructed in the world's poorest country. The point is exactly the opposite. The people of Dhakka are understandably proud of their building. Every local designer and planner has picked up little themes from it and has used them for lamp shades, for the street lighting system, and so forth. In other words, this is an instance where a building created by a foreigner in an alien medium for a debatable purpose (Pakistan imposed it on Bangladesh for tactical reasons) has become a true sign of a country, with images that are used in all expressions of the country.

Sadam Hussein tried to do the same thing with his huge international project of a state morgue. It is a mosque in theory, but it is more than a mosque: it was to have become the focus of the whole life of the city, the place to which the whole city would gather for collective activities. It is interesting in a sense that it would have been built not around death, not around the memory of the defeats, victories, destructions, killings, and so forth, but around a civic building with religious and social aspirations.

The last example is a project done by a British firm for a quarter in Baghdad. This was a great project in which every part of Baghdad was going to be rebuilt, restored by different architectural firms. What is interesting about the project is that if you look at its details, all the countries in the world are depicted on its focal buildings. It had maps of the world all over it, so that it was as though the whole world was present in this little quarter of the city.

The interesting thing that I derive from this experience of the new countries is that whenever they have sought to commemorate in public the same themes that the West has used, with its tradition derived from Rome, they have made a pastiche of foreign things. Or else they have had to invent forms that have not caught on or may not catch on because their language is one nobody understands, or only architects admire, but nobody else can feel. The purpose of the monument is to find an affinity with the aspirations, needs, feelings, and life of a society, as in a center's eating quarter or the large mosque in a government building. If a sufficient quality is given to these monuments, as clearly happened in Dhakka and might have happened in Baghdad, the impact of the building becomes enormous. So then there is a possibility of creating a monument out of life and not only out of death, and this is the lesson we can learn from new countries.

12. Brookgreen Gardens: Monument to American Sculpture

Joseph Veach Noble

Brookgreen Gardens is a museum of sculpture in South Carolina which was founded in 1931 by Archer Milton Huntington and Anna Hyatt Huntington. Archer was the son of Collis Huntington, who had built the Central Pacific Railroad and the Newport News Shipyard. Archer was his only son and sole heir. Anna Hyatt was a sculptor in her own right, and the two married late in life. They had no children.

The Gardens are located about ninety miles north of Charleston, South Carolina, along the coast on Route 17, about 20 miles south of Myrtle Beach. It is the biggest museum in America: nine thousand acres, 400 of which are landscaped. On entering Brookgreen from the main highway, which bisects the property, visitors first see the piece of sculpture, which is used as a trademark, the *Fighting Stallions* by Anna Hyatt Huntington (Fig. 12–1). She loved horses, and many of the pieces that she did involved horses. Her *Diana of the Chase* is also at Brookgreen (Fig. 12–2). It was originally in the Huntington's home on Fifth Avenue in New York City, which now houses the National Academy of Design. Archer Huntington gave the house to the National Academy.

Anna Hyatt Huntington laid out the initial plan of the garden and the sculpture installation. We have been expanding the collection so that now it's more than twice the size the Huntingtons left us. The property runs inland 5 miles, so it covers about twenty square miles, which is quite a lot to administer. Originally, it was four independent plantations: Brookgreen, Springfield, Laurel Hill, and The Oaks. They had been granted to the early settlers not by King George III, but by King George II.

Brookgreen is certainly one of the very few big and successful sculpture gardens. We have 526 pieces of sculpture, of which more than half are life-size or colossal in scale, up to 40 tons. They are by 232 sculptors, all of whom are Ameri-

Figure 12–1 *Fighting Stallions*. Anna Hyatt Huntington, sculptor. Aluminum. 1950.
Brookgreen Gardens.

Figure 12–2 *Diana of the chase.* Anna Hyatt Huntington, sculptor. Bronze. 1922. Brookgreen Gardens.

Figure 12–3 *Narcissus*. Adolph Alexander Weinman, sculptor. Marble. 1923. Brookgreen Gardens.

can. Some may have been born abroad, but eventually they became naturalized American citizens.

Each piece of sculpture is carefully displayed within the landscape setting to enhance its formal properties. Adoph A. Weinman's *Narcissus*, for example, stands before the great avenue of live oaks leading to where the original plantation houses used to stand (Fig. 12–3). The four manor houses were all destroyed during the Civil War or by fires. Weinman also created *Riders of the Dawn*, a major sculpture group, surrounded by dogwoods (Fig. 12–4). We attempt to design appropriate settings for each piece of sculpture. Thus, *Nature's Dance* by Stirling Calder is displayed with azaleas, dogwood, and flowering magnolias in the background (Fig. 12–5). Stirling Calder's father was the great sculptor who did the statue of William Penn on top of City Hall in Philadelphia, and whose son was Alexander Calder, famous for his mobiles.

A beautifully sited group is *Nymph and Fawn* by C. Paul Jennewein (Fig. 12–6). It is the only other casting of the Darlington Memorial Fountain group, which is in Washington, D.C. The *Seaweed Fountain* by Beatrice Fenton is a personal favorite of mine (Fig. 12–7). I was born in Philadelphia, and this is one of the first fountains I

Figure 12–4 *Riders of the Dawn*. Adolph Alexander Weisman, sculptor. Limestone. Brookgreen Gardens.

Figure 12–5   *Nature's Dance*. Alexander Stirling Caulder, sculptor. Bronze. Brookgreen
Gardens.

Figure 12–6 *Nymph and Fawn.* Carl Paul Jennewein, sculptor. Bronze. Brookgreen Gardens.

Figure 12–7   *Seaweed Fountain*. Beatrice Fenton, sculptor. Bronze. Brookgreen Gardens.

remember as a child in Fairmount Park. Of course, Fairmount Park also contains one of the great outdoor collections of sculpture.

Brookgreen is blessed with clean air. We have neither air pollution nor acid rain. Most of the property is kept as a wildlife preserve and as the Huntington Beach State Park, which we permit the state to administer for public bathing. It has about four miles of beach, a beautiful beach like Jones Beach or the Atlantic City beach. The staff works very hard on preventive conservation, not overt conservation. For example, all of the marbles and limestones are coated with silicon twice a year, and the bronzes are waxed four times a year.

We have an active collection. For example, on November 30, 1990, we bought Hirman Powers' *The Fisher Boy*, a lifesize marble, about five feet tall, which Hiram Powers cut in Italy in 1846. Two months before that, we bought a *Diana* in bronze by Augustus Saint-Gaudens, nine feet in height, which he created in 1892 (Fig. 12–8). It is identical in size to the one in The Metropolitan Museum of Art's American Wing courtyard. In addition to collecting historically significant sculptures that go back 150 years, we are constantly commissioning new pieces and annual medals.

One of our guiding principles states that art is a form of communication. It is the function of the artist to communicate ideas to his or her audience. Artists must be clear to be understood, and if the work of art is not understood by the pubic, then the public rightly considers it to be a failure. In Chapter 11 of this text, Professor Grabar refers to this lack of understanding of certain modern images in architecture as: "an architectural language that nobody understands." So it is with sculpture. The problem is similar in many respects for authors and public speakers. If they do not express their ideas clearly, or if I as a public speaker mumble and you can not understand what I say, you are certainly entitled to consider the presentation worthless.

Some examples of sculpture bear out this dedication to clear communication. For example, a scupture well-known to New Yorkers is *The Fountain of the Muses* by Carl Milles (Figs. 12–9 to 12–11). If you have wondered what happened to *The Fountain of the Muses* at the Metropolitan Museum of Art, after twenty-eight years of exhibition it was put in the basement in 1982 because of the weight of the pool area. I was then able to purchase it for Brookgreen Gardens. The theme of the fountain is one that Milles suggested to the director of the museum. *The Fountain* represents artists and the arts. In the front is the poet with the bluebird, followed by the architect with the column. Behind him come the musician with a sort of crazy trombone, and then the painter. I guess sculptors are always considered to be slightly to the left, so behind the painter and off to the left you have a sculptor reaching for his inspiration. At the end of the pool is *Aganippe*, the nymph of the fountain. As she waves to the artists, they rush down the pool, which I insisted on being exactly the same size as the pool in the Metropolitan Museum. It has the same black granite edging because that is the way Carl Milles designed it. We have landscaped it so that the artists rush toward the *Pegasus* by Laura Gardin Fraser, the inspiration for all artists and sculptors.

Another piece of sculpture that has a story to tell is *Time and the Fates of Man* by Paul Manship (Fig. 12–12). He created it for the 1939 World's Fair in New York.

Figure 12–8 *Diana*. Augustus Saint-Guadens, sculptor. Bronze. Brookgreen Gardens.

Figure 12–9 *Fountain of Muses.* Carl Milles, sculptor. Bronze. Brookgreen Gardens.

Figure 12–10   Detail of Fig. 9.

Figure 12–11 Detail of Fig. 9.

Figure 12-12   *Time and the Fates of Man.* Paul Manship, csulptor. Bronze. Brookgreen Gardens.

Fugyre 12–13 *Into the Unknown*. Hermon Mcneil, sculptor. White Marble. Brookgreen Gardens.

Figure 12–14 *Man Carving His Own Destiny*. Allbin Polasek, sculptor. Limestone. Brookgreen Gardens.

The gnomon, which cast the shadow for this working sundial at the World's Fair, was done in plaster and was eighty feet in length. This bronze version, which Paul had cast, is forty feet for the gnomon. The three fates sit under the gnomon, and the tree of life is full of leaves over the first two fates. The first spins the thread of life, the second one measures it, and the third, sitting under the barren tree with the raven overhead, cuts it.

Into the Unknown by Hermon A. MacNeil is a sculpture that was created near the beginning of the century, and it seems to have so much meaning that the National Sculpture Society adopted it as their symbol (Fig. 12–13). A winged female figure is carving into the unknown and is creating the future. A similar theme is one by Albin Polasek, *Man Carving His Own Destiny* (Fig. 12–14). The sculptor uses his mallet and chisel to carve himself free from the encompassing block of stone. This is one of my favorite pieces because it encompasses all of us carving our own destinies. It is also a fitting image to conclude this brief discussion of Brookgreen Gardens, Monument to American Sculpture, created by the love and dedication of Archer and Anna Huntington.

13. Bees on the Tomb of Urban VIII

Howard McPharlin Davis

Since the Barberini coat of arms has a set of three bees as its central element, works commissioned by Pope Urban VIII include the family coat of arms and occasionally bees in a variety of less formal roles. The handling of bees on Bernini's tomb for the pope in the apse of Saint Peter's is nonetheless distinctive and calls for interpretation (Fig. 13–1).

There are three sets of bees on the tomb (Fig. 13–2) two to them in very large scale. Though cut off in most photographs,[1] a papal coat of arms barely overlaps the arch enframing the niche containing the tomb. In it are three gilt bronze bees on a soft red marble shield, arranged heraldically, with one bee centered below and two symmetrically placed above.

On the monument below, only slightly smaller in size and also in gilt bronze, are the bees in the second set . The lowest of the three here measures 5.5 inches in length (14 cm.), larger in scale than the human figures, which are heroic in size. Caritas, at the left, is about 2 inches shy of 10 feet tall (284 cm) and does not stand erect. Referring to this set, Hibbard has noted: "A number of Barberini bees have alighted capriciously on the sarcophagus and statue base—Bernini liberated heraldry as he did everything else."[2] The bees are not arranged in a formal pattern. Two are high on the statue base, close to the figure of the pope, as if moving toward him. The third bee in this set is seen against the black marble sarcophagus; it seems more stationary than the other two.

The bees in the third set are the most surprising; they are "life-sized," each one three-quarters of an inch long (2 cm). These may have been mentioned in the Bernini literature, but I have not been able to find any explicit reference to them.[3] Lower on the monument than any of the above mentioned bees, these life-sized bees are also in gilt bronze. They are four in number, one on each leg of the sarcophagus. The number 4 is probably symbolic; for centuries, the idea that the world consisted

Figure 13–1 *The Tomb of Pope Urban VIII.* Gianlorenzo Bernini, sculptor. Marble. St. Peter's, Rome.

Figure 13–2 Detail of Fig. 13–1.

of four elements had made the number 4 useful in indicating the earthbound, here-and-now character of things or beings.

The most eye-catching of the small bees is the one high on the decorative vertical strips of the left front leg, light against the dark bronze of the flat strip framing the concave vertical groove ("flute"?) toward the left. A black spot at this point in the etching mentioned above indicates that at least for the late seventeenth-century designer of this print this tiny bee seemed worthy of note.[4] On the right front leg, the bee is lower and centered, at the top of the gilt cabling filling the lower part of the center vertical "flute," light on light and, therefore, less prominent even though it is closer to the viewer. On the back legs, the bees are on a plain, undecorated surface, gold on gold; one is low, centered on the left back leg, and the other is off-center to the right and near the bottom of the right back leg. The bee on the back right leg has a faint linear circle around it.

The positioning of the small bees seems aimed at suggesting that they have been attracted to the sarcophagus and have come to rest on it in a random pattern. Without detracting from other possible allusions that may be discerned in these bees, I submit that Bernini is here suggesting that from this sarcophagus there comes a fragrance, one that is familiarly known as the "odor of sanctity."[5] In this, the lowest of the large bees also plays a role, for it is placed just below the point at which the lid of the sarcophagus comes to rest on the lower part, the point at which a fragrance from inside the sarcophagus would emerge. I suggest this in spite of the fact that it has recently been discovered that the pope's remains are not in the sarcophagus and in all probability never were.[6] Fehl suggests that the pope was perhaps buried in the statue base. I am attempting, however, to interpret the forms of the tomb as they address the viewer, who would naturally assume that the pope's remains were and are in the sarcophagus.[7] Bees are attracted to those fragrant things called flowers and from them produce another fragrant, and sweet-tasting, substance—honey. Bernini associated with Jesuits, went daily to the church of the Gesù for vespers, and practiced the *Spiritual Exercises* of Saint Ignatius. The sense of touch had been emphasized in many works of his very early years: it was to be expected that he would welcome an opportunity to use the sense of smell to refer to spiritual qualities in his intimate friend and patron, Pope Urban.

In the above, I am not suggesting that Bernini perceived in the pope qualities and achievements that would ultimately lead to canonization. Rather, he seems to be using the response of the bees to a fragrance issuing from the sarcophagus as a subtle and sophisticated compliment to the pope, implying saintliness in Urban—a kind of personal nomination on the part of his friend and "official" artist that the pope should be considered for that highest honor.

The importance of the small bees in this regard is that their "evidence" could not be readily faulted. The large bees, after all, are appropriately called "Barberini bees," since their number and preternatural size relate them to the figure of Urban, the coat of arms, and the large supporting figure in the tomb monument. In contrast, the small bees, even though they are on the supports of the sarcophagus, are scaled to the world of the viewer, ordinary bees, not limited in time to the period immediately following the death of the pope, bees whose superior olfactory

senses draw them to this sarcophagus from which fragrant odors continue to issue.[8]

The small bees, and their ambivalent sense of being part of the image and also
part of the world of the viewer, relate to a tradition of trompe l'oeil realism described by Pliny and Philostratus as part of the practice of painters in ancient
Greece and Rome, later revived in the Renaissance (and even attributed by Vasari
to Giotto). As Panofsky has pointed out, Philostratus in his Narcissus chapter "de-
lightfully describes how the painter, 'enamored of verisimilitude' had depicted a
bee sitting on a flower in such a manner that it was impossible to decide whether
'an actual bee had been deceived by the picture or a painted bee deceived the beholder.'"[9] Three paintings used at the symposium in honor of Professor Wittkower to illustrate the revival in the Renaissance of this ancient conceit are the Petrus
Christus portrait of a Carthusian of 1446,[10] Carlo Crivelli's Madonna and Child—
both showing a fly close to life size on a parapet and both in the Metropolitan Museum in New York—and Sebastiano del Piombo's portrait of Cardinal Bandinello
Sauli and three other figures (1516) in the Washington National Gallery, a much
larger work (about 4′ x 5′) in which a fly painted as if alighted on the white vest-
ment of the sitter is again of a size where it might be mistaken for a real fly on the
surface of the painting.[11] Bernini would enjoy the challenge of using a motif tradi-
tionally reserved for the medium of painting in a very large, formal sculptural
work, anticipating the pleasure a viewer might have in recognizing with surprise
the play with reality and the play with media.

A likely source for the "capricious" spray of the large bees on the statue base and
the sarcophagus of Urban's tomb is a title page for a book of Maffeo Barberini's
poems designed by Ruben.[12] The pope's given name is used on the title page because, as the wording indicates, the poems were written when he was a cardinal
prior to his elevation to the papacy in 1623, even though the volume was printed in
1634. The Rubens design has a specific Biblical sources—Judges 14—in which
Samson first kills a young lion with his bare hands, returns later, and finds a
swarm of bees and honey in the carcass of the lion, and, following this, formulates
a riddle for the Philistines: "Out of the eater came forth meat, and out of the strong
came forth sweetness." Held argues convincingly that the bees represent the
poems, as well as illustrating the story and functioning as "Barberini bees" allud-
ing to the pope's family coat of arms. In the title page and in Rubens' even more
powerful preparatory drawing,[13] in addition to the swarm below, there are three
bees above the upper arm of Samson that resemble a slightly skewed coat of arms.
There is a very high probability that Bernini knew this title page and not a small
chance that here lies the first stimulus to Bernini's conception of the highly unusual handling of the "spray" of large bees on Urban's tomb.[14] I see no need, however,
for Bernini's spray of bees having a specific allusive significance beyond the role
as "Barberini bees."

Finally, there are three prints published between 1625 and 1630 (the first two
dedicated to Urban and the third to Cardinal Francesco Barberini) by two of the
founding members of the Accademia dei Lincei that may have a bearing on Bernini's sense for the properties of bees and his handling of bee imagery in works made
for the Barberini.[15] The most promising of these in terms of possible influence on

Bernini and the tomb of the pope is a large engraving entitled *Melissographia* (17" x 11.75"; 43 x 31 cm), which was issued early in December 1625.[16] Galileo had sent Federico Cesi, the prime mover of the Lincei group, a microscope on September 23, 1624. The *Melissographia*, dedicated to Urban, was clearly designed to secure papal patronage for the research activities of this intense group of scholars. Framed by branches of laurel, an emblem both of the Barberini family and of Urban as a poet, are three bees, arranged as in the Barberini coat of arms, except that they are drawn in profile, bottom view, and top view, to show the details newly discovered though examination by microscope. Francesco Stelluti, another important Lincean, signs at the bottom as the microscopic observer. A poem written in honor of Urban by Josse de Rycke, a Belgian member of the Lincei group, appears near the bottom of the engraving; in the lower corner, as if engraved on the side of the scroll on which the poem is represented as written, are details of seven members of bee's bodies in varying degrees of magnification.[17]

Panofsky, who introduced one of the "microscopic" prints of this group to the worlds of art history and Renaissance studies, noted that Pietro da Cortona, in the huge bees in the "natural" coat of arms in the ceiling of the *salone* of the Barberini palace in Rome, paints them without using any of the new knowledge gained through microscopic examinations.[18] He did this in spite of the fact that Stelluti had published an engraving with even more microscopic detail in a book,[19] which as a book probably had a wider circulation than the single-sheet *Melissographia*— and this was in 1630, three years before Cortona began to paint the ceiling. The *Melissographia*, which Panofsky does not mention, appeared, of course, eight years earlier. Bernini's bees on the tomb of Urban are not quite as innocent of the new microscopic information as those of Pietro da Cortona. Bernini's at least have stingers, a felt part of people's experience of bees. These are clearly visible on the two large bees on the statue base; that of the large bee on the sarcophagus may have been broken off, since it can be easily reached from the floor of the church. Neither Bernini's nor Cortona's bees show the marked difference between the small inner wings of bees and the larger and differently shaped outer wings, as both engravings clearly show. Bernini's bees seem to reflect the new knowledge of the large size, marked convexity, and angle with the axis of the body of the bees' eyes that the engravings show. Although he obviously did not feel constrained to follow the engravings in all aspects of the new microscopic information, Bernini seems to have been influenced by one or both of these engravings in achieving a tangibly enhanced sense of reality in the bees on the tomb of Urban.

Not really necessary to my argument, but fascinating, of very high quality, and relevant to Bernini's genuine interest in bees and variety of approach to them, is the cartouche below a portrait of Antonio Barberini, Pope Urban's great-uncle who had been murdered in 1559. The cartouche is framed by the open skin of a flayed bee, much in the manner of the flayed dragon framing the cartouche of *Apollo and Daphne*, probably slightly earlier, the text of which was written by Urban. Here one feels the aggressive aspect of the bee. And here is perhaps a basis in the new "microscopic" knowledge that had been made public in the *Melissographia* engraving.[20]

NOTES

1. For a good photograph that includes the coat of arms, see P. O. Fehl, "L'Umiltà cristiana e il monumento sontuoso: La tomba di Urbano VIII del Bernini," in *Gian Lorenzo Bernini e le art visive*, ed. Marcello Fagiolo (Rome: 1987), 193.

2. Howard Hibbard, *Bernini* (Baltimore: Penguin Books, 1966), 105.

3. I remember being startled by their size when I came upon these small bees in 1951, when I was working intensively on Bernini.

4. The etching is datable to the late seventeenth century by the dates in the life of the individual to whom it is dedicated, *Bernini in Vaticano* (Rome: 1981), 110, fig. 90, catalogue entry by Dotta. Maria Teresa De Lotto.

5. For help with the literature on the odor of sanctity, I am deeply indebted to my colleagues Caroline W. Bynum, Wert Cousins, and John Keber. See H. Thurston, SJ, *The Physical Phenomena of Mysticism* (Chicago: 1952), esp. chs. IX and X, 222–270; P. Camporesi, *The Incorruptible Flesh* (Cambridge: 1988); and A. Vauchez, *La Sainteté en occident aux derniers siècles du moyen-âge* (Rome: 1981), esp. livre III, 491 ff.

6. Fehl, op. cit., 202 and note 25.

7. It is not clear whether or not the lid and lower body of the sarcophagus are separate pieces of marble. Not having anticipated such a problem, I found on a recent visit to Saint Peter's that I did not have with me tools adequate to check this definitively. The important thing is that the prominent strip of ornament just above the lowest of the large bees, with salient, slanting, convex forms angles toward the center of the sarcophagus, *is* clearly in design terms the ornamental form designating the bottom of the lid.

8. According to the literature, the recorded duration of saintly fragrances varies greatly (see note 5, above). In the legend of Saint Mark, centuries passed between his burial and the opening of his tomb by the Venetians who came to Alexandria to remove the body of their patron saint and take it to Venice. When the tomb was opened, the entire city of Alexandria was filled with an "odor soavissimo"—an "olfactory sign" that this, indeed, was the corpse of Saint Mark. See David Rosand, *Painting in Cinquecento Venice: Titian, Vernones, Tintoretto* (New Haven and London: Yale University Press, 1982), 191–2 and note 25; I am indebted to David Rosand for this striking example of the odor of sanctity.

9. Erwin Panofsky, *Early Netherlandish Painting*, 2 vols. (Cambridge, Mass.: Harvard University Press, 1953), I, 310, note 5 (488, 489).

10. Ibid, II, Fig. 405.

11. I am again indebted to David Rosand, who called my attention to the Sebastiano painting.

12. Once again I am indebted to David Rosand, who called my attention to the similarity in the handling of bees in Rubens' book title page and Bernini's tomb of Pope Urban. See *Rubens and His Circle: Studies by Julius S. Held*, ed. A. W. Lowenthal, D. Rosand, and J W. Walsh, Jr. (Princeton, N.J.: 1982), 182, 183, and fig. XV 26. See also ibid., 177, 178, and fig XV 18, a 1632 title page to a book of poems "honoring Urban VIII written by a Polish Jesuit, Mathias Casimir Sarbiewski." Held connects the child in the cradle in the lower right to Pindar, "the sweetness of whose poetry was attributed to the honey which bees had left on his tongue when he was a child." Held also calls attention to the linkage between the spray of bees above the mouth of the child Pindar and those of Urban VIII at the top center of the same title page.

13. The drawing is in the Plantin-Moretus Museum in Antwerp; see G. Glück and F. M. Habeditzl, *Die Handzeichnungen von Peter Paul Rubens* (Berlin: 1928), fig. 215.

14. Again, see *Rubens and His Circle*, 89, 90, and figs. VII 6, VII 7. Held here had earlier pointed to a book title page by Rubens as having influenced Bernini's handling of the Virtue figures in the tomb of Urban and their relationship to the sarcophagus. This enhances the probability that the Rubens title page of 1634 for Urban's poems influenced Bernini in the handling of the bees on Urban's tomb, as suggested above.

15. See the excellent article by Dotta. Enrica Schettini Piazza, "Teoria e sperimentazione nell'*Apiario* di Federico Cesi," in *Atti dei convegni Lincei* (Rome: 1986), 231–249, for the chronological sequence, character, and relationship of these prints to one another and the learned Linceans who produced them. It is a tribute to Wittkower's scholarship that he was elected a member of the Accademia dei Lincei.

16. Ibid., 232–235 and fig. 1.

17. Two enlarged hind legs of a bee form what at first looks like an ornamental frame just above Stelluti's signature.

18. E. Panofsky, "Artist, Scientist, Genius: Notes on the 'Renaissance-Dämmerung,'" in *The Renaissance* (New York: Harper Torchbooks, 1962), 178–180 and figs. 26, 27. Panofsky, who seems not to have been aware of the *Melissographia*, also does less than justice to Cesi. It is true that Cesi did not publish prints reflecting new visual "microscopic" discoveries. In a prolegomenon to a planned major book on bees, however, he did include references to this new knowledge in the form of an immense engraving consisting of four separate plates, which when combined produce an engraving 41" x 25.5" (1,040 x 646 mm.), consisting almost entirely of text in minute script, but also bearing Urban's coat of arms and reproductions of four ancient coins with images of bees. It is entitled *Apiarium* and bears the date 1625, although it may not have been finished until January 1626 (Piazza, 235–241 and fig. 2). Cesi died prematurely (Aug. 1, 1630) without having completed his work on bees.

19. Francesco Stelluti, *Persio tradotto inverso sciolto e dichiarato* (Rome: 1630), into which he found an excuse for squeezing two and one half pages (pp. 51–54) of descriptive text about bees and this engraving (Piazza, fig. 4; Panofsky, fig. 27). I am indebted to Joseph Connors, who first called my attention to this print, to the *Melissographia*, and also to the Panofsky essay.

20. R. Wittkower, *Gianlorenzo Bernini*, 2d ed. (London: Phaidon Press, 1966), 191, 192, fig. 30. Maurizio and Marcello Fagiolo dell'Arco, *Bernini* (Rome: 1967), pl. 16. The same plate contains the cartouche on the pedestal of the *Apollo and Daphne*.

PART II

14. Statues of the Tsars and the Redefinition of Russia's Past

Richard Wortman

The erection of a public monument in the nineteenth century had implications far beyond the acts of its planning and construction. The monument was the center of a major public event. Ceremonies of dedication dramatized its historical importance. Engravings, lithographs, and later photographs, defined it as an example of national art. Explanatory texts, sometimes written by the artists themselves, made its meaning explicit and known, and placed it within a national tradition of monuments.

The original Latin sense of the word "monument" is "to remind," just as the Russian word *pamiatnik* contains the meaning of reminding. By creating reminders for the future, nineteenth-century regimes created an illusion of permanence, of becoming part of an evolving history that was moving ineluctably to a great destiny. Today many of these monuments are gone. Many of those that remain are regarded as artistic fixtures whose original meanings have been lost or transformed. But for the historian they remain significant events whose expressions allow us to understand a world that found meaning in a bronze or stone image. From this point of view, a monument is not a mere physical object, but a specific political statement that evoked feelings, comments, and associations among contemporaries. These are to be found in written explanations and responses, in the ceremonies that dramatized its importance, and in the illustrations that showed how it was intended to be seen. These presentations and representations reveal the monument's meaning for contemporaries and the spirit and significance of the events surrounding it. It is the purpose of this paper to try to restore the statues of the Russian emperors in the nineteenth twentieth century to their political and cultural context.

The monuments erected by European monarchs of the nineteenth and early twentieth centuries were expressions of the cult of dynasty that was ascendant after the fall of Napoleon. Monuments identified the members of the dynasty with the nation and established its members among world historical figures worthy of note. Such presentation often involved considerable reshaping of the dynasty's past, what Eric Hobsbawm has called "the invention of tradition."[1] First, the identification of the dynasty with the nation required the concealment or denial of the markedly antinational and cosmopolitan character of most eighteenth- and nineteenth-century European monarchs. Secondly, it required the creation of a tradition of shared dynastic values and smooth transitions between reigns that often were contradicted by history.

In Russia, the need for such reworking of the past was particularly acute. Russian monarchs from Peter the Great to 1825 had endeavored to demonstrate their European character and to eradicate any hint of cultural links with the Russian people or national past. Secondly, the succession problems of the eighteenth century and the political crises of the nineteenth led to sharp discontinuities between reigns that hardly sustained the myth of a unified dynasty. The statues to the tsars helped to disguise these uncomfortable truths in imposing artistic forms that created the illusion of an ongoing historical process. The tsarist statue in this respect was a calculated violation of the past in order to enhance the image of the ruling monarch.

The tsarist statue contained a political statement, but the political statement was also embodied in an artistic tradition with its own references and associations. From the start, the tsarist statue was a violation of the past in a primal sense, for it transgressed against the Orthodox Church's prohibition of graven images. Peter the Great placed half-naked classical figures in the parks near his palaces in Petersburg and Peterhof, thus blaspheming both the esthetic and moral tenets of Orthodoxy. By the end of the nineteenth century, the imperial family had become so inured to Western values that they had lost touch with earlier teachings and sensibilities. Nicholas I (1825–1855) even placed a statue of St. Vladimir, the "enlightener of Rus'" who had adopted Eastern Christianity in 988, on a hill over the Dnepr at Kiev. During the construction, the Metropolitan of Kiev remarked drily that the statue had only "civic significance" and won his approval to begin collecting donations for a cathedral to honor the saint.[2] During the nineteenth and twentieth centuries, statues continued to carry connotations of alien, pagan, and even menacing bodies.[3]

The prototype of nineteenth-century tsarist statues was Étienne-Maurice Falconet's monument to Peter the Great, "the Bronze Horseman," on Senate Square, now Decembrist Square, in St. Petersburg (Fig. 14–1). Falconet's statue, completed in 1782, explicitly transformed the image of Peter the Great (1682–1725) to fit the image of monarch presented by Catherine the Great (1762–1796). Catherine had no hereditary ties to Peter; she came to the throne by ousting her husband, Peter III. Her claims to rule were based on her aspirations to be an enlightened monarch, the bestower of law and prosperity on Russia. The statue was her attempt to show Peter, an enlightened monarch, as her spiritual forbear.

Figure 14–1 *Equestrian Monument of Peter the Great.* Etienne Maurice Falconet, sculptor. Bronze. St. Petersburg.

An enlightened monarch was hardly the dominant image of Peter in eighteenth-century Russia. More current was the image of Peter as ruthless commander who had transformed Russia by his force of will. Carlo Bartolommeo Rastrelli's equestrian statue of Peter the Great presents this view of Peter. The Emperor is in Roman dress, wears a laurel wreath, and holds a scepter in his right hand. He is implacable in his strength and there is a fierce, intimidating look in his eyes. Cast in 1745, it remained hidden in a shed beside the St. Isaac's cathedral until Paul I placed it before the Mikhailovskii Palace in 1800, where it now stands.[4]

Falconet's statue accomplished the feat of transforming Peter from a martial figure to what H. W. Janson called "a hero of virtue." The monumental equestrian figure in Roman toga, similar to a statue of Louis XIV by Bernini, soars skyward, trampling a snake, triumphant over evil and human weakness.[5] The inscription *"Petro primo, Catarina secunda"* declares both Catherine's assumption of the Petrine heritage and her presumption to reshape it. Falconet shared this intention and made clear in his correspondence with Catherine that his statue was to be a symbolic embodiment of Catherine's conception of rule. He wrote that he did not exclude the possibility of allegory, but thought that the hero himself should express it. He had in mind, he wrote to Diderot, "not the victor over Charles XII, but Russia and her reformer." He wanted to fashion "the person of the founder, legislator, benefactor of his country." He therefore put no scepter in Peter's hand and clothed him as a Roman emperor.[6] The dedication of the statue on August 7, 1782, was a major ceremonial occasion. Catherine was deeply moved, feeling the spirit of Peter passing to her. She wrote to Baron Melchior Grimm that Peter's image "had a look of contentment which also passed to me and encouraged me to do better in the future."[7]

Falconet made the base of the statue a statement of the relationship between Peter and the nation. Stone symbolized the triumph of reason over crude nature. Falconet wrote, "He extends his beneficent hand over the country he travelled across. He rises at the top of the rock that is his pedestal. This is an emblem of the difficulties he conquered." The metaphor was a reference to Peter's own return to one of Peter's favorite symbols. Peter had taken the motif of Pygmalion and Galatea as his own personal emblem—a sculptor reshaping Russia, which was emblazoned on his standard and his seal. "The whole of Russia is your statue, transformed by your superb craftsmanship," the archbishop Feofan Prokopovich declared in a famous sermon.[8]

Falconet himself made clear that the finding, hauling, and placement of the stone had "emblematic meaning," turning it into a symbol of nature subdued.[9] The technological feat in extracting and moving a monolith weighing 1,600 tons and towering over twenty-four feet high was a central part of the achievement. The construction of the statue demonstrated the transformation of Russia, raw nature, by the rational mind of the monarch. It showed that Russia had joined and perhaps surpassed the classical tradition of the West. The eighteenth-century versifier Vasili Ruban wrote:

Oh, Collossus of Rhodes,
Humble thy haughty gaze,
And tall Pyramids of the Nile,

No longer think yourself such marvels!
This Russian mountain untouched by hands,
Having heard God's voice,
Came to Peter's city along the Neva,
And stood beneath the feet of the GREAT PETER.[10]

Falconet's statue was an act of willful redefinition and violation. It turned Peter into a symbol of virtue and reason, ignoring the ruthless force of destruction that had accompanied his reign. It asserted the irresistible will of the monarch who, armed with reason, accomplished prodigies; it was a statement of pagan pride. The achievement of a German princess, it reaffirmed the triumph of Western aesthetic values and a disdain for Orthodox misgivings about statuary. It was this tradition that was taken up by official tsarist statuary in the nineteenth century.

The opposite perception of the statue, as an inimical, menacing figure, is better known to us from Alexander Pushkin's poem "The Bronze Horseman" and other works of Russian literature. Pushkin's poem transforms the statue into a symbol of Peter's remorseless, inhuman capital, built on a swamp. The poem's central figure, Evgenii, is left ruined and alone by the great flood of 1824, and is chased by the vision of the Horseman, galloping after him to his death. Emperor Alexander I, no master of nature, watches bewildered and sorrowful from the palace balcony and says "It is not for Tsars to tame God's elements." Pushkin's poem introduced what Jakobson called "the myth of the destructive statue" that reappeared in such works as Velimir Khlebnikov's "Monument" and Andrei Belyi's novel *Petersburg*. As perhaps its most horrifying evocation, the Bronze Horseman appears in a vision before Belyi's phobic Nietzschean revolutionary Alexander Dudkin, returns to its molten state, and pours itself down his throat.[11]

* * *

The column dedicated to Alexander I (1801–1825) on the Palace Square in St. Petersburg was the first public monument expressing the cult of the Romanov dynasty. The cult brought a major change in the official conceptions of the past. Russian rulers of the eighteenth century had sought to distance themselves from their predecessors and to condemn the previous reign as an era of darkness and despotism preceding a dawning Age of Gold. Similarities and continuities were submerged in an effort to justify a seizure of power as an act of political deliverance. After Nicholas I's accession in 1825, Russian emperors proceeded in the opposite manner: they tried to conceal the considerable discontinuities between reigns by creating an illusion of continuity. The statues enshrined each emperor's values and goals as those of his predecessor.

Nicholas I (1825–1855) ascended the throne after crushing a rebellion of guards' regiments demanding a constitution, the "Decembrist" uprising. His accession ushered in a period of political conservatism, militarization of government and society, and police repression. Nicholas's anti-revolutionary policies continued those of the last years of his brother Alexander I's reign (1801–1825), when Alexander was under the influence of Metternich. But through most of his reign, Alexander had retained hopes for major reforms of the Russian political system. The conservative views of the close of his reign, moreover, were based on a vision of religious rebirth of all mankind, a Christian religion inspired by the reading of the Bible. In this respect, he remained true to the eighteenth-century faith in human perfectibility and the existence of universal truths for all nations.

Nicholas I, on the other hand, conceived of autocratic rule as the ideal form of government for Russia, necessitated by historical conditions, and requiring only a strong ruler, a firm hand, and consistent laws—all of which were lacking in 1825—to work well. The slogan "Autocracy, Orthodoxy, and Nationality" expressed what came to be known as the doctrine of "official nationality," which presented autocratic government as the expression of Russia's distinctive national heritage. The highly Western cosmopolitan monarchy was thus defined as a distinctively Russian institution and Russian autocracy as the highest development of monarchy and empire, capable of resisting the inimical forces, "the revolutionary bacilli" weakening and destroying the monarchies of the West.

The artist chosen to create the Alexandrine column, Auguste Ricard de Montferrand, had been brought to Petersburg by Alexander to design and direct the construction of St. Isaac's Cathedral. A representative of French late Neoclassicism and eclecticism, Montferrand continued the project of turning Petersburg into a simulacrum of Rome. A simple statue, he claimed, would not fit the vast proportions of the palace square, and at the directive of Nicholas I he chose the form of the column. The column is crowned by an angel with the features of Alexander I, the work of the sculptor Boris Orlovskii.[12]

The monument presents Alexander I as a hero in the ongoing process of perfection of autocratic government. Montferrand described this conception in a lavish folio volume, filled by his own drawings, reproduced by lithography, and published in Paris. His opening dedication to Nicholas I establishes the connection between contemporary Petersburg and the traditions of Peter. The dedication opens with a glorification of Peter's work for the general good, for introducing science to Russia, and above all for embellishing St. Petersburg. After Peter's death, "thanks to the care of his successors everything became more perfect according to his views." Nicholas I had brought this process to its culmination. St. Petersburg had even begun to rival the ancient capitals of the world "not so much by useful institutions, its temples, monuments and riches, as by its inhabitants' urbanity, the mildness (douceur) and the regularity of their morals, which are owing to Your Majesty, and the fine arts that [St. Petersburg] shelters."[13]

The arts were the visual expression, the symbol of this process of perfection, and Montferrand envisioned his column as the symbol of its culmination. For this reason, he chose what he believed to be the perfect example of the column, Trajan's Column in Rome, following the example of the Napoleon Column in Paris, now the Vendôme Column. He wrote that he sought "to approach this sublime model of antiquity as closely as possible." But while imitating the Trajan Column, Montferrand was determined, undoubtedly with the emperor's encouragement, to surpass his model as well and recent copies, like the Napoleon Column, and to make his column the largest in the world.[14] At 154 feet, it was in fact higher than the Napoleon Column, registering another victory of Russia over France. Lest doubts linger, Montferrand included a scale drawing showing the Alexandrine higher than the Napoleon, Trajan, Antonine, and Pompeian columns.

Montferrand had no humble opinion of the significance of his work. He saw it continuing and consummating the endeavor of Peter, and he makes his point explicit at the close of his text with a parable illustrated by a vignette. His drawing shows Petersburg covered by the sea. Two monuments, the Bronze Horseman and the Alexandrine Column, and the ruins of an ancient temple are the only surviving structures. Montferrand imagines a traveler venturing into this "ancient northern sea" and stopping to survey the ruins of the great city. Having passed through remains of the temple, the traveler "will behold alone, erect in the midst of the tumultuous waves, the Alexandrine Column, still attesting to the imperishable glory of the immortal sovereigns of Russia."[15]

For Montferrand, stone remained the symbol of Russia's progress and the medium whose transformation exemplified the force and the allure of art. Most of his text and illustrations are devoted to the discovery of the slab of red granite in Finland and the feats of extraction and transportation to the capital. The act of mobilizing great numbers of laborers was a demonstration of the power and effectiveness of the autocracy, which Montferrand describes with great admiration. Six hundred workers labored for two years alone to extract the monolith. Montferrand describes at length his feat of organizing three thousand workers to hoist the column into place and added an illustration of the massive scaffolding, with the Imperial Family awaiting the dramatic moment. He writes "If our imagination transports us to the platform of the works, we would see a great nation represented by three-thousand of its children lifting a monument to their father. The Emperor, his son, and his brother, stand in the middle of these fine men who give an example of work."[16]

The Column was presented as a metonym of the perfect state of Russia. It expressed feelings of pride for a completed achievement that were quite different from the spirit of Alexander I, who despaired about the state of Russia and the failure of his efforts to reform his country. Court poet Vasilii Zhukovskii, describing the scene of the dedication in the newspapers *Severnaia Pchela* and *Russkii Invalid*, confesses that he was overwhelmed by the monument. He compares the base of Falconet's statue of Peter the Great, "an ugly crag," with "the harmonious column that is the only one in the world of such height." The size and majesty of the object, he writes, defied the poet's gifts. The device of metaphor is inappropriate to the occasion; his inspiration, he insists, is not the inspiration of the poet, "embellishing or transforming the substance of a thing." It is instead "an astonishing feeling of what was lofty, inseparable from the object prompting it," like the feeling he experienced when first seeing the Alps and the dome of St. Peter's in Rome.[17]

The base was decorated with reliefs designed by Montferrand that symbolized Alexander's worldly accomplishments, particularly his military triumphs. The front relief bore the legend, "To Alexander, from a grateful Russia," indicating that it was principally the Emperor who was responsible for the victory. Garlands, eagles, and laurel wreaths resembled those on the Trajan Column. Russian military insignia included the helmets of Alexander Nevskii and Ermak and a shield attributed to Prince Oleg. The front bas-relief included figures symbolizing the rivers, the Nieman and the Vistula. The other sides displayed female allegorical figures of the Virtues, Victory, Peace, Justice, Clemency, and Abundance. The figure of Victory carries a buckle with the dates 1812, 1813, and 1814.[18]

The statue of Alexander himself, if it can be so termed, is placed high atop the Column—like the Roman emperors and Napoleon on their respective columns—so high as to be visible only in silhouette from the ground. The angel, crushing a serpent with a cross, points to the heavens and peers down at the Square. If Peter the Great appears as a classical hero, Alexander assumes the incorporeal form of an angel. This angel, indeed, was the favored metaphor for Alexander during his reign. The image of the angel captured his mild and elusive personality, his otherworldly spirit, and the sense that he was above the mundane cares of the moment. Nicholas Karamzin compared Alexander to an angel in his accession of 1801, and at his death, his wife, the Empress Elizabeth, said, "Our Angel is now in Heaven," a line that was widely quoted in the memorial literature.[19]

But the angel on the Column is not a reference to Alexander's angelic traits. Orlovskii had been directed to fashion an allegory expressing the triumph of Russia. Like Falconet, he insisted that the allegory be given concrete human form. "It is necessary that the idea of this allegory be expressed clearly, characteristically, and in a form proper to our era and national idea. Those were the conditions with which I harmonized my allegory, depicting an angel crushing a serpent with a cross."[20] The angel on the statue is hardly mild and effacing, but is instead a powerful expression of a divine force, an instrument of Providence acting in behalf of the nation. It is a statement of political transcendence and destiny.

Alexander is depicted not as a hero who has accomplished worldly exploits, but as a figure whose spiritual nature brought the salvation of Europe to the greatness of Russia, a savior. In a brochure describing the dedication ceremony, Ivan Butovskii writes "He is sad to part with Russia, which he saved, which he comforted, upon which he bestowed happiness. His right hand points to the heavens, giving credit for his great exploit to God alone." The great Column, Butovskii asserts, shows Alexander's firmness at the moment of doubt in 1812. "It seemed as if the Messiah came down to earth and announced to all peoples of the beginning of eternal bliss." Enlightenment spread, luxury flourished, towns were built.[21] Zhukovskii thought Russia had entered a new period of civic development after the military triumph, "a period of internal development, of firm legality, and the quiet acquisition of all treasures." This era would bring "the rich harvest of well-being, entrusted to Autocracy," symbolized by the angel, "and his name is God's Truth."[22]

The savior theme is stated most explicitly by the poem "Feelings of a Youth at the sight of the Monument to Alexander the Blessed," printed in the newspaper *Russkii Invalid*:

Holding in your hands the sacred symbol,
You gaze on us from on high;
With the hand of the autocrat,
You bless Holy Rus'.
You are ours! In you I know
The tsar savior of the universe!

I stand as if charmed
Enraptured by the visage of the Tsar.[23]

The solemn ceremony of dedication on Alexander's name day, August 30, 1834, marked the monument as a votive object in the new cult of dynasty. As was typical of imperial ceremonies, the dedication consisted of two interconnected acts of consecration, a massive parade and a religious ceremony of thanksgiving and blessing. The event concluded with a "ceremonial march" as all the regiments filed by the Tsar and his suite before the Winter Palace. Taking place after Russian armies had crushed the revolution of 1830 in Poland, the ceremony was a celebration of Russia's triumph under the rule of the Romanov dynasty.

The central figure in this symbolic drama was, of course, the Emperor himself. At 11 a.m. Nicholas appeared on the square cannon to the sound of cannon salvos. At the third blast, columns of troops began marching toward the square to the sounds of the band music. They quickly covered the entire vast expanse. Zhukovskii described the stirring display he beheld as an emanation of the awesome personal power of the Tsar:

The heavy measured step, shaking the soul, the calm approach of a force that was at once invincible and obedient. The army poured in thick waves and submerged the square. But there was amazing order in this flood. The eyes beheld an innumerable and immense moving mass, but the most striking thing in this spectacle was something the eyes could not see: the secret presence of a will that moved and directed with a mere nod.[24]

The Emperor, now standing at the side of his brother-in-law Prince Wilhelm of Prussia, bared his head and prayed together with his entire army, "a spectacle that was at once touching and instructive," Butovskii writes. Nicholas fell to his knees, followed by the entire army. When the Protodeacon uttered the prayer of Eternal Memory, the cloth fell, baring the monument to public view. Nicholas then took command of the guard and saluted the monument to the sound of band music and general exclamations of "Hoorah" from the crowd.[25]

The newspaper accounts present the scene as an expression of the providential confidence of the triumphal Russian autocracy. After observing the scene and the monument, Butovskii exclaimed, "Who of those standing here could remain unconvinced that GOD IS GREAT, that THE RUSSIAN TSAR IS GREAT as are HIS people. . . ."[26] Zhukovskii describes the moment of common prayer as a condensed, microcosmic statement of Russian grandeur, silencing the writer's imagination:

The miraculous fusion of earthly power reduced to dust with mysterious power of the cross, rising above it and the invisible presence of that without name, expressing everything that is dear to us, something whispering to the soul, "Russia, your past glory is your future glory" and finally the touching word eternal memory and the name ALEXANDER, whereupon the drape fell from the column, followed by a thunderous prolonged Hoorah, combined with sound of five-hundred cannons, from which the air was transformed into a festive storm of glory. . . . For the depiction of such moments there are no words and the very recollection of them destroys the gift of the one who describes.[27]

The blessing of the monument took place after the prayer. This began with a procession of the cross, led by clergy, that presented an array of the Tsar's leading military and civil servants and the members of the estates who served him. They marched in a procession of the cross. The clergy in their chasubles led the members of the imperial family, ladies and gentlemen of the court, members of the State Council and the Senate, noblemen, and merchants. After the procession circled the statue, the clergy pronounced the benediction and ministered the holy water. The conclusion was the ceremonial march. For three hours, the troops filed past the Emperor, standing beside the monument, and a pavilion with the Empress and other members of the family.

For Butovskii the ceremony was an emblematic enactment of the emotional solidarity between people and monarch. The people on the square represented all the Russian people. He described a "touching scene" that took place after the ceremony. "Common people" (*prostye liudi*) gathered at the monument and looked upon it with tenderness (*umilenie*), uttering the name of Alexander with tears in their eyes. They called him "their Angel, their Benefactor, their Little Father." Others brought their children to the column and spoke of "the kindness and majesty of Russian TSARS" and the glory of the Russian armies.[28]

If the ceremony confirmed the political significance of the monument, pictures established both monument and ceremony in the mythic history of the dynasty. The two known to me, Montferrand's illustration for his volume and a painting by Vasili Raev, follow the style of the "perspectival school" of painting that received encouragement in Nicholas I's reign.[29] "Perspective painting" sought to present the image of perfect geometric and spatial order. It marked the final development of the perspectival bias of absolutism, what Jean-Marie Apostolids refers to as the "oculary imperialism" of Louis XIV's reign, the gaze of the monarch that puts everything in hierarchical perspective.[30] The mortals on the Square are turned into objects of art, their order and submission reflecting the creative will of the monarch. They are arranged in neat quadrilaterals over the expanse, the Square surrounded by monumental classical edifices. The scene fades into the distance, giving the impression that it continues indefinitely. Butovskii's brochure also presents the Square as a metonym of the empire as a whole. The buildings of the Square represent "the foundation stones upon which our empire rests. The happiness and well-being of Russia flow from the marvelous buildings bordering the Square."[31]

* * *

The monument to Nicholas I on Mariinskii, now Isaac's Square in St. Petersburg, was built under quite different historical circumstances. Alexander II succeeded his father on February 19, 1855, in the midst of diplomatic and political crises. Nicholas I armies had suffered a humiliating defeat at the hands of a small British and French expeditionary force in the Crimea. The war had shown the state bureaucracy riddled with corruption and incompetence. It left Russia, a few years before the most influential of European monarchies, in diplomatic isolation. The

Treaty of Paris, concluding the Crimean War, inflicted the further humiliation of barring Russian warships from the Black Sea.

Alexander II then embarked on the "Great Reforms": the emancipation of the serfs (1861); the introduction of a new court system (1864); and institutions of local self-government, the *zemstva* (1864). A devoted son who continued to worship his father, Alexander broke with the very principle of bureaucratic rule and authoritarian morality that Nicholas I had exemplified. But Alexander remained faithful to the fundamental principle of autocratic rule and presented his reign as a continuation of his father's. The monument to Nicholas I was his declaration of filial and dynastic devotion, even as he embarked on a period of liberalization and humanitarian change. He ordered a statue that would render "the features of his immortal parent in the military outfit [*vooruzhenie*] in which the late *Tsar* was most majestic." Alexander proceeded swiftly with the execution of the statue: the cornerstone was laid in June 1857, and the monument was dedicated in June 1859.[32]

The reduced circumstances of the post-Crimean War period brought forth a problem of style that would confront all late nineteenth-century sculptors of royal monuments. How was a monarch to be given a proper monumental aspect when the heroic idiom had been largely abandoned, and in any event would be inappropriate for a ruler whose claims to omnipotence and omniscience had been discredited? The designer of the monument was again Auguste Montferrand, who completed his plans shortly before his death in 1858. But this statue has none of the grandiose pretensions of the Alexandrine Column. Nicholas is depicted as if from life; there is little heroic or otherworldly about him. The humiliation has produced a sense of humility, reflected in a turn to realism.

Montferrand chose an equestrian statue, presumably to place the monument in the tradition of Falconet's Bronze Horseman. But this statue is not a timeless superhuman figure. Instead, Nicholas appears as if on ceremonial display, in the uniform and eagle helmet of the Horse Guards, one of the most aristocratic and ceremonial of the regiments. The statue establishes an acceptable continuity with Nicholas' reign by emphasizing the *ceremonial* elegance of Nicholas' bearing rather than the stern, awesome manner that made him a terrifying figure at public occasions. Alexander himself shared Nicholas' taste for magnificent parades and fine posture, and this presentation of his father clearly pleased him.

Indeed, Alexander II dictated the style and decided the final appearance of the statue, which very much relects his own image of his father. He rejected an earlier plan for a standing horse. He wanted the more animated pose of the Bronze Horseman, or Klodt's horses on the Anichkov bridge. But those horses did not have riders and the sculptor, Peter Klodt, had to find a way to support the 3,600 pounds of this horse's body on its slender rear legs. The feat was one of balance and calculation, with the aid of internal supports. The problem, as described by the journal *Russkii Khudozhestvennyi Listok*, was "to present the rider properly seated in his saddle, on a thoroughbred bob-tailed stallion leaping into an exercise gallop, that is to reinforce the bronze mass, twenty-four feet high, on the two rear legs of the thoroughbred horse."[33]

With his usual fussiness about dress—also characteristic of his father—Alexander asked for additional changes after the first revisions, "to change the gait of the horse from left to right, to make the plume on the helmet smaller, to place the helmet farther back on the head, to make the boots softer, the epaulets and right sleeve fuller."[34] He continued to watch over the work, as depicted by Vasilii Timm's engraving in *Russkii Khudozhestvennyi Listok* showing Alexander inspecting the statue in Klodt's studio in 1857 with Montferrand, Klodt, and several officials.[35]

The emphasis on ceremonial style satisfied Alexander, but the impression that Nicholas was performing a fancy riding exercise hardly gave the statue a majestic aura. The look is rather one of parade performance than of majesty, and Nicholas' gaze, not strong and piercing, as it had been in life, is averted fastidiously. An Emperor who never was a skillful rider and did not like to ride appears to posterity performing an equestrian stunt. The monarch who overpowered people with his presence here appears effete. H. W. Janson comments "Clearly something has gone wrong here for this statue strikes us a mere display of horsemanship by a military man who knows how to put his mount through its paces." Scoffers in the nineteenth century remarked that Nicholas I was galloping after Peter the Great but couldn't catch up.[36]

The late Emperor's personal quality glorified by artists was his love of family. The cult of domesticity had been a prominent feature of Nicholas's public life; he had presented himself as an affectionate and doting husband and father. Accordingly, the sculptor Robert Zaleman executed allegorical virtues representing Justice, Strength, Faith, and Reason with the features of Nicholas' three daughters and of the Dowager Empress, Alexandra Fedorovna. The statue thus expresses Nicholas' identification of virtue with the family and his cult of the pure and idealized woman, which his son shared, at least in principle.

The pedestal of the statue also reflects the retreat from earlier lofty aspirations. It too employs Finnish granite, but the mass does not call attention to itself and it is placed under a layer of white Italian marble. The pedestal was intended to be twelve feet higher than it now stands, but a comparison with Christian Daniel Rauch's statue of Frederick the Great in Berlin and other foreign monuments led Montferrand to reduce its height and to increase its width by a few feet. Indicatively, he now used foreign models to moderate rather than increase the proportions of his monument.[37]

The bas-reliefs, the work of Nicholas Ramazanov and Zaleman, Ramazanov's teacher, depict Nicholas' achievements. They present him principally as protector of the dynasty and defender of order against the forces of revolution. Initially, three of the four reliefs were devoted to this theme: the Decembrist uprising, the cholera insurrection of 1831 in St. Petersburg, and the surrender of the Hungarian troops to the Russians in 1849. The philosopher Peter Chaadaev observed to Baron A. I. Delvig, who oversaw Ramazanov's work, that it was unfortunate to leave so sad a recollection of the past for the future and that the subjects would probably be changed. Indeed, an order soon came from Petersburg eliminating the Hungarian scene and commissioning two new scenes more in keeping with the new civic spirit—one by Ramazanov of Nicholas' opening of the Vereiskii Railway bridge, a second by Zaleman of Nicholas decorating Speranskii with a star from his own chest for the completion of the Digest of Laws. The latter relief shows special attention to historical accuracy and depicts all those present at the ceremony.[38]

Nonetheless, the other two reliefs are extraordinary in depicting the emperor's own heroism in terms of the suppression of rebellion among his own subjects. Nicholas strikes theatrical poses on both occasions. There is no allegory, only the Tsar's display of courage before his guardsmen and the people of St. Petersburg. In the first relief, Nicholas presents Alexander to the Saper battalion on December 14, 1825. This portrayal links Alexander II with his father's defense of monarchy and celebrates the political bond between father and son. Nicholas stands in the center, tall and imposing in his uniform, making a grand gesture toward Alexander, held in the arms of several officers. The others look on with the rapt engagement of the observers in historical paintings, indicating the significance of the moment by raising their hats, extending their arms, or falling to their knees. The relief on the cholera insurrection depicts the moment in 1831 when Nicholas rode through the square demanding the obedience of his subjects. He stands huge and triumphant on the carriage; peasants grovel at wheels beneath him and raise their hands, abjectly beseeching forgiveness. Others are at the feet of the tall, haughty officers in his suite.[39]

The dedication of the statue on June 25, 1859, was celebrated with the usual complement of guards regiments and publicity.[40] The tone of the presentation, however, is considerably more humble than that of 1834. The account emphasizes the public character of the event. It describes how stands were erected around the Square and tickets sold for seats; rooms viewing the Square went for one-hundred and fifty rubles per window. The account gives the impression of a motley tumult; there was no glorification of the mobilization or the disciplining of the population. Crowds of people followed the guards' regiments into the Square. "The stands were covered by a solid mass of spectators, the windows of the adjoining houses turned into little ampitheaters, even the roofs were ornamented as if with beads, by multicolored parasols, and above everything shone the burning summer sun."[40] Timm's illustration provides a sense of animation rather than restrained order.

The Emperor arrived on horseback accompanied by the Grand Dukes and his suite. After reviewing the troops, he returned to the palace to escort the Empress, Maria Aleksandrovna, and the Grand Duchesses, who rode to the Square in carriages. The clergy in their holiday vestments moved in a procession of the cross from St. Isaac's Cathedral to the statue. A hush fell over the Square. Only the sound of a choir was heard from the church, and they gave the impression, in their brilliant chasubles, of "a ribbon of gold." When the protodeacon had declaimed the prayer for eternal rest, the troops, at the Emperor's command, saluted, a salvo came from the guns of the Peter-Paul fortress, and the boats lined up along the Neva, which echoed the firings of the troops on the Square.

There was no effort to suggest that the event resonated with political meaning, nor did the anonymous author suggest that it had prompted exalted feelings defying description. It was a festive but hardly significant moment, and the emphasis was on the picturesque scene rather than the great symbolic moment of the ceremonies. After the salvo the members of the Family, followed by the ladies of the court in their holiday "Russian dress" and the leading officials and members of the merchantry, proceeded to the statue. "At this moment, the Square took on another, but no less solemn character. The measured procession of the Imperial Family, the thousands of people, all in silence, the uninterrupted salvoes, and the ringing of bells, all fused in some kind of extraordinary picture, full of majesty." After the regiments passed by in ceremonial march, the Imperial Family returned to the Winter Palace.

The monument and the ceremony of dedication had redefined the meaning of the dynastic tradition to fit the circumstances and values of the time. This tradition could no longer be understood in terms of the heroic conquest of nature described by the Petrine myth. Nor could it be understood as embodying the providential imperial destiny of Russia. Now the tradition was expressed in personal and familial bonds with the past. Alexander understood the ceremony as a filial act of devotion to his father. In a letter to his mother, the Dowager Empress, he described sentiments that he would express throughout his reign. Everyone was overwhelmed with tears, he wrote. "As for me my heart was choking from [the ceremony] and at the same time I was happy to be able to achieve this holy design in memory of my Emperor, of my Father, of the one who treated me not as a son, but as a true friend, and whom I continue to serve in my heart as if he were still alive."[41]

* * *

The problem of finding a suitable artistic model for a statue to Alexander II proved still more complicated. It was generally agreed that the Tsar who had sponsored the Great Reforms should be memorialized, but how this was to be done became a matter subject to considerable disagreement. Alexander did not cut a majestic, heroic figure, and the political conflict and the family scandal of the last years of his reign made him a public embarrassment to the royal family. In addition, by the 1880s national sentiment demanded a monument that had a distinctively Russian character. The concept of a national art in Russia, unlike Germany, ruled out classical models, which were regarded as Western borrowings. But the actual character of Russian art remained unclear, and another controversial matter, combined with the open nature of the discussion, made agreement on a model especially difficult to achieve.

The search for an appropriate national idiom for a dynastic statue prompted varied and contradictory solutions, many of them grandiose and bizarre. This problem was most eloquently stated by a September 1880 article published by the literary critic Constantine Leont'ev about a half-year before Alexander II's death, on the twenty-fifth anniversary of Alexander II's accession.[42] Leont'ev contends that the principal problem in designing such a monument is to give elegant artistic expression to the civic achievements of Alexander's reign, which were, he acknowledges, prosaic in character. One should not "disfigure a national monument of gratitude with European frock coat and tails," he writes. He suggests presenting the reforms and political progress of Alexander's reign in an allegory surrounding the Tsar. The Tsar, himself, however, would be depicted on his coronation throne: "The Tsar crowned and in broad purple is not *allegory*: he is truth, he is real."

Leont'ev's monument was not to be a personal monument to the Tsar, which presumably could not do justice to the achievements of his reign, but an expression of the national imagination. He insists that it be situated in Moscow, the national capital, "since Petersburg must lose its contemporary significance." It was to be a "historical cathedral [*khram*]" filled with glittering decoration that stunned the eyes. The ornamentation would be the work of Russian craftsmen, wood carvings "in Russian taste," gold and silver work. He envisions walls covered with mosaics and pictures against a gold background. The mosaics should be executed in old Russian style, but not necessarily on religious themes. The glass windows would be draped in Russian embroidered cloth or costly silk, with red, blue, and gold lacework and design, "in the taste of Russian towel cloths." Byzantine floral columns and multicolored cupolas like Vasilii the Blessed's would add to the national character. But Leont'ev's conception of the national is clearly eclectic. He asserts that nothing could be described as specifically national. "The national has been only *unique combinations* of what is common to all mankind [*obshchecheleve-cheskogo*]." He urges that the sculptures imitate ancient Greek statues in ivory, gold, and enamel.

Leont'ev's answer to the problem of memorializing Alexander II was to surround the Tsar with a large and elaborate structure that would convey the majesty lacking in Alexander's character. The profusion of ornamentation was to evoke a national glory. Historical elements were to be used, but the monument was to have an unabashedly contemporary style and appeal. For Leont'ev, as for many of his contemporaries, ornateness provided the national idiom. The monument would be dazzling rather than uplifting, a political kaleidoscope. And while neither of the great memorials to Alexander II, the Alexander II monument in Moscow and the Cathedral of Christ the Savior "on the blood," followed his suggestions to the letter, each shared the inspiration of Leont'ev's aestheticism in its final form.

The assassination of Alexander II on March 1, 1881, made the problem of memorializing the Tsar immediate. The new Tsar, Alexander III, moreover, had repudiated nearly everything his father stood for. He distrusted the institutions produced by the reforms and disliked his father's Westernized, Germanophile tastes. He was a stern believer in family morality and a pious believer who looked to the nation's historical past in the seventeenth century as the grounding for Russian autocracy. The memorials he envisioned transformed Alexander II into a figure who fit his own neo-Slavophile narrative of power. The Cathedral of Christ "on the blood," which contained the pavement stained by Alexander II, presents him as a Christian martyr suffering for the good of his nation. Plans for a statue in Petersburg were discussed, but not encouraged, and Alexander II remained the only nineteenth-century Russian emperor not to be honored with a statue in the capital.[43]

The leaders of the town government and society of Moscow, Alexander II's birthplace, took the initiative in building the monument. The mayor, a merchant named S. M. Tretiakov, announced upon his return from the funeral a proposal to erect a monument to Alexander in the Kremlin, "the Russian shrine," before the palace in which the Tsar was born. Oppressed by grief, Tretiakov had seen "an image of angelic kindness with the marks of a martyr's death." D. F. Samarin, a representative in the Moscow *zemstvo*, hoped that the monument would embody Slavophile ideals. "May it be a manifestation of the Russian national spirit, of the cherished and unbreakable union of the Russian people and their tsar." Alexander III's rescript expressed his approval: "In days of joy as in the years of painful trials, all layers of the Moscow population have always reciprocated the feelings of their tsars."[44] The rules of the competition were announced in July of 1881. The style was left to the artists' discretion, "but the monument should be a faithful and clear representation of the personality, great deeds, and events of the glorious reign of the deceased monarch." The materials were to be granite, marble, and bronze.[45]

But a design that could unite monarch and nation proved an elusive goal. The site of the memorial in the Moscow Kremlin, opposite the Small Nicholas Palace where Alexander had been born, raised special difficulties. The statue had to fit into the medieval landscape of the Kremlin, the symbol of a religious tradition inhospitable to three-dimensional images. The result was a succession of abortive competitions. After the third, the Grand Duke Vladimir Aleksandrovich, president of the Academy of Arts, issued the severe judgment: "Not one of the submitted projects has proved worthy of execution as a monument to the deceased Monarch, for they lack monumental appearance, originality, and the character that penetrated the entire reign of the late Emperor."[46]

The Grand Duke demanded a monumental figure, but the artists could not find a suitable idiom. Five prize winning entries for the second competition give a sense of their quandary. Reproduced in the journal *Vsemirnaia Illiustratsiia*, they present Alexander in three poses: standing in general's uniform and mantle; seated on the coronation throne; and in the classical equestrian pose. The national character was displayed by decorative forms of the "Russian style," such as the tent (*shatrovye*) roofs and tiara, *kokoshniki* designs on the canopies and pedestals, and particularly Alexander Opekushin's project, which won fourth place.[47]

The first prize submission, the work of Vladimir Sherwood—the architect of the Slavic-Revival-style Historical Museum in Moscow—sought rather to make a specific political point. Sherwood bluntly stated the meaning of the statue. He rendered Alexander in general's uniform and mantle to show the persistence of respect for autocratic government. The uniform represented the Emperor's role as leader of his nation. The mantle was necessary because

the monument, first of all should express the feelings of the people, and the Russian people are accustomed to respecting not only the person of the Tsar, but the very principle of power, second in spite of all his acts of liberation and indeed because of them the late Tsar revealed himself as a true representative of autocratic power.[48]

His monument, Sherwood writes, aimed to show that the principles of autocratic rule and emancipation were complementary. According to Sherwood, the Tsar's pose expressed the theme of liberation. "The Tsar, his head bent, looks down with love and points with his right hand to the sacred Kremlin cathedrals. With this movement, we have expressed the religious feeling inspiring him and making up the true source of freedom."[49] The base continued the theme of liberation and combined it with a characterization of the expansion of empire. Groups of standing figures represented the emancipation, the liberation of the Slavs, and the sub-jugation of the Central Asian khans and the Caucasus.

Despite the competition and the public discussion, the final choice of project for the Moscow monument was made by the Tsar himself. In 1890, Alexander III asked the official architect Nicholas Sultanov, and the artist P. V. Zhukovskii, the son of the poet Vasilii Zhukovskii, to submit a project. Sultanov and Zhukovskii submitted the design of a large monument with a statue by the sculptor Alexander Opekushin. The Emperor gave his approval after a few modifications and formed a special commission, chaired by the Grand Duke Sergei, and consisting of archi-tects and representatives of the estates. Alexander himself kept close watch over the entire project. He reviewed the accounts, visited the site, and approved of each step of the construction.[50] As a result, a memorial conceived as an act of popular gratitude was realized as an official memorial of a son to his father.

Sultanov, an exponent of the "Russian style" in church architecture, explained his artistic principles and described his work in a long article published in the jour-nal *Stroitel'* (*The Builder*) and which later appeared as a brochure. Like Montfer-rand, he bluntly informs the reader of the extent of his technical and aesthetic achievement. Sultanov explains the problem of fitting a monument into the medi-eval setting of the Kremlin. He concludes that a large enclosing structure was nec-essary if the statue was not to be dwarfed by the imposing edifices nearby, the tower of Ivan the Great and the Spasskii Tower. He therefore designed a massive wall like structure, set on a bluff above the Kremlin wall and commanding a view of the Moscow river. In fact, the monument was taller than the Ivan the Great tower (128 meters in height, compared to 97 of the tower) though it was set on a lower level. The monument's most striking feature was its overwhelming size, and it would have been still larger, but for the objections of the Moscow Governor-Gen-eral of Moscow. Photographs from the beginning of the century show it dominat-ing the Kremlin's southeastern vista and competing with the ensemble of cathedrals to the west. Louis Leger describes it as "assuredly one of the most colos-sal monuments ever dedicated to glorify a sovereign."[51]

Sultanov sought to combine the Italian and Russian elements of the Kremlin ca-thedrals and walls. The general outline, he claims, was Russian, and the details Italian.[52] The three tent roofs over the canopy and the ends of the gallery stressed the Muscovite traditions now central to autocratic ideology. But the columns and gallery were strikingly Italian. Indeed, Sultanov in his explanation makes sure to indicate the provenance of the different motifs, the Florentine doors, the Venetian pilasters. The tent roofs of the entry matched the Kremlin towers but also derived from the campanile of Italian churches, among them St. Marks, and the ribbing and ornamentation followed an Italian model. The gallery vaults were covered with a mosaic, he wrote, "that recalls in its motifs the mosaic of the 'Galla Placidia' in Ravenna."[53]

The ceilings of the gallery presented the history of the dynasty in Venetian mo-saic portraits of Russian princes and tsars, based on drawings of Zhukovskii. If the embellishments were meant to fit the statue into the surroundings, the portraits were intended to "explain the historical meaning of the monument." The portraits began with St. Vladimir as the first Christian prince, shown wearing a Byzantine crown and holding a cross, and ended with Nicholas I. The historical meaning was embodied in the ruling house, and Alexander II's achievement was presented as an extension of the dynastic heritage.

The artists were particularly proud of the ornate canopy they designed to enclose Alexander's statue. Sultanov points out that such a structure would help to overcome the national suspicion of statues:

> The Russian people, having been weaned by the Orthodox Church away from sculptured images of the divinity and saints, have completely lost the ability to understand *sculpture* alone in its pure form, and so a statue alone does not speak to its mind and heart. This alone may explain the desolate emptiness near all our monuments.

A canopy, on the other hand, "gives the monument a sacred character in the eyes of the people completely appropriate to the late Emperor, for our people is used to seeing a canopy only over especially sacred spots, as in churches over altar thrones, over Tsar's and Patriarchs' places, and in palaces over the throne."[54] But Sultanov's solution was hardly peculiar to Russia. Placing statues within canopies that would presumably protect them from the elements was a common practice in the second half of the nineteenth century. Perhaps the best known example is George Gilbert Scott's Gothic covering for the Albert Memorial, completed in 1872, which Janson describes as "by far the largest monument dedicated to an individual up to that time."[55] Scott too makes clear that such a structure lent greater significance to the subject of the monument. He endeavored to give "this overshadowing structure the character of a vast shrine, enriching it with all the arts by which the character of preciousness can be imparted to an architectural design, and by which it can be made to express the value attached to the object which it protects."[56]

Sultanov and Zhukovskii also employed size and "preciousness" to create a shrine that would exalt their subject's person and at the same time lend him a particular historical significance. The canopy is massive, 36 meters in height. Just as Scott had utilized the Gothic, which had become the British "national" style, Sultanov utilized the now emblematic tent form, which evoked the Muscovite traditions Alexander III endeavored to call upon. The tent, crowned with a double-headed eagle, was made of pink granite decorated with gilded bronze and green enamel work. Sultanov claimed that it gave the impression of "a colossal piece of brocade forming a tent. It is a replica of those luxurious cloths that were always used to make the tents of the tsars."[57]

The Alexander II monument in Moscow submerged the subject of tribute in a historical-political statement. Sultanov incorporated the statue into a structure that was both Muscovite and Italian, and the Tsar into a dynastic continuity that reached back to the beginnings of Rus'. It was ornate and ostentatious decoration that provided the sign of majesty and expressed what Leont'ev called the national imagination. Like Leont'ev's scheme, the monument sought to exalt the contradictory elements of the autocratic tradition and produce a sense of majesty by dazzling the senses.

It earned little praise for artistic merit. A guide book of 1917 remarks on the excellent view from the gallery but that "the memorial itself does not have an artistic effect." The canopy is "of very expensive materials, with a mass of gilt that is already tarnished and a Venetian mosaic that is tasteless and devoid of ideas."[58] The Bolsheviks tore it down shortly after they moved the capital to Moscow in 1918 and, as far as I know, it remains unlamented.

Only Opekushin's bronze figure of Alexander won admiration. Opekushin presented Alexander as he had appeared at his coronation, in full general's uniform, wearing the imperial mantle. His right hand pointed outward, to the people, according to Sultanov, "signifying the good deeds bestowed upon them." His left hand held the scepter, the symbol of rule, and rested on a cushion supporting the imperial crown. This was hardly an idealized image of Alexander. Opekushin had seen Alexander many times in life and had executed other statues of him. "I could sculpt a statue of the late Emperor with my eyes closed, so alive is his image in my memory," he said during an interview.[59]

There was general agreement that the likeness was extraordinary. Alexander's features were true to life; his face had the intense, pop-eyed expression that the Tsar maintained in public appearances. He stood with his customary stiffness; there was neither ease nor naturalness in his bearing. Opekushin captured Alexander's straining to assume the pose of noble leader, the benefactor of his people, who evoked not awe but affection. He was not a hero, but an emperor struggling to be a civic leader. The pedestal carried the inscription "To Alexander II, with the love of the people."[60]

The dedication of the statue took place only in 1898, four years after Alexander III's death. Reports in the press had little to say about either the monument or Alexander II himself. The account in *Novoe Vremia* described the reception in the Kremlin, and the procession to the Assumption Cathedral, then jumped to the monument itself. The author, one V. Prokof'ev, glowingly describes the beautiful uniforms of the guards regiments that Alexander II himself had commanded. Stands erected near the monument were filled with rows of eminent officials wearing glittering parade uniforms, but there was no mention of the public. The Tsar, Nicholas II, in the company of his suite, inspected the troops. Then he returned to join the imperial procession, which moved with a procession of the cross to the monument for the actual dedication. All kneeled and the Metropolitan pronounced a prayer of thanksgiving. The prayer was "touching," Prokof'ev writes, when "the entire square of people led by Tsar prayed under open sky at the monument to the Tsar-Empancipator."[61]

The ceremony became another occasion to emphasize "the unity of Tsar and people," which had been a leading theme in official rhetoric since 1881. A lead article in the nationalist, monarchist newspaper, *Moskovskie Vedomosti*, describes the dedication as one of those holy events "that united the Russian national family at the foot of the throne of the Russian autocrat over the course of centuries." It was a sacred moment "of unity in prayer between the soul of the people and the Tsar, crowned by God."[62] The prayer, the common religious experience inspired by all the tsars, overshadowed the secular achievements of Alexander II, represented by the monument, which the article virtually disregarded.

Alexander II's achievements received their true tribute in the statues erected to him in towns and public institutions across the empire. While the Moscow monument hid his figure, these placed it forward for all to see. They stood in court houses, before hospitals, and in the squares of provincial towns. Alexander appears in various poses, holding the emancipation edict, holding the declaration of war against Turkey, or simply resting his hand on a sword. In Walter Runeberg's famous statue in Helsinki (1894), he wears a military uniform and stands nobly over allegorical depictions of justice, peace, science, and labor. The date 1863, when he opened the Finnish Diet, is inscribed on the base. Newspapers published reports of villages of peasants making collections for their own statues to the tsar-liberator.[63] These statues expressed the gratitude of moderate society and the hopes for a revival of the spirit of reform.

* * *

Nicholas II's accession after his father's death in 1894 proceeded without crisis or visible break from the preceding reign. Nicholas, 26 years old at his father's death, made it clear that he would be faithful to the conservative and national policies of his father. At his wedding reception, he uttered his famous rebuff to the pleas for a constitution, dismissing such "senseless dreams" and declaring that he would "maintain the principle of autocracy as firmly and steadfastly as did my unforgettable father." The two statues erected in memory of Alexander III, Paolo Trubetskoi's in St. Petersburg, and Alexander Opekushin's in Moscow, were efforts to express admiration and adoration rather than to redefine the dynastic tradition. Both were designed and approved at the end of the 1890s, but their completion and dedication were delayed by the Revolution of 1905. By this time, the meaning of the past and the dynastic tradition had become obscured in conflicting images that reflected the political crisis of the moment.

The problem of style was a central one, but in contrast to the early period it seems to have prompted little serious discussion during the planning of the projects. Nicholas II, like his father, looked to pre-Petrine culture and institutions for a national Russian tradition. But both were examples of the cosmopolitan culture of royalty at the close of the century, dressed in European style military uniforms, though these were given a more national cut by Alexander III. Alexander, moreover, hardly presented a heroic image. His principal achievements were the maintenance of peace for the thirteen years of his reign, for which he was called the Tsar-Peacemaker: the successful suppression of the revolutionary movement; and most of all, the beginning of a policy of rapid industrialization, which, however great its benefits, won the regime little popularity at the time.

The final projects of both statues appear to have been chosen by the members of the Imperial Family, with the Dowager, Maria Fedorovna, and the Tsar's uncle, the Grand Duke Vladimir Aleksandrovich, exercising the decisive influence. Although the monuments were in different styles, both presented Alexander III as a symbol, reversing the tendency of the previous century to humanize the statue and to make of it a representation of the figure of the monarch himself.

Alexander Opekushin's statue was placed before the great Cathedral of Christ the Redeemer in Moscow, which Alexander had dedicated after his coronation in 1883. It is the only statue of a Tsar in full regalia on his coronation throne. Alexander sits impassively, immobile, defined by the vestments and insignia of power.

The statue expresses a purely sacramental notion of autocratic power. There is no allusion to Alexander's achievements; he is Tsar because of the blessing of God conferred at the coronation. His personal character and his contribution to the life of the people are not featured in this glorification.

The statue was dedicated in April 1912. Before then, the Tsar was afraid to return to Moscow, the scene of so much bloodshed in 1905, including the gruesome assassination of his uncle the Grand Duke Sergei, the Governor-General of Moscow. These premonitions were well founded. The situation was tense. The guards' regiments were met with cries of "butchers, Praetorians."[64] The monument did not stand long. It was demolished in 1918, its fall immortalized in Eisenstein's film *October*.

The meaning of Paolo Trubetskoi's equestrian statue of Alexander III was not so clear. The Emperor sits in military uniform, swollen and ungainly, on a small, heavy, bob-tailed horse, its head lowered as if balking. The statue was set on Znamenskaia Square (now Revolution Square) before the Nicholas (now Moscow) train station, the starting point of the Trans-Siberian Railroad, the construction of which began under Alexander III. The very appearance of the statue outraged the members of the Imperial Family and members of the court, who found it ugly and crude. Yet the project and models were approved by the Tsar himself and the Grand Duke Vladimir. Baron N. N. Wrangel, in the first edition of Igor Grabar's *History of Russian Art*, suggests that the casting of the full size statue produced distortions that were not present in the original.[65]

Critics have remarked that the monument is atypical of Trubetskoi's work. Trubetskoi was known as an impressionist, influenced by recent trends in Western Europe and associated with the avant-garde World of Art group. Indeed, despite his name, he was more Italian than Russia. The illegitimate son of an impecunious scion of the ancient Trubetskoi family and an American mother, he was raised and educated in Italy. He had achieved recognition primarily for his impressionistic rendering of animals with their offspring: a horse and foal, a fox and cub. He had also executed portrait statues, such as one of the Minister of Finances, Sergei Witte, who initially was in charge of building the monument. Trubetskoi's combination of modernist, art-nouveau, and impressionist influences was characteristic of new trends in Russian art. Such styles had appeared in official publications as well, for example, Nicholas II's Coronation Album, published in 1898.[66]

The unveiling and dedication of the statue on May 23, 1909, took place in the tense atmosphere of the post-revolutionary years. Nicholas left his palace at Tsarskoe Selo, where he had resided since the revolution of 1905, to make a rare visit to the capital. He travelled on the Tsarskoe Selo filial of the railroad that arrived and departed at the Nicholas Station, so that his sojourn was no longer than the ceremony. The newspaper account mentions the official participants, the court, the estates, and the brightly dressed guards regiments who attended. The troops formed a barrier of three lines, the fourth side being the station itself, keeping the onlookers at a safe distance. Nicholas himself commanded the regiment after the unveiling of the monument. The ceremony was brief, official, and had little gala spirit. Trubetskoi was not informed in time of the date of the ceremony and arrived two days late.[67]

The initial response to the statue was one of disappointment or derision. One M. Menshikov, writing in *Novoe Vremia*, calls the monument "an event in Russian life, and sad to say, another unhappy event, it is such a failure." The absense of a tail on the horse was the source of much concern and some mirth. *Moskovskie Vedomosti* remarks that the statue "leaves an impression of preposterousness. The simple people say that such a work-horse, [*bitiug*] should have a tail that's a tail." They joked that the tail had been cut off for economy's sake and talked of starting up a collection to make a new one.[68] There were rumors that Nicholas considered exiling the sculptor to Siberia. In the streets of Petersburg it was called a "scarecrow" and prompted an especially crude bit of doggerel:

> On the square, there stands a chest of drawers,
> On the chest, there stands a hippopotamus,
> On the hippopotamus, there sits a bum.[69]

Most of the statue's admirers understood it as a powerful attack on the Tsar as a symbol of the tsarist regime. Ilia Repin, called it "a reactionary monster in soldier's dress." Alexander Benois praised the courage of an artist who issued "a cruel sentence on the Tsar-Peacemaker." The belief that the statue was a satirical statement on the monarchy was shared by the Bolsheviks, who preserved the statue unharmed on the Square until 1937. At that point, Stalin, concerned to restore respect to authority, had it removed to an inconspicuous courtyard of the Russian Museum, where it now stands. Trubetskoi, however, denied such political content, insisting that he had depicted only "one animal sitting upon another."[70] When Sergei Diaghilev compared the statue to the Bronze Horseman, Trubetskoi replied that his statue was better than Falconet's. Indeed, he had originally conceived his statue in the Petrine tradition and had sought a boulder to use as a base. But he could not find an appropriate stone. Instead, he substituted the box-like form, which presumably recalled a catacomb, for the original plan.[71]

Donald Carlisle offers the interesting opinion that the statue presents Alexander in the form of a medieval Russian knight, the *bogatyr'*.[72] The *bogatyr'* was a popular theme in contemporary art, particularly in the paintings of Michael Vrubel' and Victor Vasnetsov. The statue does present the Emperor, himself large and imposing, with the massive, bearlike lines of the *bogatyr'* and captures something of his artlessness and implacable will. On the other hand, the Emperor on Trubetskoi's monument is a rather ponderous and it seems inactive *bogatyr'*, who is unlikely to intimidate the enemy or inspire confidence in his people. Although *bogatyr'* images were common in the art of the period, few contemporaries made this association. The reporter for *Moskovskie Vedomosti* quite aptly observes that the monument lacks the aspect of "tranquil, tsarist might."[73]

Vasilii Rozanov, the irreverent and eccentric monarchist philosopher, replied to the criticism by arguing that the statue was a tribute to the autocracy and the Russian people. The statue, he claimed, was an answer to Falconet. Falconet's statue was "an opera, a fairy-tale"; Trubetskoi's was "something kindred, 'mine,' 'ours,' 'all-Russian.'" The fact that it did not resemble a horse, or in any event an elegant horse, seemed completely appropriate to him. "What kind of stallion is Russia; Russia is a pig, not a stallion."[74] Rozanov perceived Trubetskoi's statue as a repudiation of the imperial tradition of magnificence. He writes that William II should build magnificent statues; Russian statues were not supposed to be magnificent: "Our mother-natures are ugly. They are old and ill and naked but we won't trade them for anything." The monument to Alexander III in this sense is an anti-statue, an antithesis to the sublime, a rebuff to the soaring aspirations of Neoclassicism.

Trubetskoi's statue also expresses a repudiation of the thematics of the tsarist tradition of statuary. The celebration of dynamism and will of the rulers has ended in a state of immobility. For Rozanov, the balking horse and the stolid rider captures the actual relationship that prevailed between the autocrat and Russia: "The horse is a horrid liberal. He doesn't know whether his head is on his front, back or side." The horse refuses to move. There is a misunderstanding between the two: the horse does not understand the benevolent horseman and suspects him of evil intentions to ride him into an abyss. "The horse is so dumb that he doesn't see that he will fly with the horseman and that the horseman can have no 'evil intention.'" For Rozanov, the statue symbolizes the standoff between the autocracy and Russian society.[75]

Without accepting Rozanov's acidulous monarchism, we can see in Trubetskoi's statue the expression of a new relationship between dynasty and nation. Previous statues had presented the dynasty as the embodiment, the epitome, or the savior of the nation. But both Trubetskoi's and Opekushin's monuments presented Alexander III as the epitome of the dynasty at a moment when the dynasty was at odds with the nation. Both made clear the dynasty's determination to rule regardless of the will and the good of the nation. Opekushin expressed this by returning to the image of a divinely ordained monarch whose preeminence was prior to and independent of his political activity. Trubetskoi turned the classical equestrian figure into a statement of mutual distrust.

The statues to Alexander III mark the end of the pattern of violating and redefining the past to express the goals of the present. This pattern had provided the dynamic of tsarist statuary, preserving the illusion of continuity while permitting the creative adaptation of official imagery. The statues of Opekushin and Trubetskoi accurately expressed the desire to defend the uncompromising autocracy of Alexander III's reign, a stolid refusal to adapt. The continuity they evoked was no longer an illusion, no longer Falconet's "fairy-tale," but a reality, an unchanging and inflexible image of the past presented to an uncomprehending and hostile public.

The poets of the time took the Trubetskoi statue as a symbol of foreboding conflict. The soaring ambition of the Bronze Horseman slowed to the measured movement of the Nicholas I statue, then to the stubborn immobility of Alexander III's in Valerii Briusov's "Three Idols" (1913):

> With frenzy the Bronze Horseman gallops,
> The other stallion rides not too fast,
> And severely, with all inherited might,
> The third cavalryman stands frozen over the crowd.[76]

The ominous cadences of Velimir Khlebnikov's "Monument" tell how the mounted figure of Alexander III leaves its pedestal to appear mysteriously before the doomed Russian fleet in the Pacific during the Russo-Japanese war. The statue descends to the depths among the corpses of Russian sailors. The disappearance is noted and a prophetic voice makes known that this is an apparition of Evil. The rider reappears in St. Petersburg and is interrogated by the police, who order him to resume his position on his pedestal. The "prisoner" feels "close and cramped on the square." The crowd stirs, "like the fur of a beast." People are speaking French, and a loud laugh is heard.[77] The first violence of the February revolution, when the troops fired on the Square, took place on Znamenskii Square. A photograph of the time shows the crowds milling about, oblivious of the stolid figure looming over them.[78]

NOTES

1. Heinz Dollinger, "Das Leitbild des Brgerknigtums in der europischen Monarchie des 19.Jahrhunderts," in *Hof, Kultur, und Politik im 19.Jahrhundert*, ed. Karl Ferdinand Werner, (Bonn: 1985), 330–1, 345–57; Eric Hobsbawm and Terence Ranger, eds., *The Invention of Tradition*, (Cambridge: Cambridge University Press, 1983).

2. G. B., "Khram sv. Vladimir v Kieve," *Stroitel'* (1896), 23: 937.

3. On the perception of statues in Russian literature, see Roman Jakobson, *The Statue in Pushkin's Poetic Mythology* (The Hague-Paris: 1975), 40–1.

4. I. Grabar', Istoriia russkoyo iskusstva (Moscow: 1989) 5: 468–73; B. N. Kalinin and PP. Iurevich, *Pamiatniki Leningrada i ego okrestnosti* (Leningrad: 1959), 124–6.

5. Robert Rosenblum and H. W. Janson, *Nineteenth Century Art* (New York: Harry Abrams, 1984), 98.

6. I. Grabar', Istoriia russkoyo iskusstva (Moscow: 1960) 6: 370–2.

7. David L. Ransel, *The Politics of Catherinian Russia: The Panin Party* (New Haven: 1975), 262.

8. Iu. M. Lotman and B. A. Uspenskij, *The Semiotics of Russian Culture* (Ann Arbor 1984), 62–3; V. Iu. Matveev, "K istorii vozniknoveniia i razvitiia siuzheta 'Petr I—vysekaiushchii statuiu Rossii'" in *Kul'tura i iskusstvo Rossii XVIII veka* (Leningrad: 1981), 26–43.

9. N .N. Erofeeva, "Pamiat' i pamiatnik v kontseptsiiakh XVIII veka," in *Vek Prosveshcheniia; Rossiia i Frantsia, Vipperovskie chteniia* (Moscow: 1989), 22: 222–36. As N. N. Erofeeva has shown, the statue is a monument to culture as well as to Peter. By turning stone into a historical embodiment of a historical figure, Falconet, following La Bross, made statuary a form of memorial or monument, *pamiatnik*, that took on the role previously fulfilled by poetry.

10. V. Ruban, *Nadpisi k kamniu naznachennomu dlia podnozhiia statuii Imperatora Petra Velikogo* (St. Petersburg: 1770).

11. Jakobson, op. cit., 5–12, 38–43.

12. A. Ricard de Montferrand, *Plans et détails du monument consacré à la mémoire de l'Empereur Alexandre* (Paris: 1836), ii–iii. His initial plan for an obelisk was rejected by the Emperor.

13. Montferrand, op. cit., n.p.

14. Ibid., iii; N. P. Nikitin, *Ogiust Monferran; proektirovanie i stroitel'stvo Isaakievskogo Sobora i Aleksandrovskoi Kolonny* (Leningrad: 1939), 243.

15. Ibid., 40.

16. Ibid., 5, 27.

17. The unsigned "Vospominanie o torzhestve 30ogo avgusta 1834 goda" appeared in *Severnaia Pchela*, Sept. 8, 1834: 807–08; and *Russkii Invalid*, Sept. 9, 1834: 906–8. It is printed in V .A. Zhukovskii, *Sochineniia* (St. Petersburg: 1902), 10: 28–32.

18. Montferrand, op. cit., 27–29; Nikitin, op. cit., 243, 254.

19. N. M. Karamzin, *Polnoe sobranie stikhotvorenii* (Moscow-Leningrad: 1966), 261. Nikolai Mikhailovskii, *Dukh ventsenosnykh suprugov v boze pochivaiushchikh Imperatora Aleksandra Igo i Imperatritsy Elizavety* (Moscow: 1829), 1: iii–iv. Karamzin wrote:

    > You shine like a divine angel
    > With goodness and beauty,
    > And your first words promise
    > Catherine's golden age.

20. U. E. Grabar' et. al., *Istoriia russkogo Iskusstva* 8: 2 (Moscow: 1964), 415.

21. Ivan Butovskii, *Ob otkrytii pamiatnika Imperatoru Aleksandru Pervomu* (St. Petersburg: 1834), 6–7, 33–34.

22. Zhukovskii, "Vospominanie o torzhestve 30ogo avgusta 1834 goda," in *Severnaia Pchela*, Sept. 8, 1834 :808; Zhukovskii, *Sochineniia* (St. Petersburg: 1902), 10: 32.

23. *Russkii Invalid*, Sept. 12, 1834: 920.

24. Zhukovskii, "Vospominanie o torzhestve 30ogo avgusta 1834 goda," in *Severnaia Pchela*, Sept. 8, 1834: 807; Zhukovskii, *Sochineniia* (St. Petersburg: 1902), 10: 29–30.

25. Butovskii, op. cit., 21–3.

26. Ibid., 27.

27. Zhukovskii, "Vospominanie o torzhestve 30ogo avgusta 1834 goda," in *Severnaia Pchela*, Sept. 8, 1834: 807; Zhukovskii, *Sochineniia* (St. Petersburg: 1902), 10: 30.

28. Butovskii, op. cit., 23, 28.

29. Montferrand, op. cit., pl. 44. The Raev painting is reproduced in small format in V. M. Glinka, *Russkii voennyi kostium, XVIII-nachala XX veka* (Leningrad: 1988), 16. It is in the collection of the Russian Museum in St. Petersburg.

30. Jean-Marie Apostolids, *Le roi machine; spectacle et politique au temps de Louis XIV* (Paris 1981), 47. Foucault writes of "the economy of visibility," most strikingly exemplified by Napoleon, that turned individuals into objects. Michel Foucault, *Discipline and Punish: The Birth of the Prison* (New York: Vintage Books, 1979), 187–9, 217.

31. Ivan Butovskii, *Ob otkrytii pamiatnika Imperatoru Aleksandru Pervomu* (St. Petersburg: 1834), 8–12.

32. *Russkii Khudozhestvennyi Listok*, 21 (July 20, 1958); 1: 3 (Jan. 20, 1858), 1.

33. *Russkii Khudozhestvennyi Listok*, July 1, 1859, 61; Aug. 1, 1859, 70.

34. Janet Kennedy, "The Neoclassical Ideal in Russian Scuplture," in *Theofanis George Stavrou, Art and Culture in Nineteenth-Century Russia* (Bloomington: University of Indiana Press, 1983), 205–6.

35. *Russkii Khudozhestvennyi Listok*, July 20, 1857.

36. H. W. Janson, *The Rise and Fall of the Public Monument* (New Orleans: 1976), 29; Louis Réau, *Saint Petersburg* (Paris: 1913), 41. Later in the century, when the Kiev City

Duma announced a competition for a monument to Nicholas I, they insisted that it not be an equestrian statue: "It is required that the monument be an exact expression of the deeds of the late Emperor, and in so doing, the Emperor should not be represented on a horse," *Moskovskie Vedomosti*, Nov. 7, 1886.

37. *Russkii Khudozhestvennyi Listok* (Aug. 1, 1859), 69.

38. A. E. Leonov, ed., *Russkoe iskusstvo; ocherki o zhizni i tvorchestve khudozhnikov; seredina deviatnagtsogo veka* (Moscow: 1958), 327–8.

39. *Russkii Khudozhestvennyi Listok*, 3 (Jan. 20, 1858), 2; 19 (July 1, 1859), 62; A. I. Del'vig, *Polveka russkoi zhizni* (Moscow-Leningrad: 1930), 2: 52–3.

40. *Russkii Khudozhestvennyi Listok*, (Aug. 1, 1859), 70–1.

41. *Tsentral'nyi Gosudarstvennyi Arkhiv Oktiabrskoi Revoliutsii*, 728–1–2496, 97.

42. Constantine Leont'ev, *Sobranie sochinenii* (Moscow: 1912), 7:451–7.

43. There was mention of plans for the Petersburg statue in the press. *Moskovskie Vedomosti*, Oct. 6, 1885.

44. N. Sultanov, *Pamiatnik Imperatoru Aleksandru II v Kremle Moskovskom* (St. Petersburg: 1898), 609–11.

45. *MV*, July 31, 1881.

46. Sultanov, op. cit., 615–9.

47. Sketches of the projects were reproduced in *Vsemirnaia Illiustratsiia* (June 11, 1883), 468.

48. Ibid. (Sept. 23, 1882), 3.

49. Ibid. (Sept. 23, 1882), 3–4.

50. Ibid., 620–32.

51. Sultanov, op. cit., 623–4; K. Baedeker, *Russland* (Leipzig 1901), 241; Louis Leger, *Moscou* (Paris: 1904), 41; the photo is shown in *Pamiatniki arkhitektury Moskvy; Kreml', Kitai-gorod, Tsentral'nye ploshchadi* (Moscow: 1982), 296–7.

52. Sultanov, op. cit., 571–2.

53. Ibid., 574–5.

54. Ibid., 571.

55. Rosenblum and Janson, op. cit., 320.

56. Elisabeth Darby and Nicola Smith, *The Cult of the Prince Consort* (New Haven: 1983), 46–50.

57. Sultanov, op. cit., 584–5.

58. N. A. Geinike, et al., eds., *Po Moskve* (Moscow: 1917), 187.

59. *Moskovskie Vedomosti*, Aug. 10, 1898; Sultanov, op. cit., 569–70.

60. Geinike, op. cit., 187.

61. *Novoe Vremia*, Aug. 17, 1898.

62. *Moskovskie Vedomosti*, Aug. 21, 1898.

63. Accounts and pictures of Alexander II statues are scattered through the press. There are many examples in the journal *Zodchii* and D. N. Loman, *Tsar' osvoboditel', tsar'-muchenik, Imperator Aleksandr II; chtenie dlia naroda* (St. Petersburg: 1898).

64. Spiridovitch, op. cit., 2: 225–6, 230–1; Richard Wortman, "The Problem of Political Center in Tsarist Russia, 1881–1914," in *Rites of Power: Symbolism, Ritual and Politics Since the Middle Ages* ed. Sean Wilentz, (Philadelphia: 1985), 244–71.

65. I. Grabar, *Istoriia russkogo iskusstva* (Moscow: 1909), 5: 384–6, 400–2. The section on sculpture was written by N.N. Vrangel'.

66. V. S. Krivenko, ed., *Koronovanie v Moskve; 14 maia 1896*, 2 volumes, (St. Petersburg: 1899); Edward Kasinec and Richard Wortman, "Imperial Russian Coronation Albums," *Biblion*, Volume 1, No 1, Fall 1992, pp. 95–97.

67. *Novoe Vremia*, May 24, 1909; S. I. Vitte, *Vospominaniia* 1:461–2.

68. *Novoe Vremia*, May 28, 1909; *Moskovskie Vedomosti*, May 28, 1909.

69. Donald C. Carlisle, "V poiskakh propavshego 'mednogo vsadnika,'" *Obozrenie*, 9 (April 1984), 25.

70. Carlisle, op. cit., 26.

71. Witte, op. cit., 1: 459.

72. Carlisle, op. cit., 27–9.

73. *Moskovskie Vedomosti*, May 28, 1909.

74. V. V. Rozanov, *Sredi khudozhnikov* (St. Petersburg: 1914), 310, 313–4.

75. Ibid., 314–7.

76. V. Briusov, *Izbrannye sochineniia v dvukh tomakh* (Moscow: 1955), 1: 362–3.

77. Velimir Khlebnikov, *Sobranie proizvedeniii* (Leningrad: 1930), 85–8.

78. Richard Pipes, *The Russian Revolution* (New York: Knapf, 1990), 277.

15. Monument to the Russian Martyrs under Stalinism

Ernst Neizvestny

Right after Stalin's death in 1954, I began to work on the subject of a monument to the victims of Stalin's repression. Only during the post-Perestroika period did building of this memorial become a reality.

The vast space of Russian land presents a unique opportunity for the creation of what I call the Triangle of Suffering, where memorials can be geographically placed in three locations: Ekaterinburg, Vorkuta, and Magadan.

Ekaterinburg, on the border dividing Europe and Asia, was a transfer point for the prison camp system. From here, prisoners were sent on to Siberian and the Far-North camps. Magadan and Vorkuta are in the Russian consciousness as dreadful as Aushchwitz and Buchenwald.

Pericles once said that we erect monuments to the good and evil that we do, but in Soviet and Russian history there has been no monument to an evil deed, as yet. For this reason, my task transcends the limits of merely a professional decoration of space. This is a monument of rectification through penance, a message from the past to the present and from the present to the future. Precisely for this reason the three monuments of the Memorial should unite the traditional with the modern, the old and the new. They should also represent the passage of time, and therefore all elements of shallow political and superficial fashion should be eliminated.

The placement of an ancient monument has always been in close connection with geography and even the universe: the elements of fire and water, present in all three monuments, are the most ancient, esoteric, and modern archetypes of folk art and ritual. Relatively large scale structures have to do with the spaciousness of the Russian land and with my notion that scale is poetry. The artist is always a Gulliver who lives and befriends giants and dwarfs. The very small and the very large are poetic if we have not lost a child's wise way of seeing or the wisdom of great folk cultures, whose plastic music is always based on the contrast between great and small.

The monument in Ekaterinburg will be two fifteen-meter-tall masks made of Ural granite—the images of sorrow that I have conditionally named Europe and Asia. In essence, the Memorial can be named The Tears of Stone. Images of sorrow, weeping tears of stone, petrified into human faces. Europe is facing Asia, Asia is turned toward Europe. The reverse side of the monument presents two masks that are negatives of the front images. The one facing toward Asia will be hollow and, seen from behind, barred with a burning Russian Orthodox cross that also resembles the bars of a prison. This cross symbolically unites victims of Europe and victims of Asia, representing the full scale of our tragedy and our sorrow.

From the top of the Vorkuta Memorial, named The Pain of Living Memory, the monument will resemble a human face with eyes looking toward the sky. The memorial will be a cement structure of one huge face composed of other faces that become smaller and smaller, down to life size. Each mask will indicate a dead soul. I don't want portraits, only masks, masks of the souls, generalized human images. Each mask will have a torch on its forehead. The entire monument will be a blazing island of light. The two large hollows on the top of the hill—the face—will be eyes brimming with tears. The tears—water—will be flowing down the mask. Only the smallest masks will be without torches. Every visitor can place a lighted candle near the mask. Any visitor will be able to write a name of his lost one in chalk on the cement stone and choose his own mask in order to associate his lost one with it. Inside the hill will be a memorial museum, with stairs going underground. Here computers will process the accumulated data. The display will be constantly changing. The task of the computer center will be to determine who are missing, who are buried, and where they are.

The Magadan Memorial will continue the theme of weeping established in The Tears of Stone. A fifteen-meter-tall mask with a huge cross extending over the nose and the eyebrows will be crying tears of human faces. In the left side of the forehead there will be masonry masks of the perished victims. In the right side of the mask's cheekbone there will be stairs leading inside the monument. A visitor will enter from the stairs into a reconstructed prison cell for the condemned man. The opposite side of the monument will be a temple space where a 5-meter-high crucifixion will be suspended over the spectator's head. On the floor of the temple, directly below the crucifixion, there is a small statue of a little girl mourning over the dead.

All three memorials form an indivisible monument that will be located in a space where a global tragedy became an anthropological crime.

16. Monumental Revisions of History in Twentieth-Century Germany: An Ongoing Process

John Czaplicka

In this century political transformations and border changes brought about as a result of war have twice redefined the country we call Germany. The revolutionary change from an Empire to a Republic following World War I led to the establishment of the conflicted Weimar Republic, whose weaknesses gave way to the Nazi regime of the Third Reich. In the aftermath of a world war instigated by that regime, the Allies divided what remained of Germany and as part of the Cold War scheme these parts evolved into two separate states, the German Democratic Republic and the Federal Republic of Germany. Finally, the end of the Cold War marked by the Fall of the Berlin Wall, led to the reunification of these two German states in 1989 to form the fifth successor state to the unified nation-state formed in 1871. This last version of "Germany" is defined by perhaps more permanent borders, but much as its predecessors, it still seeks its identity as a nation.

That search corresponds in many ways to the successive political and geographical redefinitions of Germany as a state and involves the official attempt to formulate a historical identity by selectively appropriating aspects of Germany's political and cultural heritage and by inventing and cultivating certain traditions. This essay considers one concrete aspect in this history-defining process that was meant to produce very public, concrete, and ostensibly longer lasting results conforming with the ideologies of the respective governments: i.e., the setting, dedication, conservation, and destruction of monuments. Specifically I will discuss the ongoing transformation of what is sometimes called the *Denkmallandschaft*, the ensemble of monuments occupying a landscape, and after a more general consideration of monument building and destruction in Germany during this century, I will focus on the most recent reconfiguration of that landscape within the territories of the former German Democratic Republic.

My premise is that in general the constantly transforming constellation of public monuments within Germany tell us how the various German governments and political interest groups have selectively sorted out their respective images of German history (*Geschichtsbild*), and how they have instrumentalized history in a manner conforming with their particular ideologies by privileging certain persons and events through their respective patterns of public commemoration. If we survey the changes in this monumental *Geschichtsbild*, we note how variously the setting, renaming, and removal of monuments were employed to shore up the authority and historical legitimacy of the diverse governments and political interest groups controlling Germany during the twentieth century. If we interpret these transformations further, we may note how the official *Geschichtsbild* evinced by a *Denkmallandschaft* conflicts or corresponds with the "image of history" shared by each generation of Germans. Furthermore, because this shared image of history constitutes an important facet of German collective identity, in surveying the monuments which provide official historical coordinates for that historical construct, we might note how tenuous and changeable any fix on German identity has been in the twentieth century.

After World War I the first official shift in the constructed image of German history takes place. In 1919 Edwin Redslob, the first minister of culture (*Reichskunstwart*) appointed by a democratic government in Germany, was directed to remove the insignia of the fallen Hohenzollern dynasty and now defunct German Empire from all public buildings. He was also empowered to design new border markers, coins, postage stamps, and monuments that would symbolically serve the newly founded Republic by distinguishing it from the autocratic and imperial government that preceded it. This proved a more problematic project than it seems, for Redslob had few indigenous symbolic precedents from which he could draw, and nationalist sentiment within the government and from veterans groups prevented him from employing foreign devices. Disputes broke out in the Reichstag about the use of the flag and about symbolic commemorative practices. Almost until its demise, the representatives of the Weimar Republic would continue to seek a common public symbolism for the first democratically elected government on German soil.

In 1924 Friedrich Ebert, the first president of the Republic called publicly for a memorial to the fallen of World War I (*Reichsehrenmal*), asking that a republican commemorative monument be built at which all Germans regardless of political persuasion might mourn their common loss and reaffirm their common national identity. The public debate about the site and about the symbolic form of this monument mirrored the fractionalism and disunity of the German Republic; that debate continued unabated for almost ten years until a decision was finally made to carve out a sacred memorial grove from a forest near Weimar and to forbid political demonstrations or even so much as the wearing of political insignia at that site. Though this peculiar republican-national compromise for a unified commemorative practice in a "natural" setting was never realized, the question of a central commemorative site for the fallen of World War I was finally resolved by fiat in

1934, when the German Reichskanzler Adolf Hitler declared the military monument at Tannenberg the *Reichsehrenmal* (Fig. 16–1).

Tannenberg had been erected in 1927 by right-wing veterans groups to commemorate the great victory of the German Imperial army over the Russians in World War I; it had the form of a fortress and occupied a site on the former battlefield in East Prussia, the province that had been separated from Germany by the creation of the Polish corridor. Deriving its form from the ancient Teutonic sites of communal gathering, *Thingplätze*, from the Castel del Monte (the fortress of Kaiser Friedrich II in Italy), and perhaps from castles appearing in Fritz Lang's film version of the *Niebelungen* (1923/24), this commemortive edifice resonates with the idea of an extended and original German Reich. The fortress type of monument signified military strength and commemorated military prowess, expressing the attitude of the "undefeated." It lent itself less to mourning the dead than to a call for vigilance or even aggression. So in designating this memorial the official *Reichsehrenmal*, Hitler appropriated the right-wing interpretation of World War I and focused the official mourning of the nation for its dead at the site of victory in World War I. Tannenberg embodied and located a defiant attitude of a Germany in the landscape and historical geography of Europe. It signified a call to revanchism. Hitler instrumentalized the historical and hallowed ground of that site and the commemoration and the ceremony that took place there for the purpose of his own aggrandizement and investiture with power.

The German monument at Tannenberg celebrated the victory of Field Marshall Hindenburg over superior Russian forces in 1914 and came to exemplify the myth of German armies, undefeated on the battlefield but betrayed by traitors on the Home Front (*Dolchstoßlegende*). Because it was located near the site where the Teutonic knights lost a "first" battle of Tannenberg to the united Polish and Lithuanian armies in 1410 (thereby putting a stop to the expansion of the Germans to the East), this German monument reoccupies the site as a species of revenge some 500 years later. On the border to Poland and in East Prussia, that monument also stood for the defense of the *Vaterland* and the claims of the Germans on territory historically disputed by Poles. The multiple historical resonances and complex symbolism of the memorial-monumental fortress at Tannenberg was enhanced in 1934 as Hindenburg was interred there in a solemn state ceremony. Adolf Hitler took that occasion to enhance his own power by having the officers of the German army swear a personal oath of allegiance to him as he literally stood at the place where the body of Hindenburg had lain in state. This was a high ceremony of investiture. *Hoc est corpus meum*: figuratively Hitler succeeded Hindenburg as the embodiment of the continuity of the unified German state offering the promise to do as Hindenburg had done in the battle fought at Tannenberg in 1914 to save the German nation.

Hitler began his Third Reich with various other appropriations and redesignations of monuments. A monument similar to Tannenberg had been erected originally by the volunteer right-wing militias (*Freikorps*) at Annaberg in Silesia as early as 1921, where they had defeated a Polish garrison in the fight for that province (Fig. 16–2). Under the Hitler regime Annaberg gained the status of a national pilgrimage site, one dedicated to the predecessors of the Erhebung or uprising, and the site was developed to a commemorative complex that included a theater

Figure 16-1 *Reichsehrenmal Tannenburg.* (Tannenburg National Monument.) Walter and Johannes Kruger, designers. Tannenburg.

Figure 16–2 *Reichsehrenmal Annaberg.* (Annaberg National Monument.) Annaberg.

(*Thingplatz*), a sports field, youth hostels, and a memorial resembling a fortress. Another major memorial site was appropriated by the Nazis near Dusseldorf, where, in 1931, a monument had been dedicated to Albert Leo Schlageter, a right-wing revolutionary and martyr-hero to the German national cause in the liberation of the Rhineland from the French. The commemoration of that one-time Nazi was built into a cult during 1933. Göring rededicated the Schlageter memorial and had it augmented by a historical museum. Although the Nazis constructed their own commemorative sites for other heroes in their political Pantheon, such as Horst Wessel or those who died in the Nazi-Putsch attempt of 1923, it remained more typical for the fascist regime to appropriate extant memorial sites by renaming, rededicating, and redesigning them so that they conformed with their ideology. In this way the Nazis mobilized the historical symbolism transported by each monument for their cause. The ideological "occupation" of commemorative sites at Tannenberg, Annaberg, and near Dusseldorf, sites located strategically in the contested and conflicted provinces of East Prussia, Silesia, and the Rhineland, allowed the Nazis to fabricate a historical genealogy of their movement in a struggle to maintain the territorial integrity of the German nation. That genealogy situated in the landscape of occupied or border regions had as its leitmotif, the idea of liberation—liberation of former German lands from Poland and the liberation of the Rhineland from the French occupation.

The pendant to this project of appropriation was one of destruction. After January of 1933 those extant monuments foreign to the Nazi cause such as the one Mies van der Rohe dedicated to communist leaders Karl Liebknecht and Rosa Luxemburg in 1919 or the monument to the workers who fell resisting the right-wing Kapp Putsch ("To the Fallen of the March Revolution") erected by Walter Gropius in 1921, were destroyed (Fig. 16–3). Even memorials to the dead of World War I were removed or transformed by the Hitler regime. The war memorial executed in 1930 by Ernst Barlach on the Rathaus Square in Hamburg, was reconfigured by the Nazis so that the image of a suffering woman and child, the victims of WWI on the home front, became a phoenix-eagle which symbolized the ascendant national cause rising from the ashes of the lost war (Fig. 16–4). Other monuments to cultural personages who could not be integrated into the Nazi hagiography (e.g., those to Heinrich Heine, Walther Rathenow, and Friedrich Ebert) were removed with remarkable precision after the Hitler takeover. The Nazis would have no truck with leftist enemies of the state, "defeatist" memorials, or "racially impure" effigies.

Because this destruction of monuments by the Nazis took place on a local and sometimes unofficial level, it is often difficult to document. In contrast those monuments such as the Wagner monument in Leipzig that had been commissioned earlier but were then financed or redesigned by the Nazis have left paper and pictorial trails which provide us with vivid examples of political aggrandizement through the appropriation of cultural symbols and heritage. In the case of the Wagner monument, Mayor Goerdele of Leipzig approached the Nazi government for funding in 1933, and Hitler gladly met this request with the stipulation that it become the first national monument of the Nazi regime. Hitler personally laid the cornerstone of the monument in March of 1934 as part of his propagation of a Wagner cult. After the Nazi defeat, this first national monument lay finished but

Figure 16–3 *Denkmal für die Märzgefallenen.* Walter Gropius, designer. Harvard University Art Museum.

Figure 16–4 *Hamberger Memorial Stele to Fallen of WWI/Relief "Grieving Mother with Child."* Ernst Barlach and Klaus Hoffman, designers. East Berlin.

unassembled far away from its designated site on the grounds of a marble supplier in Upper Bavaria (Fig. 16–5). Very few monuments were completed during the Third Reich, though many were appropriated and destroyed.

In fact, to provide raw materials for their armaments industry the Nazi war-machine had stockpiled thousands of bronze monuments and bells gathered from the territories of the German Reich and all of Europe at the harbor in Hamburg by the end of World War II. After their capture by the Allies most of these monuments and bells were repatriated. However, those effigies of famous Germans the Allies thought too closely associated with authoritarian regimes and ideas were subsequently melted down. In a related instance, the monuments to the Hohenzollern dynasty that had stood along the Siegesallee (victory allee) in Berlin were seen as being too closely allied with militarism and were therefore buried on the grounds of the Belvedere palace at the order of the Allied High Command. Only recently have these emblems of dynasty been excavated. They are now stored in an old pump house that serves as a provisory lapidarium for historical figures currently out of use and fashion.

With the defeat of the Third Reich came the removal of all its insignia from public buildings, the renaming of streets, and the redesignation of buildings. Denazification, if ineffective on the private level and with regard to the functionaries of the regime, was very effective on the symbolic level that removed the physical traces of the old regime from public view. One even legislated against the symbols of the Nazi regime, so that bearing the sign of the swastika became a crime. A very questionable "Out of sight and out of mind" resolved the German need to confront their immediate past and their own complicity with a criminal regime.

The eradication of commemorative and symbolic elements of what the Communists called a "reign of terror" was accompanied by selective returns and additions to the monumental composite of cities and towns of a reduced Germany soon to become two separate states, the communist German Democratic Republic and the democratic Federal Republic of Germany. The opposing ideological tendencies predominating in these states led to a distinctive reoccupation of the public spaces and the public consciousness with new and old monuments that supported each state's respective revisions of German history. In the GDR this revisioning entailed an emphasis on the personages and events of the antifascist resistance and on the memorialization of the victims of fascism; these became the two constituent elements in the mythology concerning the origin of the state that claimed to be the "first socialist state on German soil." Propagating this mythology, that state claimed to be free of Nazi war criminals (the official claim was that all the old Nazis had settled in the West) and proceeded to construct its historical genealogy by selectively commemorating only the progressive strains in German history.

Fritz Cremer's strident sculptural ensemble representing inmates liberating themselves at the Buchenwald concentration camp exemplifies the attempt of the GDR to legitimate itself through the appropriation of a very selected German history (Fig. 16–6). It became official state policy to recognize such instances of leftist resistance and to honor its perpetrators. As a result, resistance monuments can be found throughout the GDR. Coupled with an obligatory and generalized recognition of the "victims of fascism," this pattern of commemoration extends down to

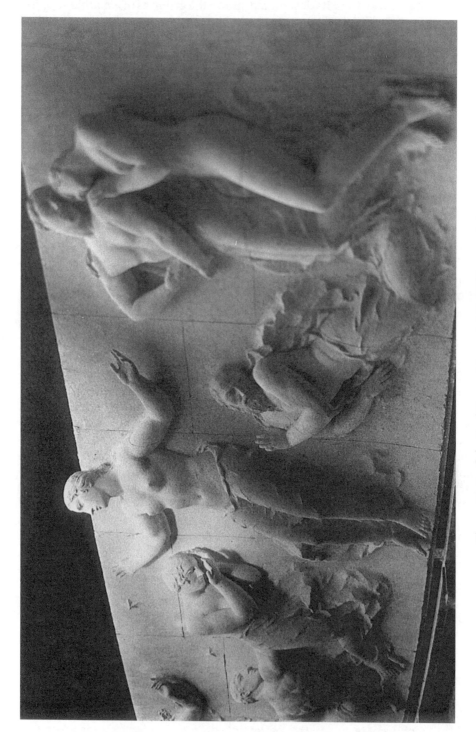

Figure 16–5 *Salvation/Wagner Monument.* Emil Hipp, sculptor.

Figure 16–6 *Buchenwald Monument.* Fritz Cremer, sculptor. Weimar.

the local level. Almost every town or village in the GDR has monuments and
plaques commemorating the anti-fascist resistance and the victims of fascism.
With the historical legitimation of their rule in mind, Communist officials had local histories (*Heimatsgeschichten*) rewritten to allow a prominent role for leftist or
working-class resistance to facism. Although there is, I think, something highly
commendable in maintaining the memory of the brave and generally unknown
"little" heroes; still the cultivation of their memory as a means to rationalize and
extend the authority of a totalitarian state deserves censure. One must also note
that the Jews, Gypsies, homosexuals, religious persons, and other victims of the
Nazi regime disappeared behind these generic images of the ideologically correct
resistance fighter or simple "victim of fascism." Communist resistance was given
a priviledged treatment.

Conforming with a larger pattern of ideological correctness in the Communist
bloc, the government of the GDR paid only selective respect to the liberators of
Germany from Nazi tyranny. Soviet cemeteries, often occupying the very center of
small towns and villages like the one in Juteborg in the province of Brandenburg
were cared for and became the sites for public rituals to reassert the friendship of
the German and Soviet peoples. After World War II the Soviet authorities marked
the cities, parks, and landscapes of their occupation zone in Germany with grandiose monuments and monumental funerary complexes dedicated to the victorious Red Army, which had borne the brunt of the fighting in the war. Some of these,
such as the Stalinist funerary complex built near Berlin in Treptow from 1947 to
1949, were carved into the landscape with forced labor. For obvious ideological
reasons, this pattern of official public commemoration of the "liberation of Germany from the Fascists" in the GDR privileged the idea of *Völkerfreundschaft* between the Russian and German people; the "other" allied liberators were
acknowledged only for the destructive effect of their air raids on German cities.
Mourning for the loss of historical substance in cities such as Jena, Dresden, and
Magdeburg was done at memorials for the "Victims of Anglo-American terror"
that were erected throughout the GDR.

Beside the cultivation of the myth and history of state origins involving the privileging of antifascist resistance, the generalized commemoration of the victims of
the Facism, and the selective celebration of the liberation from tyranny, the Communists controlling the German Democratic Republic propagated a cult of personality typical for all state-socialist regimes. The *uomini famosi* through which the
state fixed its identity included the standard bearers of Communist doctrine such
as Marx, Engels, and Lenin as well as local propagators of the faith such as the first
president of the GDR, Wilhelm Pieck. The commemorative pieces to these figures
ranged in size from wall plaques to enormous monumental sculptures such as the
ones of Lenin or Ernst Thalmann in Berlin (the leader of the Communists during
the Weimar Republic). The effigies of these ideological standard-bearers were
among the first to be removed from public sight once the Berlin Wall had fallen. At
a local level and for its everyday ritual purposes, the Communist Party in the GDR
(i.e., the SED or Socialist Unity Party), installed bronze plaques and other small
markers at sites to commemorate where this or that notable gave a speech or spent
a night or where the forced unification of the SED and the SPD (Socialist Party of

Germany) took place under the auspices of the Soviet administration occupying Germany in 1946. With such "little monuments," the SED construed the history of a "popular" political movement that had led to the establishment of a one-party state. This myth of popular origins helped legitimate the German Democratic Republic.

Another myth allied to the doctrines of that Communist state posed the working class as the motive force in history. Thus it was incumbent on the state to honor its workers, and one manner of doing this was through the erection of public monuments to that class. Generic sculptural ensembles in the style of socialist realism depict working-class families, construction or factory workers, or just "the worker" at various sites in the GDR. For example, statues of working women who helped rebuild Germany after World War II (*Die Aufbauhelferin*, 1958) were erected in the 1950s (Fig. 16–7). Unlike the Federal Republic of Germany, this pattern of public commemoration recognized the achievements of the "common (wo-)man," which, despite all of its ideological trappings, is an accomplishment of the cultural politics of the GDR, even if the aesthetic execution of these figures often left much to be desired. In contrast, where the working class appeared as a massed military force marching off to war, as it does in the monumental complex erected in Berlin to honor thirty years of the paramilitary national guard (*Betriebskampfgruppen*, 1983), one cannot but recall the equally strident military monuments erected by the Nazis (Fig. 16–8). Here the masses appear as ornaments of the regime that organized them as instruments of power. This particular monument was justly removed in 1991. Seen together, all these commemorative devices— whether referring to ideological forefathers, the antifascist heroes and victims, or the industrious and militant working classes—helped construct the history of the first "socialist State on German soil." Beyond this peculiar "German" history, the representation and commemoration of the more general history of Germany proved problematic in the GDR.

Under the Communists that more general history receded in the official histories, which primarily focused on a prehistory of a German state based on socialist principles. When visiting Magdeburg in 1990, I asked the director of the cultural history museum to loan me a recent GDR history of that city, the *Magdeburg Chronik*. Magdeburg's history before 1919 was reduced to an outline of "oppression" and in the more substantial part of the book (fully two-thirds of it) one could read the local version of the working-class struggle fashioned by party ideologues for their purposes. The historical figures and events chosen helped formulate a prehistory of the socialist state and provided ideologically correct exempla for emulation by the general populace. The course of this history projected through successive stages toward the inevitable victory of the proletariat and the Communist party. This prescribed image of German history presented the SED regime as the sole inheritor of all the progressive elements in German history.

An analogous fabrication of the historical can be observed in the policies of the GDR with regard to the erection and removal of monuments. Under the SED regime, monuments destroyed by the Nazis but consistent with the logic of the Communist regime were rebuilt or, if they were still extant, they were returned to their places. For instance, the memorial to the Fallen of the First World War by Ernst Bar-

Figure 16–7 *Ausbauhelferin*. Fritz Cremer, sculptor. Bronze. Berlin.

Figure 16–8 *Betriefskampfgruppendenkmal.* Gerhard Rommel, sculptor. Berlin.

lach was returned to its site in the Magdeburger Cathedral in 1948 (Fig. 16–9). Walter Gropius' monument to the Fallen of the March Revolution was reconstructed in Weimar. Even though the abstract quality of the Gropius monument must have made it suspect to those propagating a style of social realism, this rare public artwork honoring the workers who fell defending the Weimar Republic against its right-wing foes during an attempted putsch demanded respect. In another instance of restoration, the government of the GDR sought to rebuild Mies van der Rohe's equally abstract monument dedicated to the communists Rosa Luxemburg and Karl Liebknecht on the Friedrichshain in Berlin, but the famous architect objected to this and thus prevented it. Beyond these selected and famous examples, one could cite many other instances of the restoration and return of monuments that were in accord with the state ideology.

In contrast, the anti-imperialist position of the regime condemned the extant monuments of the German Empire. Official policy demanded they be eradicated or left to decay. There were exceptions to this rule such as the *Volkerschlachtdenkmal* in Leipzig, a grand national and imperial monument in Leipzig which commemorated the liberation of Germany from Napoleon. It had been exploited successfully by the two authoritarian regimes, one imperial and one Nazi. The third one of communists made the most of the fact that the *Volkerschlachtdenkmal* implicitly commemorated the Russian-Prussian military alliance that defeated Napoleon. In this case, mere reinterpretation sufficed to make an "inherited" monument useful. The more typical monuments referring to the first unification of Germany under Wilhelm I and Bismarck, such as the many Bismarck towers, were removed, rendered anonymous, renamed, or left simply to decay. Sometimes monuments associated with the German Empire met a violent end at the urgings of communist officials. To give one example, in a ritualized act of vandalism during the early 1970s a group belonging to the Communist youth movement decapitated a neoclassical statue of Queen Luise of Prussia that stood in a Magdeburg park and threw its broken body into fresh concrete for the foundations of a construction site. Many bronze effigies of Hohnzollern rulers that still decorated town squares in East Germany were melted down for their metal. In contrast to the imperial monuments, the memorials to the fallen of World War I suffered a benign neglect—they were neither officially sanctioned nor included in any of the historical traditions propagated by the state, yet they were not destroyed. The monuments of the Weimar period, as noted, were selectively rebuilt and those of the Nazi period—with exceptions—eradicated.

During the last decade of the German Democratic Republic the setting of monuments suggests a slow but steady revision in the reception of German history. Historical figures and especially those of Prussian lineage re-entered public space and consciousness in the form of monuments. In 1983, during the Luther year, a museum dedicated to the great church reformer was refurbished in Eisleben, the place of his birth, and a "Luther way" was inaugurated in Erfurt. The statue of Luther in Eisleben began to receive as much care as its colleague Lenin just down the street. In fact, with travel agencies offering special "tours of the 'Luther-cities' Eisenach, Wittenberg, Erfurt, Leipzig, and Mohra near Bad Salzungen," the festive commemoration of Luther in 1983 seemed, in some respects, to outdo the one for Marx, the hundredth anniversary of whose death fell in the same year (this might

Figure 16–9 *The Magdeburg Memorial to the Fallen of WWI.* Ernst Barlach, sculptor. Magdeburg Cathedral.

be attributed to the investment of the Lutheran church in such celebrations and to the possibility of gaining access to Western currencies by attracting Western tourists).

In 1980 the famous statue of the Prussian king, Friedrich the Great, by Christian Daniel Rauch was returned to its original site on Unter den Linden in East Berlin at the orders of the Communist party secretary, Erich Honecker. Yet, perhaps the grass-roots story of Friedrich II's return to Letschin, a small village in the Oderbruch East of Berlin, tells us more about the type of historical revision taking place under and despite Honecker's regime. In 1945 a statue of Friedrich the Great had been removed from its socle in Letschin to make way for a Russian cemetery. That statue was to be melted down, but the village inhabitants kept it hidden from the Communist officials until 1986 on the occasion of the 650th anniversary of the village, when the statue was reinstated with a missing leg at the center of the village. State officials had it removed from public view, ostensibly for restoration, and it only returned to Letschin in April of 1990 after the demise of the GDR.

I questioned several villagers and the West Berlin policeman Werner Textor, who had raised the money for the statue's restoration concerning the reasons for returning the monument to its socle. Their answers made me realize how much Friedrich the Great belonged to local lore and tradition, how much his identity helped constitute the identity of the villagers. The sympathetic depiction of Friedrich II in Theodor Fontane's Wanderings through the March of Brandenburg still occupied a place in the collective consciousness of these people. He was the enlightened monarch, the Friedrich the "Great" of legend, who had made the land around Letschin arable by draining the marshes. Not the autocrat or warrior king defiled in the GDR, not the king with French tastes; the Friedrich of local lore was the one who colonized, industrialized, and furthered the arts and industry in the area. This was the ruler to whom, historically, the people of Letschin owed their livelihood. That historical figure remained in their rather selective, collective memory. The monument was returned to its socle before the history books in the GDR had been rewritten to accommodate the historical figure and before the teaching of history had revised the collective identity and memory of the Letschiner.

Just as the GDR began to revise its version of German heritage to include Luther, Frederick the Great, and even Bismarck, the Communist regime fell. In the wake of its demise the names of streets were changed and many monuments and commemorative sites were removed from the streets and squares of cities. In the Fall of 1990, shortly before East Germany became a part of the Federal Republic of Germany, it seemed my memory did not serve me well when I arrived in Magdeburg from Berlin wanting to photograph monuments which might be destroyed as Germany once again rewrote its history in the light of reunification. Although I had studied the city map thoroughly I could not find the Karl-Marx street, which I knew to be the representative way through the center of the city. The street's name had, already in September of 1990, been changed back to its prewar name. It was now "Broadway."

On Broadway an effigy of Erich Weinert, a favorite poet of Walter Ulbrich and local son of the city, had also been removed after someone had smeared it with red paint. Karl Marx himself had been taken down from the facade of the main post office. The city was being revised, historically. As the communist poet descended from his place of honor in the city center, a German hero of the American Revolution reoccupied his position of prominence in the public eye. General von Steuben, a son of Magdeburg, returned. The bronze plaque dedicated to the general as well as his bust were "rediscovered" by a local historian, Alfred Heidelmayer, and brought to the attention of the interim authorities, who had the von Steuben Bronze plaque remounted where it once hung on the main facade of the Central Post Office.

Originally dedicated in 1937 and rededicated 1990 this small commemorative plaque has a checkered history. In 1937 its dedication ceremony was attended by the American Ambassador to Germany, Mr. Dood, and delegations from the Daughters of the American Revolution and the American Steuben Society, the mayor of Magdeburg, and a Nazi SA delegation. In 1951 the city council of Magdeburg, then under Stalinist control, had the bronze plaque removed from the wall. Somehow it fell into the hands of a clergyman of the Lutheran church in Magdeburg, who concealed it for almost forty years. In 1990 the wife of the American Ambassador in East Berlin and the mayor Dr. Willi Polte rededicated the restored plaque. Mayor Polte said: "Today we Magdeburgers are helped by the great son of the city Wilhelm von Steuben to bridge the many years of forced separation to the New World, so that we might turn to the most progressive ideas in science, economics and culture of America." There was no mention of the original context in which the Steuben commemorative plaque had been dedicated. One exploited the memory of von Steuben for current purposes, attempting to build a bridge to America while abridging the past. Up main street the shell of the Johanneskirche in Magdeburg surrounded the sculpture of a grieving "Madgeburga" the female allegory representing the city and sited in the midst of its destruction. In the Fall of 1990, the refurbished tower of that church still accommodated an exhibition of photographs documenting the "Anglo-American terror attacks" that destroyed the historical core of the city in a hail of bombs in 1945.

Such contradictory instances of commemoration typify the confusion and conflict in the East Germans' renewed attempt to establish their history and identity as part of a larger Germany. These examples could be augmented with narratives of my experiences in Quedlinburg, Eisleben, Leipzig, Jena, or Erfurt, but the conflicts arising are essentially the same as monuments; those concrete historical markers are being removed, added, or returned to their original sites. Currently we see a still rather uncoordinated attempt to reconfigure the monumental landscapes of cities and towns in such a way that they conform to some new "image" of German history. What that image will be remains unresolved.

The latest monumental reconfiguration of history in Germany in the territories that were once a part of the German Democratic Republic may culminate with yet another erasure of history; Lenin statues and Marx effigies have been removed from public places; old figures such as Bismarck and Friedrich II are reappearing and being erected on their original sites. Antifascist monuments, to which the members of the Communist Youth organization, the Young Pioneers, were once led for there initiation into a Communist adulthood (Jugendweihe), have now fallen into general disuse. The concentration camps of Buchenwald and Sachsenhausen, once reserved for the more general commemoration of the Communists and Anti-fascists rather exclusively by the Socialist regime in the GDR, are now being rede-signed to include separate commemorative elements referring to the particular groups victimized by the Nazis—such as the Jews and the Gypsies—as well as to the victims of Stalinism, who also died there. This "refurbishing" of the concrete memory raises questions about relating the victims of Nazism with those of Stalin-ism, who were often Nazis themselves.

This redefinition of the monumental landscape relates to the reconstitution of the state, but, what is more, suggests a reconfiguring of a German identity through a revision of the collective memory of the populace in that part of Germany. The many monuments representing members of the Communist pantheon, those founding fathers of Communism, Marx and Engels, the martyrs of the "faith" such as Ernst Thalmann, or the embodiment of scientific progress under the Com-munists (the Cosmonauts), are being removed from the public eye as an unsys-tematic way of disposing with the past. The official history of the GDR is being revised, suppressed, and supplanted in a fashion that does not allow for a working through the past, that denies the political discourse necessary to deal with it, and that reminds of the recurrent concern of the Germans to redefine themselves and their need to finally assume an identity that derives from a critical confrontation with their past.

17. Eternal Celebration in American Memorials

Jonathan L. Fairbanks

"In the beginning was the Word."[1] Without written or spoken words, mankind would surely fail to share and transmit complex ideas about memories from one generation to another. About ten generations ago, in 1681, the first printmaker in North America, an astronomer, mathematician, and book printer, John Foster, died at the age of 33. This man, from Dorchester, Massachusetts, succumbed to a disease that progressed slowly enough to permit him to correspond with his minister, Increase Mather. Both the minister and this ingenious printer wrote to each other in Latin. The text of this correspondence is carved on Foster's headstone (Fig. 17–1). Mather to Foster: "*Astra colis vivens: moriens super aethra Foster scande, precor: Coelum metiri disce supremum.*"

Roughly translated, Mather observed that, "Living thou studiest the stars; dying, mayest thou, Foster, I pray, mount above the skies and learn to measure the highest heavens."

Foster replied in Latin, "*Metior, atque meum est: emit mihi dives Jesus nec teneor quicquam, nisi grates, solvere.*" Roughly translated: "I measure it and it is mine; the Lord Jesus has bought it for me, now I am held to pay aught for it, but thanks."

The footstone is more prosaic. It states clearly for all the unlearned to read that, "SKILL WAS HIS CASH."[2] These writings reveal two extremes of the New England mind. The headstone contains elevated or learned thoughts; the footstone represents the practical or the ordinary viewpoint. The Ideal of the headstone contrasts with footstone realities, or the ornamental versus the plain. Such polarities of thought (e.g., ideal versus real or universal versus particular) are echoed in various mutations throughout most of the history of American sculpture. Pictorially, the tympanum of the headstone shows a carved image of Father Time, who stays the hand of death (a skeleton), who, in turn, reaches out to extinguish the flame of life. This is an image that the Boston/Charleston stonecutter adopted from an early English emblem book authored by Francis Quarels.[3] The carver used it on many

Figure 17–1   *Slate Headstone for John Foster.* Dorchester.

New England headstones. Without explanation, the viewer probably could not guess that Father Time stays Death for the right moment.

Emblems must be explained in words. Most sculpture is mute and hence requires interpretation through words. The printed word was commonly shared in the highly literate world of Bible-reading Puritans. In seventeenth-century New England there was a high rate of literacy. History was written even as it was being enacted. The most famous examples of such consciously wrought histories are William Bradford's *Of Plimouth Plantation (1620–1647)* and John Winthrop's manuscript, *The History of New England from 1630–1649*, a journal that was begun with his journey from England to settle the Massachusetts Bay Colony.[4]

Popular learning through memories carried by recitation was another way to know history and the Bible, and to transfer knowledge among New England's common-folk. Yet today, oral history concerning seventeenth-century New England is infrequently encountered and unreliable. Oral traditions do not survive a dozen generations of modern society as well as they do in folk and native cultures. In 1664, towards the end of her life, Anne Bradstreet put her thoughts down in a small manuscript (now at the Houghton Library of Harvard), called *Meditations Divine and Morall*.[5] She didn't live to complete the manuscript. In the front page she wrote to her son Samuel, reminding him that he had once asked that Anne leave something to remember her that he could look upon after she was gone. She hoped that these thoughts would be treasured for their author's sake as they were her own ideas and not the ideas of others.

The Bradstreet manuscript's beautiful preamble reveals what the business of art and history is mostly about—INSPIRATION and MEMORIES! A passage from the manuscript explains the nature of the journey of earthly life; the word Pilgrim is used in its period sense. The reader is advised that pilgrims, or travelers, should not want to become too comfortable in this life lest they lose their way, destiny, or place of belonging when change from life to death will come. Bradstreet's little sayings are easily memorized. That is part of the miracle of her booklet. Through the word, visual experiences are transformed into brief sayings that are easy to remember. The memory lesson is recalled as a memorized passage is recited from the Bradstreet manuscript. The internal and the external worlds are referenced, and there seems to be a thin veil between the invisible and the visible, the spiritual and the material worlds:

> The eyes and the ears are the inlets or doores of the Soule, through which innumerable objects enter, yet is not that Spacious roome filled neither doeth it ever Say it is enough, but like the daughters of the horGlass, crys give give & which is most strange, the more it receives the more empty it finds itself, and sees an impossibility ever to be filled, but by him, in whom fullness dwells.[6]

The Word was extremely important to Pilgrims and Puritans—to reformers who were searching for patterns to illuminate God's ways. Patterns, essential for mankind to observe and understand, involved the cosmic order of things. Order for the seventeenth-century mind was of two sorts. The seventeenth century looked both backward and forward. The late medieval astrological man of science represented by Foster's woodcut (1678),[7] looked backward. At the same time there was another view of mankind as illustrated in a figure of the proportional man, pictured in a book issued by John Bate in London in 1634 entitled, *The Mysteries of Nature and Art.*[8] It was the first illustrated handbook in the English language for understanding studio practices in art. This book was read in or before 1670 by Increase Mather, the distinguished New England divine. It plagiarized the works of the sixteenth-century Bible of Mannerism, Giovanni Paolo Lomazzo's, *Tratato della Pittura* (1584).[9]

It may seem remarkable that a Puritan minister read Italian/Catholic thought about the divine order of the universe, but he was unaware of this fact. Access to world knowledge through books was much broader and deeper in seventeenth-century New England than most people realize today. The concept of the proportional body of mankind helped, in part, to unravel the magical world of astrological signs and portents in the late seventeenth-century Puritan world. Portents and replacing magic signs were replaced by symmetry, logic, and mathematical order—expressed through new concepts of natural theology. Sight was a primary instrument through which new rational systems could be understood. Rational order crept into mankind's consciousness slowly. Minister Charles Morton, who was invited to come to Boston from Oxford, England, in 1686, observed in his *Compendium physicae* (the first physics textbook of Harvard University, completed c.1680), that "sight to the mind doth bear a near relation, more matter then, affords much contemplation."[10]

Towns planted in colonial days close to the edge of harbors and the waterways soon became crowded with markets, homes, and commerce. God's plot for burial, what was once believed to be ample, became crowded in the eighteenth century. By the early nineteenth century, urban graveyards overflowed. Graveyard crowding was blamed for the great epidemics in the late eighteenth century: the yellow fever epidemics of Philadelphia of the 1790s, and the cholera plagues of 1832 that spread through the coastal states and out onto the frontier. Period literature cites the noxious of effluvia of the dead as the source of such inexplicable diseases. Philadelphia's yellow fever epidemic prompted the building of a new water works. This included a pumping station in the center of town enclosed in a handsome classical temple designed by Benjamin Henry Latrobe (1764–1820). In front of that building stood an allegorical wooden nymph of the Schuylkill River with attendant bittern (c.1809), carved by William Rush (1756–1833). This sculpture now survives as a bronze replica in the Philadelphia Museum of Art.[11]

Sculpture of the federal period was often ornamental, frequently made for ships, buildings, or furniture. A superb example of architectural adornment is the pine figure of Liberty (1746–1800) (Fig. 17–2) at the Museum of Fine Arts, Boston. It was made about 1800, not long after John (1746–1800) or Simeon Skillin (1757–1806) of Boston carved a figure of Fame on a chest-on-chest (now at the Museum of Fine Arts, Boston), for the Derby family of Salem. The Skillins are also responsible for three allegorical figures on another Derby family chest-on-chest, which is now in the Garvan collection in the Yale University Art Gallery.[12] Such figures are abstractions or ideal personifications representing Fame, Liberty, Peace, and Plenty. Within a generation (in the early nineteenth century), poet William Cullen Bryant (1794–1818) wrote his great poem about death, *Thanatopsis*. He

Figure 17–2 *Liberty.* white Pine. Museum of Fine Arts, Boston.

expressed attitudes toward death in a new way. Rather than death represented by the grim reaper or the skull, it was presented as a time of sleep or sweet dreaming. Recall the last part of *Thanatopsis*:

> So live that when thy summons comes to join
> The innumerable caravan, which moves
> To that mysterious realm, where each shall take
> His chamber in the silent halls of death,
> Thou go not, like the quarry-slave at night.
> Scourged to his dungeon, but, sustained and soothed
> By an unfaltering trust, approach thy grave,
> Like one who wraps the drapery of his couch
> About him, and lies down to pleasant dreams.[13]

A change in attitude toward death and life illuminates the new approach to cosmic order and the measure of mankind. Early in the nineteenth century the measure for sculpture is by rule and divider. A drawing by Samuel McIntire (1757–1811), an architect and carver of Salem, demonstrates the system. It is a practical method based upon provincial academic Neoclassicism. Neoclassicism may be closely linked to a search for picturesque qualities in the American landscape and paintings. Many events forged the search for the picturesque and the revival of art of the ancient classical world in America. While the cholera epidemic of 1832 prompted citizens to reform urban plans, they also discovered that the people of ancient times buried their dead outside city walls. That fact, linked with a growing interest in horticulture and the search for beauty in Nature (the picturesque), prompted the removal of burial to cemeteries into rural areas or town suburbs. At the outskirts of major cities both here and abroad, the well-to-do were simultaneously building suburban villas. A convergence of popular interest, the revival of ancient classical style, new sanitation concerns, and horticulture were but three forces at work.

The rural cemetery movement was also driven by profit motives. Joint stock companies were formed and land for rural cemeteries was secured. Share holding companies were run by speculators. They were a success. In 1831, the suburban, picturesque cemetery in Cambridge, Massachusetts, Mount Auburn, was begun, the first rural cemetery in America. Next, in 1837, Laurel Hill was established in Philadelphia. Green-Wood in Brooklyn, New York, opened in 1842, and Forest Hills in Jamaica Plain near Boston, was operating in 1848.[14] These rural cemeteries provided bread and butter for American sculptors of the Romantic/Classical generations.

Gates to the cemetery entries suggested passage to a special place. The Egyptian style was adopted at Mount Auburn to imply permanence. Egyptian architecture with its heavy, battered walls symbolized, not only death, but also power and eternity to the Victorian mind. Prisons and reservoirs were also constructed in the Egyptian style. Victorians were attuned to symbolism. The Philadelphia architect, John Notman (1810–1865), who won a competition for the Laurel Hill cemetery, designed a classical gateway and a Gothic-style chapel within the grounds.[14]

All of the three earliest rural cemeteries had chapels. They had to because the presence of a gothic-style chapel defused potential criticism by churchmen that cemetery company land was not sacred ground and hence not fit for Christian burials. All early guidebooks to garden cemeteries stress a special consecrated quality of the shaded dells and glades of God, of nature's handy work, altered slightly by man. The visitor to Green-Wood entered past an arched gate with a belfry—a suitable emblem of mourning. Such designs diffused criticism that these cemeteries were merely commercial. After passing through the arched gate of Laurel Hill, the visitor first views a structure sheltering a group of life-size stone figures: one depicts a bust of the celebrated novelist, Sir Walter Scott (1771–1832), and the other *Old Mortality* and his horse (Fig. 17–3). *Old Mortality* is a central figure in a Waverly novel by Scott of the same title. *Old Mortality* was a pilgrim whose personal mission was to restore or recut eroding inscriptions on tombs of Presbyterian martyrs throughout Scotland. The sculpture in Philadelphia is genre art, carved by an immigrant Scottish stonemason, James Thom (1799–1850), who remains uncelebrated in American sculpture history.[16]

Bodies of famous individuals who died before Laurel Hill was established were exhumed and reburied at the new cemetery. This added the respectability of age to the site. It encouraged sales of lots. Philadelphia's famous Gothic novelist, Charles Brockden Brown (1771–1810), who died twenty-seven years before Laurel Hill opened, has a finely cut stone with urn and drape. Military hero General Hugh Mercer, a native of Scotland who died at the battle of Princeton in 1771, was placed under what was then called a Roman-style memorial after 1840 when his remains were moved from the Christ Church yard on Second Street to Laurel Hill. The Saint Andrew's Society, a powerful Scottish organization in Philadelphia, sponsored the removal and memorialization of Mercer's remains as a tribute to their brother.

Figural sculpture began to flourish in American Garden cemeteries with the emergence of American sculptors who trained abroad in Italy. The earliest example at Mount Auburn is Thomas Crawford's (1813–1857) Amos Binney monument (Fig. 17–4). Dr. Binney (1803–1847) was a naturalist, a patron of the arts, and president of the Boston Society of Natural History. He died in Rome, but his remains were returned to be buried beside his parents at Mt. Auburn. The monument is now seriously eroding. It is a difficult and expensive proposition to save marble monuments from continued decline. Shelter seems to be the only sure remedy. For the Binney monument, that means disassembly and possibly replacement with a polyester resin replica. Marble poses a real problem out-of-doors. It is a soft stone, easily dissolved by acid rain. Despite erosion, Crawford's carving on the Binney monument can still be discerned. The iconography of the hooded female carrying a jar of ashes recalls Benjamin West's (1738–1820) painting now in Yale University Art Gallery's collection, *Agrippina Landing at Brundisium with the Ashes of Germanicus*. This famous work was painted in London in 1768.[17]

Crawford's sculptural debut was made at the Boston Athenaeum in 1844 with the display of his marble carving, *Orpheus and Cerberus*. The sculpture was modeled in Rome in 1839 and carved by 1843. When the Athenaeum grew overcrowded with works of art, some of its officers established the Museum of Fine Arts, which then became a repository for many of the Athenaeum's treasures. In 1975, quite unexpectedly, the Athenaeum withdrew loans anticipating sales. This prompted the noted scholars of classical art, Drs. Cornelius and Emily Vermeule,

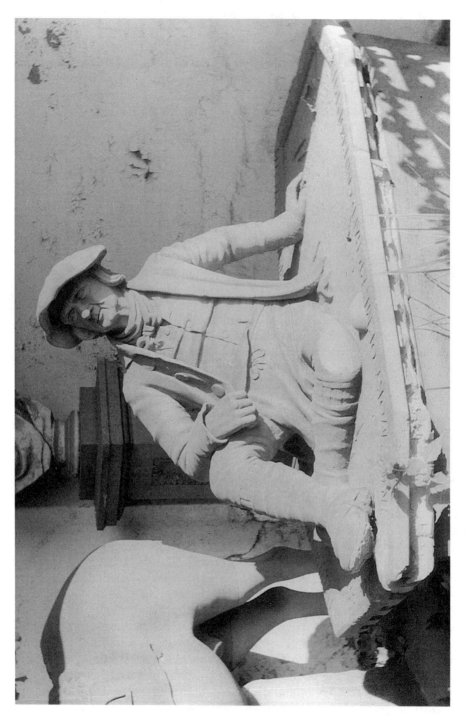

Figure 17–3 *Old Mortality,* James Thom, sculptor. Philadelphia.

Figure 17–4 *Amos Binney, M.D., Died at Rome, February 18, 1847 Age 41.* Thomas Crawford, sculptor. Cambridge.

to make a generous gift that transferred ownership of *Orpheus and Cerberus* to the Museum.[18]

In contrast to American sculptors who established their reputation with classical training in Italy, in this country a self-taught sculptor and foundryman, Clark Mills (1810–1883), modeled, and cast in bronze, the first equestrian memorial produced in this country. It was made between 1852–1853 in Washington D.C. at a furnace and studio at Fifteenth Street on Pennsylvania Avenue. The sculpture represents Andrew Jackson on a lively rearing horse, mounted on a high, stone pedestal on Lafayette Square, Washington, D.C. (Fig. 17–5). Later, in 1860, he produced a similar rendering for the Washington Circle in D.C. of General George Washington on horseback.[19]

Historical figures, modeled posthumously, are necessarily recollected or reconstructed by sculptors who make memorials. If the artist has not seen the person he or she commemorates during the subject's lifetime, then the memorial is based upon reseach and/or imagination. Early handbooks in art observed that the reason that the art of painting and sculpture was invented was to "record and perpetuate the effigies of famous men." Representation of famous deeds were likewise worthy to record in order to "stirre up men's minds with the emulation of like Glorious enterprises."[20] While this viewpoint may seem narrow today, it is not entirely forgotten in the world of public art. The most effective memorialization in sculpture conveys not just a record of the past; it also inspires the viewer with magnificent form and symbols.

However symbolic or imposing was Horatio Greenough's (1805–1852) Phidian-inspired figure of Washington (1841, displayed in the National Museum of History, Washington D.C.), it nonetheless failed to meet the needs of most Americans who wanted their heros represented in proper contemporary clothing. Idealization of this sort seemed to many viewers at odds with the current real world. Average Americans, unversed in classical visual symbols, were puzzled by Greenough's seminude Washington. Yet Americans who understood the language of classical antiquity continued to order or produce ideal marble images in Italy throughout the era of the great turmoil of the American Civil War.

Harriet Hosmer (1830–1908), an expatriot from Watertown, Massachusetts, who settled in Rome (the first American woman to achieve fame as a sculptor) carved a sleeping faun of exquisite beauty in 1865. There is little doubt that she carved it in response to the novel by Nathaniel Hawthorne, *Transformation: The Romance of Monte Beni*, which soon became a book known as *The Marble Faun*. Hosmer was mentioned by name in the preface of this book, and undoubtedly both she and the author shared a mutual admiration for the ancient Praxitelean sculpture that inspired the novel, the personage of Donatello, and Hosmer's carving. Hawthorne observed William Wetmore Story (1819–1895) as he worked on his *Cleopatra*. The author acknowledged that this experience helped to develop the plot and the fictional sculptor, Kenyon. For Hawthorne, the mood or presence of the deep past in Rome was felt far more urgently than anything modern. He introduced the reader to his novel by commenting on the mood visitors felt in Rome—a sense of ponderous remembrances of the past, "At the ruins, Etruscan, Roman, Christian,

Figure 17–5 *Jackson Monument 1852–1853. Clark Mills, sculptor. Bronze. Washington.*

venerable with a threefold antiquity, and at the company of world-famous statues.[21]

William Wetmore Story's sculpture career came about directly as a result of a commission given to him by the officials of Mount Auburn Cemetery to create a memorial to his father, the Chief Justice Joseph Story (1779–1845), which is now in the Law Library at Harvard. Prior to that commission he had been admitted to the Boston bar and had published a treatise on the law of contracts, as well as a volume of poems and a biography of his father. Now best remembered for his long career abroad as a productive sculptor, Story was also known as a poet and classicist during his lifetime. The diversity of his talents makes the assessment of his contributions difficult. Also complicating is the fact that he outlived the era in which his style of antiquarian classicism was popular.[22]

The Civil War brought a new aesthetic to American sculpture. A young sculptor from Boston, Martin Milmore (1844–1883), chose to portray the common foot soldier of the Civil War in vigorously modeled, realistic terms for a commission that resulted in an impressively simple memorial to the Union soldiers from Roxbury (Fig. 17–6). Milmore's realistic style referenced late Republican Roman genre sculpture from 60 to 30 B.C. The monument (cast at the Ames Foundry in Chickopee) was placed in the Forest Hills Cemetery in 1867, surrounded with burials of Civil War soldiers. On the base was chiseled Lincoln's words at Gettysburg, November 1865: "From these honored dead we take increased devotion to that cause for which they gave their last full measure of devotion." Another inscription ensures that the reader will know why the monument went up, erected by the city of Roxbury. "In the honor of her soldiers who died for their country in the rebellion of 1861–65." Citizens were proud of Milmore's achievement and a granite version of the foot soldier was soon placed at the center of the crossroads in Jamaica Plain. Hundreds of monuments throughout the United States imitated Milmore's foot soldier. His success with realism did not prevent him from also entertaining allegorical and symbolic concepts.

Milmore's most enigmatic work is the great granite Sphinx of 1872, which he and his brother, Joseph, carved and placed at Mt. Auburn Cemetery (Fig. 17–7). This memorial commemorated the Union dead. The sphinx makes reference to Africa and Africans and, more particularly, draws upon Victorian notions of eternal memorialization through this symbol of Egypt. The modern viewer may not understand that message. But even if the symbol is not understood today, it certainly was clear to Victorians who were sensitive to associated meanings. Milmore's Copenhagen Tomb (1874) in Mount Auburn is a more old-fashioned expression—merely a conventional angel with a trumpet. A similar concept is expressed by Milmore's teacher (from 1858 to 1863) thomas Ball (1819–1911), whose marble monument to the piano manufacturing family of chickering, "The Realization of Fatith" (Fig. 17–8), also depicts an angel. This angel holds a down-turned torch, extinguishing the flame of life, while uncovering the head of a dying Christian and releasing her to heaven.

Death as pleasant dreams had become an outmoded concept with the Civil War. Managers of garden cemeteries and thanatologists tried to sweeten death with the beauty of picturesque landscape. However, the brutal reality of unexpected death

Figure 17–6 *Union Soldier Monument.* Martin Milmore, sculptor. Jamaica Plain.

Figure 17–7 *American Union Monument.* Martin Milmore, sculptor. Cambridge.

as part of nature and the natural process was clearly becoming recognized in both sculpture and poetry. In a poem by Emerson entitled *Hamatreya*, the reader can sense a new attitude towards death:

> Bulkeley, Hunt, Willard, Hosmer, Meriam, Flint,
> Possessed the land which rendered to their toil
> Hay, corn, roots, hemp, flax, apples, wool and wood.
> Each of these landlords walked amidst his farm
> Saying, ' 'Tis mine, my children's and my names.
> How sweet the west wind sounds in mine own trees!
> How graceful climb those shadows on my hill!
> I fancy these pure waters and the flags
> Know me, as does my dog: we sympathize;
> And, I affirm, my actions smack of the soil.'
> Where are these men? Asleep beneath their grounds:
> And strangers, fond as they, their furrows plough.
> Earth laughs in flowers, to see her boastful boys
> Earth-proud, proud of the earth which is not theirs;
> Who steer the plough, but cannot steer their feet
> Clear of the grave."[23]

Figure 17–8   *Chickering Monument.* T. Ball, sculptor. Cambridge.

This realistic view of death is not unlike that which is seen in Milmore's realistic work. Milmore's greatest effort, the *Soldiers' and Sailors' Monument*, dedicated in 1877 on the Boston Common, mixes both ideal figures (a few symbolic female figures) among realistic soldiers and sailors around the base.[24] The central towering shaft is crowned by a figure of Liberty. Towered figures became a conventional device that the next generation of gifted sculptors avoided.

The mid-1870s marked a dramatic new wave of talent arriving in New York City. Boston had become outmoded as a center of innovative fashion or creativity in America. New York dominated the art scene. Sculptors, schooled in Paris, often in the École des Beaux-Arts, brought to New York a new approach to sculpture. The premier figure to emerge was Augustus Saint-Gaudens (1848–1907), who in 1876 received the commission for *The Farragut Monument* (1879–1880) placed in New York City. The monument consisted of a heroic portrait bronze figure elevated above a bluestone base. The memorial celebrates brave action in the face of danger. It marks an important transition in the history of memorial sculpture. The figure represents Admiral David Glasgow Farragut and is convincingly real. Its composition is as dynamic and alive as its surfaces. Profound understanding of the Renaissance sculptors, Michelangelo and Donatello, are evident in the composition and pose of this work that launched Saint-Gauden's career.[25] The Farragut Monument does not make the mistake of elevating the central figure on a shaft too high for ordinary mortals to see. The base contains idealized female figures in low relief, while the compositional focus remains centered on the realistically portrayed Admiral. At least partial credit for the success of this composition is due to the design collaboration of architect Stanford White (1853–1906), who provided the design for the base.

Undoubtedly, the most moving collaboration between Saint-Gaudens and White is the disarmingly quiet *Adams Memorial* (1890–1891) in Rock Creek Cemetery near Washington, D.C. (Figs. 17–9a,b). After the death of Henry Adams's wife, Marion, artist John LaFarge and Adams traveled to Japan and studied oriental art and philosophy. On their return, Adams asked LaFarge to request that Saint-Gaudens create a suitable memorial to his wife. Adams offered no instructions to the sculptor and apparently did not wish to see it until completed. Saint-Gaudens struggled with this unusual problem of creating a worthy memorial without consultation with the client. After five years, the masterpiece was finished. It challenges, but defies explication.[26] The sculpture must be experienced in its place and setting to understand its emotional power. It is sparely sited and enclosed with shrubbery. The sculpture's solitude and pensive mood is enhanced by both plantings and simple architectonic setting (Fig. 10).

In contrast to the personal yet universal sculptural statement for Henry Adams, by 1884, Saint-Gaudens had already embarked on his greatest masterpiece—a memorial in Boston. This was to commemorate, in high relief, the heroism of the Fifty-fourth volunteer infantry Regiment of Free Blacks in a monument known as the *Memorial to Robert Gould Shaw* (Fig. 17–10). Completed in 1897, this thirteen-year project recalls sacrifices of lives made by the Fifty-fourth Regiment at Fort Wagner, near Charleston, South Carolina. Robert Gould Shaw is the central figure in the composition. On horseback, he leads his troops, as they paraded down Beacon

Figure 17–9a *Untitled Memorial for Adams Family Plot.* Augustus Saint-Gaudens, sculptor. Bronze. Washington.

Figure 17–9b   *Adam's Memorial*. Detail.

Street, off to war. They are guided by a hovering, symbolic female figure overhead. At the dedication of the monument, some thirty years after the battle, Saint-Gaudens witnessed the return of the balance of the troops. They were then aged, mounted on horseback, marching back in the direction opposite to their departure. Saint-Gaudens proclaimed that witnessing this was, for him, a consecration. The sculpture magnificently expresses the solemnity of the event with many figures in both high and shallow relief. It is arguably the finest piece of memorial sculpture in America today.[27]

Daniel Chester French's *Milmore Memorial* erected at Forest Hills Cemetery in 1893 (Fig. 17–11), probably would not have looked the same without some knowledge of what was taking place with the Shaw Memorial. Yet, unlike the Shaw Memorial, the Milmore figures are fully three-dimensional, seeming almost detached from the relief. The figure of death is represented by a great hooded female with poppies in one hand; the other hand stays the chisel of the young sculptor, Milmore, as he works on the Mount Auburn Sphinx.[28] Saint-Gaudens and French both inspired at least three subsequent generations of American sculptors who either knew them personally or who were otherwise in touch with them or moved by their works. The studio assistants, clients, materials, equipment, and casts of models of and by French and Saint-Gaudens also disseminated their influence across the nation. Many of the next generation of sculptors came from the Far West.

One of these was my late father, Avard T. Fairbanks (1897–1987) (who admired the art of and knew both French and Saint-Gaudens). In 1911 he studied animal sculpture in the Bronx Zoo where he met many other sculptors of note. As a fourteen-year-old, he modeled a charging buffalo based on a captive animal, which, I am told by zoo officials, is the sire of many bison on the plains today. At the zoo, Fairbanks met James Earle Fraser (1876–1953), Anna Hyatt Huntington (1876–1973), and Solon Borglum (1868–1922), all of whom encouraged him and offered constructive criticism. He also met Alexander Phimister Proctor (1862–1950), who in 1914/1915 placed the great bronze Bisons in Washington, D.C., at the ends of the Dumbarton Bridge.

Memorialization extended to species at risk at that time, not just mankind. It also extended to (what, at that time, was believed to be) vanishing races such as the Native Americans. Examples of this genre were the impressive works that Solon Borglum made for the Louisiana Purchase Exposition, St. Louis, Missouri, in 1904. Borglum's sculpture represented universalized figures rather than portraits of particular individuals. Cyrus Edwin Dallin (1861–1944), who, like Borglum, was born in Utah, also modeled idealized Indians. His most famous bronze, "Appeal to the Great Spirit" (1909), stands at the Huntington entrance of the Museum of Fine Arts, Boston.[29]

Figure 17–10, page 180 *Shaw Memorial to the Fifty-Fourth Volunteer Regiment.* Augustus Saint-Gaudens, sculptor. Bronze and Stone. Boston.

Figure 17–11, page 181 *Milmore Memorial.* Bronze. Jamaica Plains.

The next generation of sculptors whose works grace the building of the Museum of Fine Arts include the late Richard H. Recchia (1888–1983), of Rockport, Massachusetts. He was encouraged and assisted in his career by French. His mastery of modeling is represented in a private memorial, a bronze relief of 1910 depicting his father, Frank C. Recchia, carver (Fig. 17–12). Recchia made in the same year an equally masterful relief of Bela Lyon Pratt, a fellow sculptor and mentor whose work, with Recchia's, ornament the Museum's Evans Wing. Recchia became something of a recluse in his old age, but, through advice of the sculptor, Walker Hancock, he made it possible for some of his finest works to come into the collections of the Museum of Fine Arts, Boston.[30]

In 1933, as my father's reputation was gaining worldwide, his massive *Winter Quarter's* memorial was dedicated near Omaha, Nebraska. This bronze (Fig. 17–13), was erected to remember the trials and demise of many Mormon pioneers at their winter encampment of 1846 after their removal from Nauvoo, Illinois.[31] At that encampment, several Fairbanks family members perished. All the pioneers are buried in unmarked graves but are memorialized and named in handsome bronze relief panels at the foot of the monument. The monument and reliefs were commissioned by The Church of Jesus Christ of Latter-day Saints. Also, they represent the sculptor's personal testimony. The two windswept bronze figures burying their child compellingly recalls the high infancy mortality in that year of decision to relocate in the Far West.

Conventional histories too often forget the thousands of craftsman-artists who served the needs of sculptors as casters, modelers, chasers, carvers, and many more who are necessary for sculptors to perform their work. Pietro Caproni of Roxbury, Massachusetts, who came to Boston from Italy in 1879 was the leading member of a great plaster casting dynasty, with galleries located on Washington Street in Boston. He was not to be forgotten. His imposing granite tombstone designed by architect Ralph Adams Cram (1863–1942), and set in 1929 in Forest Hills Cemetery endures (Fig. 17–14). A sleeping granite lion guards one side and an awake lion on the other. Clearly Italinate in composition, the tomb lions are modeled after Antonio Canova's tomb to Pope Clement the XVIII in Rome.

The Caproni tomb is an effective memorial for person, family, and nation of origin. Not so effective, however, are later tombs. Sadly, picturesque cemeteries of the nineteenth century began to change in the 1940s—the sculpture changed, but not for the better. With the war years a decline engulfed garden cemetery aesthetics. The nation's romance with technology and industrialization encouraged a faith in efficiency and economy rather than in humanistic expression. Profit-making tendencies in those years encouraged the crowding of many old, dignified cemeteries with undistinguished and uniform stones. Tablets began to line plot upon plot like decks of cards. Mechanized design eroded even the overall layout of garden cemeteries. Yet memorials of high artistic merit do occasionally continue to be made.

Walker Hancock (b. 1901) was the sculptor who in 1950 made the *Pennsylvania Railroad War Memorial* at 30th Street Station, Philadelphia (Figure 17–15).[32] The original model for the head of the angel in that memorial is in the collection of the Museum of Fine Arts, Boston. In his ninety-first year, Hancock continues to produce sculpture. For this paper I visited him in his Lanesville, Massachusetts, stu-

Figure 17–12 *Bronze Relief of Frank Recchia.* R. H. Recchia. Bronze. Museum of Fine Arts, Boston.

Figure 17–13 *The Tragedy at Winter Quarters*. Avard Tennyson Fairbanks, sculptor. Florence, NB.

Figure 17–14 *Caproni Monument.* Ralph Adams Cram, Architect. Granite. Jamaica Plains.

Figure 17–15 *Pennsylvania Railroad War Memorial.* Walter Hancock, sculptor. Plaster. Lanesville, MA.

dio. He was working on a very large monument to be dedicated at West Point. I took some photographs, but Hancock later said, "If you show the slides, Jonathan, just show them momentarily because I've really improved it a lot since your visit." Hancock's West Point figure is an ascending, lyrical work with an eloquent message. It was commissioned to remember all graduates of West Point who, in pursuing their careers, perished in flight.

Eloquent memorial sculpture, both public and private, can and should still lift the human spirit with new expressions, drawing upon the timeless and universal theme of human mortality and memory. It is hoped that the few examples cited and illustrated here will serve to link the golden chain of memories into future generations and sculptural possibilities.

NOTES

1. *The New Testament*, The Gospel According to Saint John, Chapter I, verse 1.

2. Jonathan L. Fairbanks et al. *New England Begins: The Seventeenth Century*, Vol. 2. 3 Vols. (Boston: Museum of Fine Arts, Boston, 1982), 318–20.

3. Francis Quarles, *Hieroglyphiques of the Life of Man* (London: Printed by M. Flesher for I. Marriot, 1638).

4. Fairbanks and Trent, op. cit., Vol. 3, 553, 569.

5. Ibid. Vol. 2, 128–129, no. 107.

6. Ibid. Vol. 3, 422.

7. Ibid. Vol. 2, 346, no. 363.

8. Ibid. Vol. 3, 423.

9. A citizen of Milan, Lomazzo (1538–c.1600) was a painter and keeper of Cosimo de Medici's picture gallery in Florence. His monumental *Trattato della Pittura* summed up precepts of cosmic harmony and mannerist art theories which were translated into English by Richard Haydocke of Oxford in 1598.

10. Fairbanks and Trent, op. cit., Vol. 3, 448. Morten's original manuscript book, his *Compendium*, has not yet been discovered. Yet it is known through several manuscript copies made by Harvard students, one of which, The Metcalf mss., is in the Dedham Historical Society Collections. See Morison on Charles Morton in *The Collections of the Colonial Society of Massachusetts* Vol. 33 (Boston: University of Virginia Press, 1940).

11. Milton W. Brown, et. al. *American Art* (New York: Harry N. Abrams, n.d.), 156, fig. 191.

12. Gerald F. R. Ward, *American Case Furniture in the Mabel Brady Garvan and Other Collections at Yale University* (New Haven, Conn.: Yale University Art Gallery, 1988), 171–7.

13. George F. Whicher, ed., *Poetry of the New England Renaissance, 1790–1890* (New York and Toronto: Rinehart and Co., 4th ed., 1959), 15. *Thanatopsis*, a youthful work, published in 1816, has long been regarded by many as one of Bryant's finest poems.

14. Period guidebooks for visitors to the first three rural cemeteries offer insights into the salesmanship and original intents of the founders: Jacob Bigelow, *A History of the*

Cemetery of Mount Auburn (Boston and Cambridge: James Munroe& Co., 1859; reprinted by Applewood Books, Chester, Conn.: The Globe Pequot Press, 1976); R. A. Smith, *Smith's Illustrated Guide to and through Laurel Hill Cemetery* (Philadelphia: Willis P. Hazard, 1852); and N. Cleavland, *Green-Wood* (New York: R. Martin, 1847).

15. At least two architects competed against Notman for the Laurel Hill commission. Both William Strickland (c.1787–1854) and Thomas U. Walter (1804–1887) proposed gateways in the Egyptian style. Their proposal drawings are preserved in the collections of the Library Company, Philadelphia.

16. The figure of *Old Mortality* was carved abroad, but the Pony and Scott were cut from a redstone obtained in New Jersey. According to contemporary accounts, these works by Thom attracted more praise than sculpture by celebrated sculptors Flaxman, Nollekens, or Chantrey. This may, of course, be marketing hyperbole. Thom went on to execute stonework for Richard Upjohn (1802–1878) in Trinity Church, in New York, completed in 1846.

17. Theodore E. Stebbins, Jr., et al. *The Lure of Italy: American Artists and the Italian Experience, 1760–1914* (Boston: Museum of Fine Arts, 1992), 152–3, figure 2, entry by Carol Troyen.

18. Jonathan L. Fairbanks et. al., *Collecting American Decorative Arts and Sculpture, 1971–1991* (Boston: Museum of Fine Arts, 1991), 57. Stebbins, op. cit., 166–9, fig. 9, entry D. Strazdes.

19. Mills also cast two additional versions of the Jackson Memorial: one for New Orleans in 1856, and another for Nashville, Tennessee in 1880. James M. Goode, *The Outdoor Sculpture of Washington, D.C.* (Washington: Smithsonian Institution Press, 1974) 377–8.

20. John Elsum, *The Art of Painting after the Italian Manner* (London: Printed for D. Brown and C. Kina, 1704), 9.

21. Hawthorne, *Transformation: The Romance of Monte Beni* (Leipzig: Bernhard and Taushnitz, 1860), 2.

22. Jan Seidler Ramirez, *A Critical Reappraisal of the Career of William Wetmore Story (1819–1895), American Sculptor of Letters.* Ph.D. diss., Boston University, 3 Vols., 1985.

23. Ralph Waldo Emerson, *Poems* (Boston: Houghton Mifflin and Company, 1895), 35.

24. Jan Seidler Rameriz, et. al., "Martin Milmore," *American Figurative Sculpture in the Museum of Fine Arts, Boston* (Boston: Museum of Fine Arts, Boston, 1986), 192–5.

25. For an assessment of Saint-Gaudens and the sculpture of his times see Kathryn Greenthal, *Augustus Saint-Gaudens, Master Sculptor* (New York: The Metropolitan Museum of Arts, 1985).

26. The subject is handled well by Greenthal, op. cit., 130–1.

27. The most moving publication about this memorial is by Lincoln Kirstein, *Lay This Laurel* (New York: Eakins Press, 1973). See also Lois Goldreich Marcus, "*The Shaw Memorial* by Augustus Saint-Gaudens, A History Painting in Bronze," *Winterthur Portfolio*, 14 (Spring 1979): 1–23.

28. The development of the design of the Milmore monument is complex but superbly documented by Michael Richman, *Daniel Chester French: An American Sculptor* (New York: The Metropolitan Museum of Art, 1976), 71–9.

29. Rell G. Francis, *Cyrus Dallin: Let Justice Be Done* (Springvale Museum of Art, 1976), 48–9.

30. Ramirez et al., op. cit., 416–26.

31. Ibid., 450–4. Other heroic memorial sculpture by Fairbanks include the *91st Division Memorial* at Fort Lewis, Washington (1928); *Pioneer Mother Memorial*, Vancouver, Washington (1930); *Pioneer Family*, Bismark, North Dakota (1947); and the Albert Woolson portrait memorial to the last survivor (age 107 years) of the Grand Army of the Republic. Two versions of this bronze were cast; one was placed at the Gettysburg Battlefield and another in the City Hall of Duluth, Minnesota. This writer met Mr. Woolson and spent the summer of 1957 in Salt Lake City making molds for this sculpture.

32. Fairbanks, et. al., *Collecting American Decorative Arts and Sculpture, 1971–1991*, 60.

18. Evergreen Cemetery and Its Memorials*

Jean-Rae Turner

The Evergreen Cemetery was established by clergymen and businessmen from Elizabethtown Borough and the City of Newark in 1852, under the rural cemetery act of 1851. The tiny churchyard cemeteries were full and at least two Elizabethtown churches wished to expand their sanctuaries.

The thirty–one–acre site of the John Teas property along the Upper Road (to Newark or Elizabethtown, depending on your direction) was purchased for this purpose. Dr. Isaac Moreau Ward selected his gardener, a Mr. Sayre, to plan the landscape. Mr. Sayre served only a short time when he was replaced by Ernest L. Meyer, a young surveyor who later became the Elizabeth City Engineer.

Mr. Meyer served the cemetery for 49 years and designed 90 of its present 115 acres in the rural cemetery style of his day. The Rural Cemetery movement was a cultural phenomenon of mid-nineteenth-century America. It arose out of a new appreciation of the countryside in a reaction to the rapid urbanization of society of that era. Beginning with Boston's Mount Auburn Cemetery in 1831, progressive civic leaders sought to replace overcrowded, often unsightly and unsanitary city churchyards with large, picturesquely landscaped cemeteries located beyond the city's edge.

Meyer, a native of Germany, adopted the precepts of the picturesque style. This style emphasizes a naturalistic approach to landscape design and was developed in England during the eighteenth century. The Picturesque style replaced the Baroque's rigid formality. Nineteenth-century designers sought to create a pastoral environment that capitalized on the irregularities of nature.

---

*Jean-Rae Turner's research into Evergreen Cemetery led to the cemetery being placed on the National Register of Historic Sites.

In planning the grounds, Meyer saved the trees. Among them is a white oak, which unlike more famous white oaks in New Jersey is unsupported by cables. The cemetery still contains the remains of fruit orchards planted by the early farmers, as well as a row of linden trees planted by the cemetery along the Upper Road (now North Broad Street), Norway and sugar maples, horse chestnuts, American beach, pin and read oaks, sycamore, white ash, catalpa, English elm, weeping willow, magnolia, dogwood, Norway spruce, yew, and cedar. There are also decorative shrubs and trees such as privet, rose, azalea, forsythia, wisteria, ivy, and myrtle, all planted by plot owners.

There are some five buildings on the grounds and approximately thirty-five mausoleums in various architectural styles. The John Teas farmhouse originally served as an office, while the barns housed the horses and sheep used on the grounds. All have since been removed. Two of the private mausoleums are partially built into the sides of hills. One constructed in 1854 for the VanBuskirk-Jaques family has the Egyptian sunburst above the door. The present public mausoleum, in the Classical Revival style, was erected in 1912 as a receiving vault and was transformed into a mausoleum in 1976.

The present Administration Building, designed by C. A. Oakley in the first decade of the twentieth century, was scheduled to be a barn. Midway through construction, the trustees decided they needed more space. The first floor contained a chapel, rest rooms, and office. The chapel now serves as the main office. The second floor housed an eight-room apartment. The most interesting details of the interior are its chestnut paneling and fluted columns and patterned tile floors.

The new chapel near the Dayton Street, Newark, gate was designed in 1932 by C. Godfrey Poggi, a well-known Elizabeth architect. It is in the Tudor Revival style. A crematorium was added in the 1970s. Garages complete the cemetery's buildings.

The main gate opposite Coe Avenue on North Broad Street, once a picket fence, and since the 1870s a wrought iron fence, opens onto a green from which four roads radiate outward though the property's original thirty-one-acres. Following a serpentine course through the terrain, the roads repeatedly branch and intersect, forming sections of various shapes and sizes. Tiny triangles or circles form many of the intersections.

The individual family plots vary in size and shape. Some are circular, while newer ones are generally rectangular. They may be for two, four, six, eight, or more graves. Some are provided for two caskets each. The new areas of the cemetery were designed in the twentieth century by William Henry Luster, Jr., who also was an Elizabeth City engineer, and his son, Clifton H. Luster, Hillside Township Engineer. Although their areas are more formal with central circles in each large rectangle, they blend well with the rest of the cemetery. The last parcel of land, a tannery in Newark, was added in 1926. Because of that addition, the cemetery is located in three communities—Hillside, Elizabeth, and Newark—and two counties—Union and Essex counties.

In addition to the family plots, the cemetery trustees provided areas known as "public grounds," originally divided between black and white graves. These areas are for single graves, usually for families who were unable or unwilling to purchase a plot (Fig. 18–1). They include a children's section with small single

Figure 18–1 *John B. Kunie Tombstone*. Stone. New Jersey.

graves. These too initially were divided between the black and white graves. This, of course, is no longer the case.

The original monuments were much like those found in the colonial cemeteries. Thus, the freestanding column, tablet, obelisk, or pedestal-type monuments are frequently topped by an urn symbolizing mortality, sorrow, or memory. There are many draped urns, broken columns, and draped broken columns in the cemetery, representing sorrow and life cut short.

Among the cemetary's more than 100,000 monuments are many statues. The most common statues include classically draped females and winged angels, either freestanding or in various poses of symbolic meaning. A notable example is the winged angel with bowed head and floral bouquet in hand, crowning a large and impressive pedestal.

Urns flank the monuments on the Wagner and Adams family plots. The free-standing angel at the Franz plot is positioned next to a typical monolithic monument with a true cross on its top. The Houigan plot has the angel on top of the monolithic monument, while "Our Mary" stands in front of the family monument (Fig. 18–2). The little girl was killed in Missouri in 1951 when she was only eight years old, and her life-size statue is one of the prettiest in the cemetery. The gravesite is also one of the best maintained (plot owners may pay for perpetual care or perform the work themselves). The Cullen Jacqmein family plot features two tiny cherubs or angels on either side of the signatory tablet. These, along with lambs, are especially popular on children's graves.

Of particular note is the bronze replica of the famous classical Greek statue "Winged Victory," which stands on a plain pedestal marking the grave of Georgia Lescher Schwerine, a blind woman who died when she was only thirty-five years old. Unfortunately, this statue has been the victim of vandals, and one of the wings has disappeared.

The variety of crosses in the cemetery is noteworthy. There are crosses with passion flowers and vines, Celtic crosses as well as wayside crosses, crosses on ledger stone, crosses with anchors, and Eastern crosses. The Viscount monument consists of four Tuscan columns supporting a triumphal arch with a carved, rockfaced cornice surmounted by a small cross. Adjacent to the arch are an altar-like epitaph block and a garden bench.

One of the largest and oldest family plots is owned by the Chetwood family and contains the graves of two mayors of Elizabethtown. The plot is circular in configuration, and at its center is a huge columnar monument, resting on a massive pedestal with markedly canted sides and supporting a shrouded urn. The headstone of William Chetwood, a veteran of the Whiskey Rebellion, features a round-arched epitaph panel with a molded enframement, a cornice, and a scrolled pediment.

Another large plot belongs to John Brisbin and his wife, Adelia. Brisbin was both a Congressman and president of the Delaware, Lackawanna, and Western Railroad. Their monument is surrounded by a stone wall, now prohibited by the cemetery's trustees. The trustees also removed the plot's iron fences, making the plot easier to maintain.

In 1862, the trustees allotted two areas for free burials for veterans of the Civil War (Fig. 18–3). The plot subsequently became available to veterans of the Spanish-American War and World War I. Two Spanish-American era cannon guard the site.

The trustees also provided sections to the Mendelsohn Benevolent Society, a burying society of Jewish immigrants; and B'nai Jeshurun Congregation from Newark. They have also welcomed the Home for Aged Women and the Elizabeth Orphanage, both of Elizabeth; the Florence Crittendon Home for Unwed Mothers in Newark; the Newark Baptist Home; and several church groups. By 1935, when a Ukrainian Catholic Church in Newark requested land, the trustees agreed to sell land to them and not to exclude others from the area. As a result,

Figure 18–2 *Mary Houigan Tomb Figures*. Stone. New Jersey.

Figure 18–3   *Veterans Section of Evergreen Cemetery.* New Jersey.

Figure 18–4   *Mary Mapes Dodge.* New Jersey.

tombstones are in numerous languages: English, Hebrew, Ukrainian, German, Chinese, and most recently, Spanish.

The cemetery is the final resting place of many prominent people from the Newark-Elizabeth area. Among them are the Kelloggs: Edward, the first, planned the "New Manufacturing City of Elizabethport" in 1835, while James, the last, was chairman of the Port Authority of New York and New Jersey. Steven Crane, the author and poet, is probably the cemetery's most famous person. Originally only his grave was considered to be historic enough to be included on the National Historic Sites Register (Fig. 18–4). Mary Mapes Dodge, who wrote *Hans Brinker or the Silver Skates* and edited *St. Nicholas Magazine*, lived nearby. Edward Stratemeyer introduced the series books such as *Nancy Drew, The Bobbsey Twins*, and *The Hardy Boys* (Fig. 18–5). George Wiegand was a member of the New York Philharmonic Orchestra, a conductor, and a composer. His monument contains several bars of his music (Fig. 18–6).

This nonsectarian, nonprofit cemetery, patronized by a variety of religious, ethnic, and racial groups, is a haven in New Jersey's most urbanized area. With the adjacent Weequahic Park in Newark, it offers more than 400 acres of picturesque, open space.

Figure 18–5 *Edward Stratemeyer Tomstone.* New Jersey.

Figure 18–6 *George Wiegand Memorial.* New Jersey.

19. Raphell, Paradigm of Celebration

Lenore Lakowitz

Our contribution to this book is based on a very personal experience. In 1978, Raphell, our precious daughter, died suddenly of an aneurysm. She was twenty-nine years old and our only child.

Because we wanted some meaning to come from this apparently senseless tragedy, we were determined to continue Raphell's work—her concern for the mentally afflicted. To that end, we established the Raphell Sims Lakowitz Memorial Foundation and erected a monument that would not only commemorate Raphell's work in the field of mental health but also celebrate her spirit of understanding and love. It is that spirit which is embodied in the monument and which is the essence of the Foundation's motivation for helping the mentally afflicted to live more fully.

Raphell was born on September 22, 1948. She attended New York City public schools, was an honor student, and was an active member of her student body. Responding to her innate warmth and compassion, Raphell chose to be a psychologist. As a psychology major at Queens College, Raphell was selected to participate in special seminars and research projects at Brooklyn State Hospital and Biometric laboratories.

In 1969, while at Queens College, Raphell decided it was not enough to study psychology from books. She wanted to experience what it is really like to work with the mentally afflicted. She convinced a friend to join her, and the two girls were the first student volunteers at Creedmoor Psychiatric Center. As a supervised undergraduate student, Raphell worked with all types of patients and all types of professionals. After training, she conducted group therapy sessions with chronic schizophrenics. The patients and staff loved her. During her first year, Raphell brought 62 friends from Queens College to volunteer at Creedmoor. Creedmoor now has 350 student volunteers who participate in this program from eight local colleges and universities. Raphell's idea has enriched the lives of thousands of patients over the years. Moreover, because of Raphell's leadership, a whole new way of working with patients developed throughout the field of mental health.

Following graduation from Queens College, Raphell enrolled in the New School for Social Research, earned a Masters Degree in psychology, and completed her Ph.D. course work. She was awarded a National Defense Education Act Fellowship and was one of three students nominated for the National Science Foundation Award.

As a graduate student, Raphell worked with emotionally disturbed adolescents at Hillside Hospital and the Long Island Jewish Medical Center. She was also involved in research in a Prenatal Project conducted at Harlem Hospital by the Columbia University School of Public Health's Division of Epidemiology. Her research at Harlem Hospital was published the *Journal of the Society for Research in Child Development*.

Raphell was an associate member of the New York State chapter of the American Psychological Association and a member of the society for Research in Child Development.

Following completion of her graduate studies, Raphell entered private psychotherapy practice. She was engaged in practice until 1978, when she died.

* * *

The goal of the Raphell Sims Lakowitz Foundation is to continue and perpetuate Raphell's commitment to humanity by making contributions in the fields of mental health and education, especially in areas that have been neglected.

As far back as 1980, the Foundation has cooperated with staff at Long Island Jewish-Hillside Medical Center and Nassau County Medical Center's Coalition for Abused Women in an effort to make information widely available to all members of the community. In 1980, an annual memorial scholarship was established at Queens College for undergraduate students who are required to do volunteer work at Creedmoor for two semesters. And in 1985, working with the New York City Board of Education, the Foundation developed programs to raise awareness of child sexual abuse.

When the monument to Raphell was installed at Creedmoor in 1983, Tony Beneri, police liaison officer of the 105th Precinct, was so inspired that he organized the Raphell Sims Lakowitz Basketball Tournament for girls. The foundation has continued to work in conjunction with the 105th Precinct, the Police Athletic League, and the New York City Department of Parks and Recreation in support of the Tournament. By 1991, the Tournament had grown from the original 66 girls to 248 girls ranging in age from seven to seventeen from the Queens community. The Tournament is held in the Creedmoor building named for Raphell, in recognition of her volunteer work there.

At North Shore University Hospital-Cornell University Medical College, the Foundation has since 1985 worked with the staff of the Department of Health Education/Community Affairs and has supported the Hospital's child and adolescent psychiatry research program on family violence. The Foundation joined the Hospital in sponsoring important conferences: "Depression and Suicide in Children and Adolescents" (1986); "The Abused Adolescent: Battered Bodies,

Figure 19–1 *Raphell*. Polychrome Bronze. Raphell. New York.

Battered Minds" (1990); "Extrafamilial Sexual Abuse and Pornography: A Community Disaster" (1990); and "Coping with Disaster: Minimizing Childhood Psychic Trauma" (1991). The purpose of these conferences is to bring together nationally renowned experts to alert and educate the professional community and to provide training for recognition, diagnosis, treatment, and prevention of these tragedies.

We commissioned the internationally-renowned sculptor, Bruno Lucchesi, to create a monument to Raphell (Fig. 19–1). The monument was dedicated on October 26, 1983, at Creedmoor, in Queens Village, New York, where Raphell established her innovative volunteer program. It was the culmination of my vision inspired by Creedmoor's offer in 1979 to beautify its large reflecting pool. The pool is located in front of the activities building, already named for Raphell. We felt that a bronze statue symbolizing Raphell's spirit would be appropriate in that its beauty would bring light and joy to the lives of all who viewed it. We also hoped that it would inspire more public interest in mental health.

We brought Mr. Lucchesi the concept of a figure in Raphell's likeness with her arms outstretched. The figure would be standing near rocks, and water would be flowing from the rocks onto her hands, symbolizing Raphell's radiant spirit of giving love and energy. The statue would be a symbol of Raphell in form and spirit, eternally human. The bronze rock formation would symbolize the strength of nature, while the water would symbolize love, energy, healing, and rebirth.

After the sculpture's installation, a patient said, "She gives the place class." A week later, another patient, Ted, asked me for change of a quarter. While I was looking for the change, he said, "I made prayers for Raphell's soul." Another patient asked me, "How did the statue get so large, when the artist's model was small to begin with?" I said that the sculptor, Bruno Lucchesi, created the model in full size, and I explained the process. When I related this to Bruno, his answer was, "It is too complicated to explain. Just say that it was made with love and patience." We will always be grateful to Bruno for the heart that he put into this work and for his insight, love, and patience.

Shortly before she died, Raphell wrote a beautiful poem to Barry, the young man she was about to marry. Two lines from that poem, which capture so well her spirit, were the inspiration for the design of the statue. These lines, therefore, appear on the bronze plaque, which is set into the rim of the reflecting pool. The plaque reads:

Raphell

As we give love, so shall we receive love
As we give strength, so shall we receive strength

This statue honors Raphell Sims Lakowitz (1948–1978)
A Volunteer Whose Radiant Spirit Fills Our Hearts with Love

A Gift of the Raphell Sims Lakowitz Memorial Foundation

Sculpture by Bruno Lucchesi
From a Concept by Lenore Lakowitz

20. Co-Existence?
Modernism and the Figure

Richard McDermott Miller

I'd like to begin my brief remarks by talking about one of Washington D.C.'s most popular monuments: the Vietnam War Memorial. I have chosen this example because of the way its two contrasting parts illustrate the coexistence of several quite different creatures presently inhabiting the jungle of the visual arts.

These two divergent elements of the Vietnam Memorial, springing from apparently irreconcilable artistic impulses, epitomize the schizophrenic division of twentieth-century art into warring camps. Our example, in fact, is of two handsome works which co-exist even as they play against each other. The polished black wall of Maya Lin and the realistic bronze servicemen by Fredrick Hart both meet high, though dissimilar, standards demanded by different groups to reflect their own particular public positions. It is true that this linkage was a marriage of necessity. Public sentiment and political pressures forced these unlikely bedfellows into a shotgun wedding.

However, the need is evident for both kinds of art in monuments. Our example may have intended each element to serve a different constituency, yet a great many viewers are responding to both. In a pluralistic world, two such disparate symbols can indeed resonate for many of the same people. Rivalry between abstract and figurative art, for the modern audience, is an artificial conflict. Why then does spurious antagonism between them remain so pervasive?

Figurative art has a long history. With its easily identified features, it was the conspicuous predecessor to twentieth-century modernism. But then, as now, the tendency of youth was to dissent and demand change. Thus modernism, in its infancy, made war on tradition, taking particular aim at a well-defined target which centered on depiction of the human figure. At that time, "abstraction" happened to characterize the new century, while "figurative" happened to evoke the status quo. Appearing to be diametric opposites, "abstract" and "figurative" came to connote aspects of art thought to be antithetical to each other.

The early modernists, who were combatting the familiar figure with their call to abstraction, were enormously successful. They thrived on opposition. They turned the force of those who attacked them into weapons of their own. Their radical innovations did indeed meet heavy fire from critics and public alike. But such objections only strengthened the modernist movement, bringing attention to the freshness of its ideas and the novelty of its product. With their views gaining in credibility, the modernists swept to the fore, vanquishing the stodgy academics and smothering all other dissent.

The role of sanctified revolutionary attracts artists. So it is no surprise that the pretense of being a revolutionary has become the most ubiquitous cliché of current establishment art. The order of the day is to play the rebel, to attempt to shock, to offend, or to trivialize. But few are shocked and only an occasional prude will take offense. Patrons, who would stay in the know, are ready to apologize if they feel a bit left behind. The large public simply cheers any such pseudo-subversion, whether it be entertaining or merely fashionable. Try as he will to offend, an artist today is hard put to raise the eyebrows by being merely outrageous. The hip public has been completely won over. Every new antic, however vacant or zany, is met by applause and public affirmation.

As it has become more difficult for artists to be startling, they have begun to stray far from the customary definitions of art. In doing so they have discovered that new definitions can transform dross into new art. Common items, not previously associated with art, can be redefined to become original creations. As a result, art has proliferated far beyond abstraction, branching into many new and different categories that have become the coequals rather than mere subdivisions of earlier modernist tendencies.

This is especially true in sculpture, where so many new kinds of work have been introduced: found objects, earthworks, minimalism, assemblage, constructivism, conceptualism, site specific installations, and on and on. Although none would have been recognizable as sculpture in earlier centuries, all are now established as separate and coexisting artforms. This rampant pluralism easily overwhelmed any former notion of symmetry between abstract and figurative art.

Modernism, split into many branches and weakened by decades of public adulation, has since grown nostalgic for the opposition it once inspired. There is an urge to mimic the early twentieth century. There is a yearning to again wrestle an opponent, but the opposition is gone. Thus the familiar refrain of "abstract vs. figurative" is revived to create a phantom opponent. This is the perennial tactic of counterfeit rebels: attack the figgies!

Yet the overall effect of modernism has been positive for figurative artists; it has given them a clean slate. Its new forms have opened new possibilities. Insofar as it responds to that slate, figurative art is a part of modernism and is entitled to a place in it. In this sense modernism has been a truly liberating force. It emphasizes that sculptors can do anything at all, anything they wish. Frederick Hart has brought realist sculpture to the Vietnam Memorial. Except for the old-fashioned modernists, no one questions his or any other sculptor's freedom to do the figure. Nor do any deny the beauty or appropriateness of Maya Lin's black granite wall.

The division between figurative and nonfigurative, always artificial, is no longer warranted. All art is abstract, all art is expressive, and all art is legitimate. Setting up "abstract" as the antithesis of "figurative" was once a convenient device for promoting the former at the expense of the latter. But the analogy no longer fits.

Having said all that, I must admit that to incorporate the human figure into a public monument—these days—is a difficult task. It is nevertheless a worthy task, one that must be attempted now and in times soon to come. As we have often been told, change is the only constant. Time runs forward. We cannot reenter the past, yet its resources are fair game for all.

The old adversaries, modernism and the figure, are certain to be reinterpreted in the twenty-first century. By then, our present century will have begun to look rather quaint. The outcome is unpredictable, but if we continue to create monuments, both figurative and abstract elements will most likely be required.

21. "The Lone Sailor" and "The Homecoming"

Stanley Bleifeld

The creative process grows only more intense when the government becomes involved. For sculptors flirting with the public review process, the creation of "The Lone Sailor" can provide an instructive tale.

To begin with, the process of selecting the sculptor was unusual. I remember receiving a telephone call from Sasaki Associates, an architectural firm noted for its landscape work and commissioned by the United States Navy Memorial Foundation (USNMF) to find both an architect and a sculptor. After Sasaki chose the architect, the firm put together a list of fifty sculptors for a nationwide search and requested presentations from each. Busy professionals normally ignore most requests of this kind because proposals require a great deal of work and the odds of receiving a commission are rather slim. I declined because I was occupied with other work and do not enjoy making presentations. The architects were persuasive, however, and I finally agreed, only to learn that my presentation would require at least twenty photographs of past work, accompanying statements, and documentation, all in sextuplicate! I declined again. Then my assistant said, "Listen, this is a marvelous opportunity. Let's do it. I'll get the pictures and documents together and make up the presentation." Three months later, hearing nothing, I called Sasaki and requested my photographs back. I then learned that I was one of five finalists.

After representatives of the USNMF and the architectural and sponsoring agencies visited my studio, I had a formal interview. I was asked to speak about myself, sculpture, and the project. Though well prepared, I felt terribly intimidated, and the admirals could not hide their stripes despite their civilian clothes. I spoke briefly about my experience but avoided saying anything specific about how I might proceed, since I was neither conscious of what I really wanted to do nor ready to commit myself. Perhaps sensing this, one admiral stood up and asked, "Why do you want to do a military monument?" I replied that I did not want to do a military monument: I was interested in trying to express the sea experience, not in illustrating warships or naval battles. Although I had no sea duty during my World War II naval service, I had always been impressed by the power of the sea and the seaman's helplessness at the mercy of the elements. I very much wanted to tackle these ideas in sculpture. This answer seemed to have satisfied the admiral, for he stood up again and announced that I was awarded the commission to do the sculpture for the United States Navy Memorial.

The architect had designed a very imposing monument which was, unfortunately, utterly inappropriate for the site. The design included a colossal triumphal arch over ten stories high; it would be larger than the Washington Arch on Fifth Avenue in New York. The arch was to be decorated with sculpture of naval subjects. When it was finally presented, the model inspired such loud and vituperative objections in Washington that the USNMF withdrew the presentation and brought the entire effort to a standstill. One reason for the arch's failure was that it paralleled Pennsylvania Avenue instead of crossing it, and so it could not fulfill its traditional purpose of having a military parade pass under it. Its great height and mass would almost obliterate the large open space that was to be the site of the Navy Memorial and would block views of the National Art Collection and the Archives, both imposing classical stone piles. On the other hand, it would also block much of the FBI building, one of Washington's foremost monstrosities.

After striking down the arch, the USNMF requested that both architect and sculptor come up with a new concept. Despite my wish to work closely with the architect, he felt that he should design the concept and that I should be its decorator. I argued that this arrangement would not produce a good design,[1] but I did not prevail. The architect produced a design dominated by a glass enclosure, and the USNMF found it inappropriate. The plan, however, received great praise for its originality, suitability to the site, and style from some of the approving agencies. Not surprisingly, the USNMF turned it down. The design had little to do with the Navy (indeed, it had no naval references), and without the USNMF's sponsorship the "glass house" wound up in the trash.

This protracted process gave me an education in the ways of Washington. I had won the commission in April 1980, but the first bronze would not be in place until October 1987. I saw that most of the people with whom I had to deal were unprepared and reluctant to think about sculpture and monuments; they wished to delay the memorial or sink it before it got too far. It became clear that I would need some help, since my career as a sculptor had not prepared me for this kind of battle. I turned to a friend, G. Scott Wright, Jr. Together we worked up a grand program for the Navy Memorial. The USNMF had insisted, "We don't want this to be just a statue; we want it to be a sculpture park, and we like your idea of creating a naval environment, a sea environment." To help us develop our ideas, the Navy sent us on an inspiring tour of ships and installations. That tour made a strong impression on us and continues to validate the necessity of knowing one's audience. The men and women of the naval groups with whom we lived, shared meals, and traded stories gave us a real education. We heard their views on what the memorial could mean to them, and in turn we described our ideas and the ways we might best express them. We found genuine enthusiasm.

The monument would now be a "living memorial": not a conventional monument commemorating the dead, but one honoring all the men and women who had served, were now serving, and would serve in the United States Navy. It would also be the site of the United States Navy Band's summer concerts. With these guidelines from the president of the USNMF, we embarked on a year of inspired planning.

In the meanwhile, the architect had made another unsuccessful presentation and once again had been turned down. His relationship with the USNMF cooled considerably. To complicate matters, the Pennsylvania Avenue Development Corporation, which controlled the real estate involved, hired him. His interests shifted away from working with the USNMF and the sculptor and toward satisfying the PADC. This arrangement proved unproductive.[2]

These setbacks threatened to halt the momentum we had so dearly gained. We could invoke no laws to help us, only a vague, toothless public charter issued during the Carter administration. Nevertheless, the Foundation decided to push forward and asked me to keep the ball rolling. Scott and I sketched out many ideas, but I soon realized that I would need models in order to make some impression. Surprisingly, I found that models were not enough; many found it difficult to regard a model as a schematic conceptualization of the full-sized product. I decided to complement the models with realistic renderings that would be clear and dramatic enough to get my point across. Burton Silverman, my friend and one of America's foremost painters and illustrators, had the genius to come up with the necessary visualizations. His watercolors of my sculptural and architectural concepts made a strong impression on the board of directors.

I envisioned the memorial plaza's back wall presenting a sea environment, replete with icebergs and giant breakers carved in granite, with water falling over it all. This one hundred foot carving would symbolize, and indeed graphically express, the power of nature and the sea. Rising out of the plaza before it would be an 18-foot sailor holding signal flags and dressed in work clothes and a watch cap. He would be a working "salt," not a decorated officer. I meant him to be taken seriously: he would not be a glorified model but a strong, mature, experienced, rough and ready seaman. As counterpoint, nearby would be some sailors lounging informally, as men at rest might appear, on board a naval vessel under way. There would also be a "swabby" chipping paint, an image so universal in the Navy that I could not omit it. Ironically, this figure—a kind of naval icon—has always been turned down by one agency or another as being too frivolous or inappropriate a Navy image! As an historical reference I devised a mid-nineteenth-century grouping at the helm of an old ship. "Homecoming," the greatest emotional event in Navy life, inspired another idea for a bronze group. The "Lone Sailor" began as a figure who would remind spectators and visitors to the memorial of those lost while serving the Navy. We envisioned a raised dais where ceremonial and memorial wreaths could be laid and where speakers could orate when occasions required. I intended the sailor to be somewhat unidentifiable, hidden in the folds of his upturned peacoat collar and seen mainly from the back, as if the viewer were bidding him farewell.

The USNMF was enthusiastic about our presentations and believed, perhaps naively, that approval to build this memorial would be forthcoming. I was to present the entire program at a hearing. It may not be too surprising to learn that we were nearly jeered out of the room. "Hokey," said a staff member of the National Capitol Planning Commission. "Too ambitious for the U.S. Navy" was a mild remark. Many of the comments noted a barrier between the Navy and the NCPC that we could not penetrate. The USNMF staff were shocked, and Scott, Burt, and I were devastated. After all our enthusiasm, we had difficulty understanding how we created such a bomb.

After some regrouping, William Thompson, a retired admiral who was the USNMF president and its driving force, got the project going again and requested still another design. We none too enthusiastically resumed our labors. This time we proposed a circular design for the formerly rectangular memorial plaza. We carefully considered one of the features that was becoming an increasingly important reason for the memorial's existence, its designation as the site for the US Navy Band's summer concerts. We also addressed the influence of the buildings projected by the PADC that would surround the memorial. (I was gradually beginning to understand that the memorial was in reality a *quid pro quo* to the public for the enormous commercial-residential space that would surround half of the plaza.) I included schematic drawings of these buildings behind the memorial in our next presentation to the NCPC.

This presentation featured a circular plaza, in the center of which I placed a fountain area of carved water in the form of breaking waves and the working "salt" of our previous presentation. The background was to be a semicircular building, divided on the 8th Street axis and rendered in classical style. Since the more than 100 windows in the 10-storey complex seemed too monotonous and disturbing to the site, I cut the number of openings in half by having one window opening span two floors. I was innocently pleased with the result. The neoclassic columns dividing the vertical rows of openings created an effect compatible with the classic style of the surrounding Federal Triangle. For some reason the commission's attention focused on the architectural suggestions surrounding the plaza during our presentation, even though I explained that our suggestions were incidental and meant only to provide an idea of the architectural mass behind the memorial plaza. The chairman of the NCPC commented that the architecture projected by the PADC had to be a 10-storey edifice and that the building he saw was only 5 stories high. Somewhat taken aback, I explained how I had used one large window to span two stories. The chairman's surprising response was that I had deceived him by trying to make a ten storey building look like one of five stories. The design was unacceptable. The plan for the memorial plaza and its sculpture, which was the presentation's real purpose, was hardly acknowledged.

For some time I had considered the dramatic possibility for a fountain and the terrifying acrobatics of tall ship sailors who climbed the rigging to set sail in all kinds of foul weather. Burt Silverman did a stunning rendering of this concept. The rigging would rise out of a heavy, breaking sea carved out of granite, which formed the base of the fountain. Water would spray all over the climbing sailors. When he saw the design, the chairman of the Commission of Fine Arts declared that carved water and real water were incompatible. They would not mix in the same fountain. His novel physical/aesthetic observation sank this proposal as well.

Though discouraged and perhaps not a little disappointed in the democratic process, the president and executive director of the USNMF did not, however, surrender. Their dedication and persistence eventually overcame resistance to a United States Navy Memorial. In some desperation, they got together with John Roach, a Naval Reserve officer who painted combat art, and combined some elements of our designs with some of their own. They combined the circular plaza with the figure of the sailor in its middle with a semi-circular wall of stone that would hold about twenty reliefs of Naval subjects. I strongly protested including these reliefs because they would be tilted about thirty degrees to the sun; anyone familiar with relief sculpture could imagine their fatal destiny. With the sun in the east or west, the reliefs would be too dark; light from the south would wash out all the modeling. Although I built a full-scale schematic model demonstrating this problem, my arguments were unavailing. The design, including this great flaw, was presented for approval. While overall it had some merit, its possibilities were never realized. By this time, however, nothing surprised me; sure enough, this proposal was accepted and passed.

The central figure was now the only fragment that I could rescue from all of our designs. Scott was particularly disappointed, and a rift nearly destroyed our friendship. No amount of rational explanation could dispel our disillusion. Somehow, however, the loyalty and dedication of Admiral Thompson and Captain Thomas inspired me to stay in the game. I began thinking about the central figure of the sailor, even though my heart still longed to create a sea environment.

My thoughts turned to building a model of a monumental thirty-foot granite wave that might serve also as the bandshell and seating for the U.S. Navy Band. It was of course "too big"; it "blocked the view"; it was "impossible." But I needed to develop it before I made serious decisions about the sailor.

The sea had to be present, even if it were in the sailor himself. The retired brass on the USNMF board of directors were placing heavy pressure on me to make the sailor a decorated officer, correctly and smartly dressed. This image would not, I felt, be widely accepted. The sailor had to be someone to whom everyone could relate: son, brother, father, husband, shipmate. I strongly defended my idea, but my early attempts to realize this concept were unsatisfactory. I found my models wanting, and I insisted on continuing my search. My penultimate model, though well received, was not really suitable for the center of a circular plaza. The model, however, turned out to be very popular with the USNMF, and I did everything possible to keep it from becoming definitive. We ultimately recognized it as being well suited to a site in Jacksonville, Florida, where there is now a US Navy Memorial.

My search ended somewhat by chance. I had asked the submarine people in New London, Connecticut, to send down a sailor who might serve as a model for me to sketch. One fine day a handsome young Machinist's Mate, 1st class, showed up with his wife and child. He had sat for me in New London and was ideal for my purpose. Casting about for a pose, I found the light in my studio inadequate, so we went down to the beach where a fine wind was blowing. As he stood there, peacoat flying, blues in the wind, all my desire to put the "sea" into the sailor became epitomized by the wind in his face and clothing. I had my concept (Fig. 21–1). It grew into the sculpture you see today. When Captain Walt Thomas, a suave and witty airman, wisecracked about the "lone sailor" in the wind, the name stuck.

I was pleased with my work, but the criticism did not end. A rich Texan (of presidential ambitions) wanted to put the sailor on a tall pedestal and be-ribbon him, press his blues, button his peacoat, and get his hands out of his pockets. The USNMF courageously resisted these suggestions. But the NCPC and the Commission of Fine Arts again turned down the presentation because of the sailor's perceived ethnicity. Who was he to be? They handed down a ruling, classic in its syntax. The sailor would be acceptable only if he resembled "less any particular ethnic group." I was so stunned that, when collared by a member of the press, I carelessly suggested (quoted on the front page of the Washington *Post*'s second section) that I take a feature from every ethnic group, mix them in a paper bag, draw them by chance (an eye from one group, a nose from another), and then stick them on the sailor's head. I fully expected the USNMF to fire me at next morning's board meeting. To my great surprise and pleasure, however, they applauded. I sensed now a solidarity, born of the rejections and humiliations we had all suffered, which restored our confidence. We were again ready to stand up to the bureaucrats. I continued to work and we finally "passed." After enlargement, casting, and still more approvals, the "Lone Sailor" was erected on its site. There was a grand dedication attended by thousands, with jet flyovers, many hundreds of uniformed Navy with large American flags, bands playing, and so forth. The event celebrated, in addition to the memorial's public significance, the conclusion of our years of emotional struggle to create this monument.

However people judge it, the memorial remains an appropriate, if incomplete, tribute to the United States Navy. Some postmortems may be in order.

While the undertaking required an impressive effort, and while all the major participants contributed to it in ways none of us could have imagined, I have many reservations about the result and the challenges it posed. These reservations are shared by many others, some of whom are qualified critics. On the one hand, the memorial is an unquestionable public success. I am told that it is one of the most photographed public monuments in Washington. It is also a testament to the persistance, loyalty, and integrity of Admiral Thompson and the USNMF, who clambered over every devastating wall of bureaucratic intransigence that appeared at every turn. On my part, my need to express a conception of the relationship of man to nature was matched by an obstinate desire to conclude such an extended and frustrating effort with some positive result, and to emerge from it with a sense of pride, no matter how battered.

But all is not well in the "art" part of the public process. A wise and sensitive high official of a key commission has argued that experience shows that without this rigorous process of distillation, Washington would be awash in "bad" art. It is difficult not to agree. Yet, in the case of this memorial, this process very nearly led to the approval of some very ineffectual or inappropriate designs. Furthermore, the concept that finally won approval is severely flawed. There is the grave error of

Figure 21–1 *Lone Sailor.* Stanley Bleifield, sculptor. Bronze. Washington.

the relief wall cited above. While I developed a coherent and expressive format that helped counteract the disadvantages of the light angles and placement, my suggestions were met with a lack of comprehension. The USNMF ignored the problems in its effort to push through the already-approved plan, and it often caved in to the inappropriate demands of the individual sponsors. My conscience did not permit me to continue with this responsibility, and I resigned my supervisory role. The resulting relief wall is a potpourri of disconnected relief sculpture. Furthermore, the proposed expressions of sea life were not realized. We were unable to convince the approving powers (PADC, NCPC, CFA, Parks, etc.) of the value of these statements. Yet it is clear to me and to the USNMF that the memorial needs dramatic fountain compositions and, in particular, a visual identification of the site from outside its perimeter. The "paint chippers" would have provided these characteristics. The memorial is unidentifiable from Pennsylvania Avenue, and even people looking for it often pass by. The "Homecoming," rejected by the Commission of Fine Arts for outdoor placement on the site of the memorial, has been placed in the entrance lobby to the adjacent Visitors' Center, a location not under the jurisdiction of the approval agencies.

Given the competitiveness for memorial space in Washington, our presentations might have seemed too ambitious for the conflicting desires of the various responsible agencies and the political climate vis-à-vis the Navy. But they were appropriate. In a more congenial atmosphere, we might have agreed on constructive compromises. We could not implement the most significant lesson of the exercise, our realization that the public should share the monument's means and goals. The invaluable inspirations that could have contributed so much to the lasting meaning of the Navy Memorial were destined to remain on the drawing board.

There are many reasons for this failure. Reasonable and necessary are the responsibilities of the Commission of Fine Arts to arbitrate competing notions of artistic propriety, those of the National Capitol Planning Commission to serve the urban interests of the District of Columbia, those of the Pennsylvania Avenue Development Corporation to refurbish the Avenue for public and private use, and those of the Department of Parks to preserve and keep the site clean. In practice however, the agencies often compete to subvert their own best intentions. I will cite one of many examples. About a year after the "Lone Sailor" had been placed on site, I learned that the beautiful patina on the bronze had become a dark black-brown opaque coating. The original patina was a beautiful, transparent, delicately variegated coppery blush on the sculpture's silicon bronze. I had learned its secrets in Italy through a long and laborious process and knew that it would protect the bronze from urban pollution by anticipating the effects of weather and time. It seems that the Parks Department, without consulting me or the USNMF, in its zeal to preserve the newly placed monument and to protect it from the ravages of the District of Columbia's pollution, treated the sculpture to a "protective" coating of a tar-like substance as impervious as it was ugly. After repeated protests on my part, Parks finally agreed to attempt the removal of the coating. They decided that they had succeeded too well in "protecting" the bronze. At least a dozen people from Parks, with tools, rags, solvents and telecameras in hand, put in many hours to remove the coating with only partial success. My beautiful patina is hardly visible. (Sculptors, collectors, and others who may have to deal with "conservators," please note.)

Given this history and the exigencies and vagaries of the public process, I hesitate to make any recommendations for the creation of a memorial. Perhaps all that I can say is that the erection of any meaningful monument on a public site might be something of a miracle. Following one strategy might soon result in the competing necessity of following another. Awareness of the possibilities and pitfalls will, of course, benefit sponsors, sculptors, and architects, and they need to be fortified with appropriate amounts of dedication, scepticism, and patience. In the long run, if an artist is moved to create public art, that creation must take place in the reality and context of the environment in which he or she must work. If that environment is, in fact, public, it is rarely ideal and may turn out to be adverse. Success is rare and, indeed, a mystery.

NOTES

1. Henry Hope Reed, "Sculpture and Architecture," *National Sculpture Society Celebrates the Figure* (Washington, D.C.: National Sculpture Society, 1987), p. 22.
2. Ibid.

22. Cathedral

Stephen Murray

Since the title of my paper would allow a multitude of possible approaches, may I begin by defining my current concerns with this all–embracing theme? I should like to address the question of how we deal with the issue of context: how we attempt to grapple with the relationship of the cathedral to the social and visual fabric of the medieval city. And how we, twentieth–century visitors, may perceive the monument—what forces come to play as we walk through the edifice. Then, finally, in a three-part structure, I will come back to revisit the problem of context.

To define context I refer to a map of medieval France and an image of the cathedral of Beauvais, just to the north of Paris. The modern scholar tends to impose his or her own social and ideological agenda upon the cathedral and may neglect aspects of the situation as it existed in the thirteenth century. We tend to "make sense" of the past in light of subsequent events, linking the phenomenon of Gothic with the "inevitable" centralization of royal power under the Capetian kings of France based in the capital city of Paris. Yet when Gothic flowered in the twelfth and thirteenth centuries, France was not yet what it was to become. The ring of great cathedrals around Paris may be understood as a sign of decentralized power—the enormous wealth and power that still lay in the hands of the secular clergy, the bishops, and chapters. Once the power of the monarchy was fully established, this wealth was soon to be diverted by means of royal taxation toward the interests of the king—above all, to the business of making war. In my recent book on Beauvais Cathedral, I attempted to portray the great monument as a project that was initiated in the teeth of energetic royal opposition to the power of the bishop.[1] It is quite impossible to construct Beauvais Cathedral as a royal phenomenon. Its founding bishop, Miles of Nanteuil, claimed to serve no lord other than the Apostle himself, Saint Peter. He was unseated in a direct confrontation with the French king, Louis IX. Gothic is, to a great extent, the expression of regional variety and regional wealth. The monopoly of power in Paris is something that belongs to a later period.

The intellectual framework that we tend to construct in order to understand the context of Gothic is an excessively limited one, derived from two strands of nineteenth-century thought. Recent interpreters have tended to impose a heavily materialist ideology, seeing Gothic as the construct of the clerical aristocracy and as necessarily destructive to the health of the economy and the welfare of the townsfolk. On the other hand, we also inherit from the nineteenth century the romantic vision of Gothic as a sign of a society able to unite in consensus in the construction of the great church that provided the visual expression of the well-being of the city. Two images will provide a visual expression of this polarity. The construction of Beauvais Cathedral was seen by Robert Lopez, the economic historian, as the destructive force responsible for the vitiation of the economic life of the city, leading to the collapse of the commune (Fig. 22–1).[2] The very image of the gigantic cathedral, towering over the rooftops of the twentieth-century city, seems to confirm the interpretation proffered by Lopez. The opposite end of the spectrum is expressed in the double image on the page from A. W. Pugin's *Contrasts*.[3] Pugin saw church architecture as a sign of the economic vitality and welfare of the medieval city. In the lower image we see the medieval urban landscape punctuated with beautiful spires. Open access to the city is provided by the graceful bridge. The upper image of the same town in 1840 shows a capitalistic nightmare. The bridge is now locked; the spires are truncated; the abbey church lies in ruins and the city is ringed by a line of satanic mills.

Here, then, is the simple opposition between opposing ideological structures; the romantic one associated with Pugin and the devastatingly destructive materialist one of Lopez. To which of these positions, finally, do we wish to subscribe? Of course, I have presented the case to you in terms of absolute black and white. I would want to take the position that we should subscribe to *neither* of these views—partly because they are constructed in ignorance of one of the most important economic dimensions of cathedral construction which involved not the city, but rather the surrounding countryside. To illustrate this point, I refer to the construction of the cathedral of Troyes in Champagne, built in a long series of campaigns from around 1200 to the 1550s.[4] The building accounts for this cathedral are unusually detailed, allowing us to establish a clear understanding of the sources of income. In the earliest surviving accounts the largest single item of receipt came not from the city at all, but from the inhabitants of the wealthy villages in the surrounding countryside. We forget that a cathedral is not only an urban phenomenon: a cathedral is head of a great diocese, which is a rural entity. And the French countryside in the Middle Ages was far more richly studded with prosperous villages than it is now. The population of thirteenth-century Picardy, for example, was greater than it is now—the excessive growth of cities like Amiens has sucked out the population of the surrounding country.

This brings me to Amiens, the site of my current research. Amiens is now a city of well over 100.000; in the thirteenth century it might have numbered 15,000. The clergy of the cathedral was not rich in urban land, but held a substantial slice of rural estates to the south and east of the city. This is highly fertile land, easily cultivable, and with the slightly warmer climate of the Middle Ages, most productive in wheat and grapes. It has been shown that the price of wheat was escalating in

Figure 22–1 *View of Beauvais Cathedral.*

the late twelfth century. We might compare the phenomenon to the increase in oil prices in the 1970s. The clergy thus found itself in command of an unprecedented source of income. In addition to this, the chapter of Amiens Cathedral controlled navigation on the River Somme. Raw wool was brought up the Somme from England and was woven into cloth in the city. In the surrounding villages woad was produced for tinting the cloth in a range of different shades of blue. Woad was also exported along the waters of the Somme. In the twelfth century the chapter collaborated with the townsfolk in the development of port facilities to handle the lucrative export-import business. The creation of new wealth lies behind the construction of the Gothic cathedral which may be understood, at least in part, as the result of a massive transfer of resources from the countryside to the town. This supply of cash, largely in the hands of the clergy, was spent in the city with the hiring of considerable numbers of masons, carpenters, and other artisans, all of whom needed accommodation and supplies. It is hard to see this as anything other than a massive stimulus to the economic welfare of the city.

Having sketched the problems faced in constructing a context—the rediscovery of lost elements of the economic infrastructure—I want to turn to the task of constructing the cathedral itself. I mean here the constructing that you, the visitor to the cathedral, would undertake when you go to the city; when you first encounter the cathedral seen in a fragmentary way across bustling streets, and when you finally enter. Each visitor will engage in a dialogue with the edifice, and will construct an intellectual cathedral. As a stimulus for your thought, I offer the intellectual cathedral constructed by Viollet-le-Duc in his *Dictionnaire*: a combination of elements from Reims, Laon, Notre-Dame of Paris, and Amiens. I am not sure that you would construct an intellectual cathedral just like this. But I am certain that the experience of the visit will involve certain kinds of memory and certain kinds of *comparison*.

The cathedral, a complex spatial and structural entity, cannot be comprehended all at once. It becomes a real force, beckoning the beholder from a distance, urging him or her to enter by the spacious portal and to explore light-filled interior spaces. In this exploration, *anticipation* is most important as questions about the unseen parts of the edifice urge us forward. And *memory* will play a vital role as the visitor moves through the edifice, fixing images in the back of the mind and comparing them both with elements yet to be seen *and* with other cathedrals that have already been seen. This process leads us to establish similarities and differences. Thus, we might note that the elevation of the choir of Amiens differs from that of the nave. When we compare Amiens with other cathedrals we note some very odd features: the towers of the west façade, for example, are not square as at Reims, Chartres, or Notre-Dame of Paris, but are distinctly rectangular.

There are many other "aberrant" features about the exterior of Amiens Cathedral—the unusual arches in front of the north transept rose window, for example. In other words, the intelligent beholder will want to enter into a kind of dialogue with the edifice, comparing what has been seen with what is about to be seen and noticing things that look different: things that do not quite correspond to our memory images or our ideal images.

Assuming that you care to adopt the methodology that I have described, the most important internal difference that you will encounter in Amiens Cathedral is between the nave and the choir. The nave of Amiens Cathedral is extremely regular: it marches seven full bays without apparent change, seeming to get no older and no younger (Fig. 22–2). You can walk up and down the nave looking for a consistent pattern in the slight differences in the sculpture of the capitals, but no such a pattern can be found.

The evidence thus points to extraordinary control over the means of production. Yet as we come to the other end of the edifice, the choir, we encounter a dramatic change (Fig. 22–3). The middle level of the elevation—the triforium—has been broken open and glazed.[6] The decorative patterns formed by the tracery of the choir triforium are quite different from the equivalent forms in the nave. Little gables, absent in the nave, have been introduced over each unit of the choir triforium. The transverse sections indicate the transformation of the aisle roof of the choir necessary to allow light to penetrate the choir triforium and the transformation of the flyers. In the nave the flyers are solid props; in the choir the mass of the flyer is voided with delicate openwork panels. The visitor to the cathedral who actually wants to spend half an hour to reflect on the significance of these differences will begin to construct a series of scenarios, inventing a range of possible explanations.

The first attempts to explain the difference between the cathedral nave and choir, made by an eighteenth-century antiquarian of Amiens, were rational.[7] Since the prevailing wind comes in from the English Channel to the north-west, it was thought that the nave, the western part of the cathedral, had to be more substantial to resist the wind-buffeting that can blow out a window or shake a flying buttress. Also established at an early date was the explanation of difference based upon problems of urban topography—for a long time it was believed that the site of the choir was blocked by the continuing existence of an older church that had to be demolished and located elsewhere.[8] It is certainly true that the old Roman wall, obsolete by the end of the twelfth century, cut through the site of the Gothic choir.

The 1980s brought to art historical discourse a passionate interest in semiotics and an antipathy to evolutionary theories. Thus, it is no surprise to find the rejection of the idea of a continuing development of style and the construction of explanations relying upon the idea of *deliberate* visual differencing intended purely to articulate meaning in the various parts of the edifice.[9] The choir, inaccessible to layfolk and the theater of the Eucharist, needed to be differenced from the rest of the cathedral. This is a seductive argument, and the visitor to Amiens Cathedral will certainly agree that the different liturgical role of the choir is very fully articulated in architectural terms. The question, however, is whether such visual differencing had been intended from the start by the builders of the cathedral, or whether it expresses changes of intention introduced only at a later point of time.

As with the opposition between the destructive materialist and the misty-eyed romantic construction of context, I would want to take the position that we are not necessarily forced to extremes. Visual differencing in the cathedral is, indeed, sometimes intended and sometimes accidental—each case must be assessed on its own merits. Amiens Cathedral offers the visitor a wonderful example of spatial

Figure 22–2 *Nave of Amiens Cathedral.*

Figure 22–3 *Choir of Amiens Cathedral.*

differencing certainly intended by the founding master mason, Robert de Lu-zarches. As you walk down the nave of the cathedral you encounter a succession of modular bays, one identical to the other. The aisle bays are close to square and the central vessel bays are double squares. All the supports are the same, and the elements of articulation, applied colonnettes, capitals, arch and rib moldings, window tracery, and so on all remain unchanged from one end of the nave to the other. The visitor, attempting to fix each bay in the mind, will be frustrated as memory breaks down under relentless repetition. At the sixth bay of the nave, however, the designer allows you, the visitor, to experience a radical spatial trans-formation as the basilical body of the cathedral is intersected by a transept (Fig. 22–4). There is nothing unusual in the presence of a transept, to be sure, but Robert de Luzarches has enhanced the spatial shock of the encounter with the transept by opening the bays contiguous with the crossing more widely than the other bays of the main arcade in nave, transept, or choir. You, the visitor, become aware of some-thing very different happening in the spatial economy of the edifice at this point, which happens to correspond to the area in the cathedral where sermons were preached.

Thus, the designer is using a kind of visual differencing (the enlarged bays adja-cent to the crossing) to announce to you, the intelligent visitor, that this is a part of the edifice with very special significance. And the study of the geometry of the en-tire cathedral plan reveals that the great square formed by the enlarged crossing (that is, the crossing bay *with* the widened arcade bay on each side: a square of 110 local feet) fixes in various ways the spatial envelope of nave, choir, and transept arms. Thus, the diagonal of the square gives the length of the nave; the half-diago-nal, the length of the choir; and half the side of the square, the projection of the transept arms.[10] You will recognize the play on the one-to-the-square-root-of-two rectangle that lies behind so much Gothic architectural planning. And I want to argue that the spatial unfolding that characterizes the plan of Amiens Cathedral is, indeed, palpable for the visitor who cares to study the question. The arrangement conveys an underlying structure of meaning for the cathedral. Thus, the statue of the *Beau Dieu*, Christ the Logos of the central west portal, the *forma formatrix*, is framed in a door aperture that conforms to the same one-to-the-square-root-of-two rectangle as the nave itself. The body of Christ *is* the Church; the shape of the Church is fixed by an underlying ordering principle or Logos.

The *idea* of the enlarged bays adjacent to the crossing that announce the presence of the great square from which the cathedral geometry is developed is a magnifi-cent one—but one that brought unforeseen structural problems. The enlarged bays of the main arcade contiguous with the crossing exercise an unusually heavy outward thrust. This problem was exacerbated by the fact that a relatively thick arcade wall was supported by very slender supports. The thrust of this thick ar-cade against the slender piers of the crossing pushed them inward, while the up-per parts of the same piers are bowed outward by the weight of the crossing tower, producing a banana-like configuration. An attempt was made in the late Middle Ages to arrest the inward deformation of the crossing piers induced by the thrust of the main arcade. In the late fifteenth century iron chains were inserted at the lev-el of the floor of the triforium. The chains run the length of nave, choir and each of

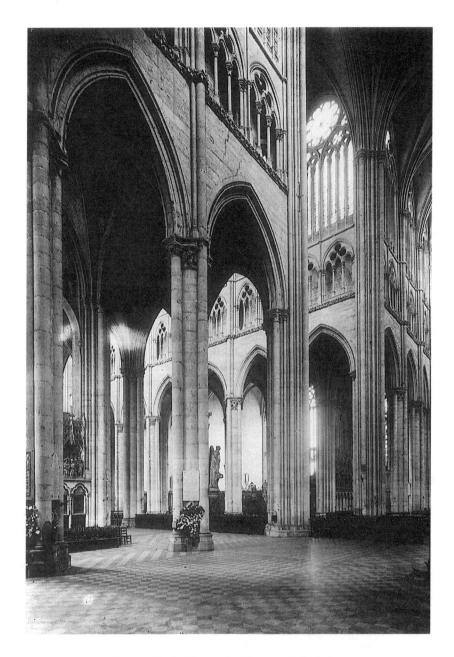

Figure 22–4 *Transept of Amiens Cathedral.*

the arms of the transept. The great piers of the crossing are pegged by means of great iron bars that resemble the cross-piece at the end of the chain of a pocket-watch.

We tend to treat cathedrals as if they are purely an expression of a rational and enlightened design process, forgetting that each of them is a battlefield of deformation and repair; each of them embodies endless possibilities for the unforeseen. A Gothic cathedral with its thrust and counterthrust contains within itself the seeds of its own downfall. This may be the result of an improperly planned buttress or a mass that has been thinned beyond the limits imposed by the laws of structure.

Thus, I invite you to enter into a dialogue with the cathedral, pursuing similarity and difference with an openness to the possibilities both of effects that are intentional *and* the possible results of accidents. Despite the current fashion that refuses to acknowledge the role of the author, and despite the Renaissance attempt to portray the medieval master mason as an anonymous and insignificant artisan, a great deal of power certainly lay in the hands of the master designer of the cathedral. In some ways, the medieval master mason held a higher social status and more real power than his Renaissance counterpart.[11] At Amiens we know that he lived in close proximity to the clergy in the episcopal manse. And the written evidence from the building accounts of Troyes Cathedral cited earlier indicates that he was highly paid and might share some of the privileges of the clergy. We should not construct an opposition (as did Viollet-le-Duc) between the clergy, on the one hand, and the secular "workshop" on the other. The master mason was the peer of a canon of the cathedral; the construction process resulted from an ongoing series of conversations between peers. Counter to current belief, the written sources of the Middle Ages (epigraphic, narrative, administrative) repeatedly stress authorship.

The identity of the master masons responsible for the construction of Amiens Cathedral is announced by an inscription placed in an octagonal plaque at the center of the great decorative labyrinth set in colored marble on the nave pavement. In the Middle Ages this labyrinth was known as the "House of Daedalus": we have an implicit comparison, therefore, between the agency of the legendary Daedalus, builder of the labyrinth on the island of Crete and the first man to fly, and the creativity of the master masons of the cathedral, Robert de Luzarches, Thomas de Cormont, and his son Renaud de Cormont. Work started in 1220 and the labyrinth was set in 1288. Within the limitations imposed by the structure of the on-going conversations with the clergy, there can be no doubt that these master masons exercised considerable control over the edifice: the power to continue the use of the same forms over the five decades of construction, producing mind-boggling repetition, or, alternatively, the power to break that repetition through the introduction of new devices. But the cathedral itself was not a passive participant in these decisions. Essentially an experimental structure, staying aloft through the interaction of thrusts and counterthrusts that were not fully understood, the cathedral had the power to surprise its builders. And the stability of the urban infrastructure itself, the consensus that must lie behind cathedral construction, was not assured. I want to turn now to some visual differencing which, I think, indicates that the cathedral was not altogether under control.

We have already noticed the remarkable differences between the nave triforium and the choir triforium; between the nave flyers and the choir flyers. Does this reflect a deliberate strategy, planned from the start, intended to introduce meaning? There is an alternative scenario—that the upper choir was the work of a young master mason in revolt against the existing forms of the cathedral, and that he pushed Gothic design to a point where structural deformation brought problems that had not been anticipated. The flying buttresses of the upper choir have clearly not been effective. They were substantially modified in the late Middle Ages when additional substantial props were inserted under the open-work units.

In order to ascertain whether the transition from the type of flyer used in the nave to the choir type was a carefully-planned and deliberate one, we should obviously study the point where the two modes of design meet. This point may be found in the angles between the nave and the west side of the transept arms. And it is quite obvious from the form of the unit to the west of the north transept arm that it was originally intended to be a massive prop, just like its counterparts in the nave. The first stones of the upper rim of such a unit were even installed, and the newfangled open-work flyer had been built against an upright intended for a more conventional flyer. At all transition points between the old and the new architectural modes, similar kinds of hesitations and dislocations take place. The first bays of the new glazed triforium to be installed were in the east side of the south transept arm. Each of the three bays of the triforium here is different, the two outermost with large trefoils at the top, and the innermost with a much more complex design with small trefoils. This is a very unstable area of the cathedral owing to the tendency of the upper transept arms to move diagonally toward the north and south. The archaeological evidence indicates quite clearly that the innermost bay of the triforium, adjacent to the southwestern crossing pier is a replacement unit—it does not fit comfortably into its framing aperture. And the same situation exists in the contiguous bay of the choir where the stones of the framing aperture and its little gable have been scorched by the flames of a fire that we know affected the cathedral in 1258, while the elements of the tracery are fresh and white. The physical evidence of the fire provides very precise dating evidence revealing the extent of completion of the upper choir in 1258. Fire-damage extends up to the enclosing arches of the clerestory windows in the eastern bays of the south side of the choir, but the stones of the high vaults were not touched.

This evidence is of particular value since we know from extraneous written evidence that the master mason of the cathedral in these years was Renaud de Cormont. Thus, the architectural revolution embodied in the upper choir with its new flying buttresses and triforium may express the work of a young master mason who, after traveling and working elsewhere, returned to Amiens and indulged in a systematic revolt against the forms of the cathedral employed by his predecessors—including his own father. The use of the labyrinth as a signing device invites us to consider the relationship between father and son within the framework of the myth of Daedalus and Icarus. Young Renaud clearly went too far with his innovations, endangering the structural stability of the cathedral. Gothic architecture may be understood as a kind of modernism—an ongoing revolt against the tyranny of existing forms. And within the human dimension of Gothic, the father–son relationship must have been a very common one indeed.

Thus, the differences that we have encountered clearly introduce meaning to the various parts of the cathedral. But the meaning may not always have been as carefully predetermined as some recent scholars have suggested. The fire-reddened stones may be considered as a natural sign left behind by the physical disaster of the fire. But the written sources indicate that the fire was no accident. This was arson, and leading members of the bourgeois were accused. This was only one of several incidents of anticlerical violence in and around Amiens in the middle decades of the thirteenth century. This brings us full circle back to our opening remarks on the problem of constructing a context for the cathedral.

The clergy of Amiens had to deal with the leading bourgeois families not as subjects but as peers. We have seen that the urban holdings of the clergy were relatively slender. Although much of the money for construction was new wealth generated from outside the city, it was vital to achieve and to maintain urban consensus. What avenues were open to the clergy in their attempt to construct a benign context for the great enterprise? Cathedral construction might actually be a force in the liberalization of relationships between clergy and townsfolk as the clergy attempted to commute dues that had been previously made in kind or in services to the cash necessary to pay for the materials and services necessary in large-scale building. The continuing effect of inflation tended to decrease the value of such cash payments, whereas the value of renderings in kind or services remained constant.

And at Amiens the written sources indicate that two concessions were made by the clergy to the townsfolk in the earliest years of cathedral construction. Each member of the bourgeois paid an annual tax to the clergy known as the "Respite of Saint Firmin." It was a respite since it represented the commutation of all previous taxes that had been paid in kind or services in recognition of the bishop's nominal status as seigneur of the city. In 1226, six years after the start of work on the cathedral, that tax was reduced by twenty five percent, from four to three deniers per annum. This is far from the Marxian scenario of cathedral construction as a heavy weight upon the urban population. Second, in an area of the city where friction existed between clerical and municipal claims to jurisdiction (the street of Nouvelle Canterraine, to the northeast of the city), the bishop in 1228 agreed to give up all pretensions.

Consensus might be achieved by a program of economic concessions or by means of references to the shared memories and myths that bound the clergy together with the townsfolk. Saint Firmin lay at the center of such a web of myths since he was patron of the city and of the cathedral. Thus, it comes as no surprise to find the story of Saint Firmin emphasized in the left-hand portal of the west façade, carved in the 1230s. Here we encounter the story of the discovery ("invention") of the saint's body which had been buried in a cemetery outside the city, the exact location of which had been forgotten. In the seventh century, a miracle led the bishop of Amiens to rediscover that lost place and to transfer the remains into the cathedral in the city. Thus, the wealth, the stones, the relics for the cathedral—

all were transferred from the surrounding countryside to the city. In the case of the transfer of the relics a miracle took place on the cold January day and for several hours winter became summer: the trees came into leaf, the flowers bloomed, and a wonderful odor filled the air. The population of the surrounding towns came out to participate in this ecological miracle. This is conveyed in the middle register of the sculpture, while at the top you can see the procession of the clergy with the relics in a steep-crested *châsse*. Legitimacy is conveyed by encoded references to the Triumphal Entry of Christ into Jerusalem. Thus, in the Amiens sculpture children climb trees; fronds are thrown into the road to the cry of "Hosanna in the highest!" In this way Amiens *becomes* Jerusalem. Behind the relic-bearing procession in the sculptural depiction we see a young man who has thrown off his coat in the heat—he is carrying it slung on a stick over his shoulder. He also carries a frond of greenery and wears a foliate crown. Many local written sources refer to the agency of the Green Man (*l'homme vert*) who would appear at the mass on the feast day of Saint Firmin (January 13) with foliate crowns for each member of the clergy. The burning of incense would recreate the wonderful odor of the miracle. This was only one of many such multisensory recreations of a mythical past that flourished at the time of the construction of the cathedral. Such continual reconstruction of a mythical past helped to bridge the potential gap between the learned exegesis inherent in the cathedral sculptural program and the participation of the people; between what is sometimes called "high" and "low" religion. Most of this common structure was swept away in the *siècle des lumières* that preceded the great Revolution.

Thus, we encounter political strategies that are familiar to the modern spectator—the construction of a benign framework through tax cuts and through the emphatic emphasis upon a structure of shared myth. There is every reason to believe that the start of work on Amiens Cathedral in the 1220s was undertaken in a spirit of cooperation. That this spirit might be a short-lived phenomenon is suggested by the arson of 1258, when leading members of the municipality attempted to burn down the unfinished cathedral. The modern spectator is all too familiar with the speed with which the urban economy can turn. We should not blame the anti-clericalism of the 1240s and 1250s entirely upon the weight of cathedral construction—heavy royal taxation for the purposes of the crusade may have played a role here. Whatever the reason, the fiscal crisis of the mid-century brought the phenomenon that we call "High Gothic" to an end. The construction of massive cathedrals like Amiens, Beauvais, and Reims became a thing of the past.

NOTES

1. S. Murray, *Beauvais Cathedral: Architecture of Transcendence* (Princeton: Princeton University Press, 1989).
2. R. S. Lopez, "Économie et architecture médiévales; cela aurait-il tué ceci?" *Annales, Economies-Sociétés-Civilizations* 8 (1952): 433–8.
3. A. W. N. Pugin, *Contrasts* (Printed by the author, Saint Marie's Grange, 1836).
4. S. Murray, *Building Troyes Cathedral: The Late Gothic Campaigns* (Bloomington: Indiana University Press, 1987).

5. E. E. Viollet-le-Duc, *Dictionnaire raisonné de l'architecture française du XIe. au XVIe. siècle*. 10 vols. Paris, 1858–1868, 2:324.

6. The triforium is the middle level of the three-story elevation where the lean-to roof of the aisle butts against the main vessel of the cathedral. A passage is generally inserted into the wall thickness. In the Amiens choir a low-pitched roof allowed windows to be inserted.

7. For the writings of Pagès, see L. Douchet (ed.), *Manuscrits de Pagès, marchand d'Amiens, écrits à la fin du 17e. et au commencement du 18e. siècle sur Amiens et la Picardie*. 6 vols. Amiens, 1856–1864.

8. I have addressed this problem elsewhere and cannot deal with it in detail here. Suffice it to say that the bishop and chapter were entirely in control at the site and were not impeded by insuperable obstacles. See S. Murray, "Looking for Robert de Luzarches," *Gesta* 29 (1990): 111–31.

9. D. Kimpel and R. Suckale, *Die gotische Architektur in Frankreich, 1130–1270* (Munich: Hirmer Verlag, 1985).

10. S. Murray and J. Addiss, "Plan and Space at Amiens Cathedral," *Journal of the Society of Architectural Historians* 49 (1990): 44–66.

11. F. Toker, "Alberti's Ideal Architect: Renaissance or Gothic?" *Renaissance Studies in Honor of Craig Hugh Smyth* (Florence: 1985), 668–74.

Index